I0132175

PICTURES

OF

SLAVERY AND ANTI-SLAVERY.

ADVANTAGES OF NEGRO SLAVERY AND THE
BENEFITS OF NEGRO FREEDOM.

MORALLY, SOCIALLY, AND POLITICALLY CONSIDERED.

BY

JOHN BELL ROBINSON.

ISBN: 978-1-63923-838-5

All Rights reserved. No part of this book maybe reproduced without written permission from the publishers, except by a reviewer who may quote brief passages in a review to be printed in a newspaper or magazine.

Printed: March 2023

Published and Distributed By:
Lushena Books
607 Country Club Drive, Unit E
Bensenville, IL 60106
www.lushenabks.com

ISBN: 978-1-63923-838-5

Entered according to the Act of Congress, in the year 1863, by

JOHN BELL ROBINSON,

in the Office of the Clerk of the District Court of the United States
in and for the Eastern District of the State of Pennsylvania.

(ii)

PREFACE.

To the people of the United States and the Christian ministry ; especially those of them who seem to have forgotten the "prize of their high calling," and have converted their pulpits into places of political, sectional strife, and rendezvous for recruiting in civil war.

I HAVE written the following chapters on the relation between Christianity, civilization, the prosperity of the universe, and negro slavery. I have long feared a dissolution of this great and glorious Union would sooner or later occur in consequence of sectional, political questions being introduced into the pulpits of the Christian church, believing it to be as much infidelity to have introduced the slave question into the church, in the way it has mostly been done, as it would be to deny that the several Epistles of Paul were a part of the Gospel.

Had I not just grounds for fears when the General Conference of the Methodist Episcopal Church divided in 1844 on the slave question, and a majority of that body deposed a bishop who stood high for his talents, zeal, and great moral worth, who had never owned a slave, though a Georgian by birth, education, and residence through his entire life, but had recently married a lady who, a short time before, fell heir to two or three little negro children, whom she had to raise up to maturity? For marrying *this lady*, Bishop Andrews was suspended from his office as bishop. Since that

(iii)

day I have feared just what is now upon us, and at
every fit opportunity since, I have tried to make ˙ ˙ose
who led that dangerous experiment (and all others ˙ho
seemed to approve of the course of that General Conference) see the ruin they would plunge both church
and State into, if they did not stop their denunciations
of slavery from their pulpits, and treat the question
as St. Paul did in his day.

I have often desired to write and publish my opinions to
the world, but being without an education, and but little
schooling, the Child's Primer, Webster's Speller, English Reader, and Bennett's Arithmetic, having been
the only school books used in those days, where I was
schooled, and any knowledge beyond the rudiments of
these branches was thought ruinous to all scholars who
should happen to pass those limits. An educated man
or woman was thought very dangerous, therefore the
children were not allowed to cross those limits, consequently I felt that I was incompetent to such a duty.
But when the John Brown raid was made in Virginia, I
was satisfied something would have to be speedily done,
or our end as a republic and a free people was near.
Knowing there was no other sectional question besides
the slave question, and that no other could jeopardize
our national Union, I thought I would write a pam-
phlet of some twenty-five or thirty pages, contrasting
slaves with free negroes, and slave negro labor with free
negro labor, showing the superiority of one to the other,
to which I have devoted Chapter III. of this book.
But I soon found I had given myself too short a limit,
and I have written some eight or nine hundred pages,
12mo., all of which was ready in the summer of 1861 ;
but finding nearly all of my old friends so directly opposed to me, and being denounced with such bitterness

by some, and ridiculed by others, that I found my moral
courage not equal to the task, so I was kept back in
that way till other circumstances intervened, which
stopped me until now, and now I only feel at liberty
to publish half of the work.

A part of the second chapter was written for the New
York Methodist in 1860, but was refused a place in
that paper, for reasons the reader will see in the correspondence between my friend, the Reverend Mr. Crooks,
and myself, at the end of the chapter; it was returned
to me in the following February; after which time I
enlarged it to its present size by discussing the points
more extensively. The first and second chapters are on
human slavery, as set forth in the Bible. The appendix and the other chapters fully sustain my position.
Then I have copied two written addresses by ex-Senator Bigler of Pa., one on the Crittenden Compromise,
the other on the only plan by which this Union can
ever be restored.

I know I shall meet with bitter opposition and severe
denunciations for my views, but knowing that with the
overthrow of this Union will end all my hopes of peace
and pleasure in this world, not only mine, but all others,
and all future generations; therefore I feel it to be my
duty to publish this much of the original now, notwithstanding the severe chastisements that may be inflicted
upon me. I appeal to Him who knoweth the secrets of
all hearts, for my sincerity.

When I say I have no sympathy with secession or rebellion, I mean just what I say. I hope no one will pass
sentence upon me until they have heard me through; then,
if I am found guilty, I must submit to the penalty.

I have written a chapter on the causes of the civil
war in this beloved country, that will, perhaps, surprise

the reader more than anything herein published ; when he comes to see the mass of evidences I have adduced, pointing out the sections, parties, and the very men, many will wonder how this great calamity was produced without their knowledge of the facts which were all around them. That, with thirteen other chapters, I intend to publish at a proper time.

I believe the Christian church could now restore peace and union to this entire country, if the Christian ministers in all the free States would speedily return to their legitimate calling ; for right will beget right, and as sure as God reigns in heaven, everything will beget its kind. If we want peace we must sow peace ; if we want war we must sow war, *"for whatever we sow of that shall we also reap."*

I had arranged eight of the following chapters in a book of twenty-one chapters, which were the 6, 7, 9, 10, 13, 17, 18, 19, therefore they will read somewhat awkwardly, as references are frequently made in those chapters to authors and chapters I have left to be published hereafter, though I altered them so as to chime in the best I could.

My Orthodox and Hicksite Quaker friends must pardon me for the chapter I have written on their connection with the causes of this bloody civil war, now devastating this great and glorious empire. I felt it a duty, as I had alluded to them in the first chapter without fully explaining my views of their character. A large part of the book was put in type in my absence from the city ; therefore some awkward blunders may have occurred in consequence, the book having been compiled from the whole manuscript a little hasty. I hope Chapter III. will be read by all good men and women.

CONTENTS.

CHAPTER I.

PAGE

Pictures of Slavery by Noah, Moses, and the other
Patriarchs 13

CHAPTER II.

Pictures of Slavery by St. Paul of the New Testament . 66

Nature of the Africans, in four letters . . . 131–155

CHAPTER III.

The Difference between Slave Negro Labor and Free
Negro Labor 168

CHAPTER IV.

ixing of blood between the White and Black Races
forbid by the Law of Nature and Nature's God . 223

CHAPTER V.

Who are Union Men and who are Anti-Union Men? . 247

CHAPTER VI.

What Connection had the Quakers or Friends with the
Instigators of the War? 293

(vii)

CHAPTER VII.

PAGE

Do as you would be done by 314

CHAPTER VIII.

Correspondence between Mrs. Mason, of Virginia, and
Mrs. Child, of Massachusetts 338

APPENDIX.

Ex-Senator Bigler's `Letters on the Crittenden Com-
promise, and Plan for Settlement . . . 374–382

SLAVERY AND ANTI-SLAVERY.

CHAPTER I.

The Moral Question of Slavery—Is Negro Slavery as it exists in the United States a Moral Evil?

THIS question has been discussed in the United States, pro and con, for nearly eighty-five years. I believe the Quakers were the first, as a Christian association, who took the idea that slavery was anti-christian. And, if I mistake not, their faith or moral notions on the subject was predicated upon a feeling that they would not (themselves) like to be slaves under negro masters. Therefore, they, as a religious society, abolished slavery among themselves in or about 1780. But the Orthodox or Foxites, as a religious association, has never interfered with other people's rights; that is, they have not united in political associations to oppose the institution of slavery as a civil institution. They only opposed it among themselves as a religious society; but left other people to do as they pleased. There was a split in the Society of Friends in 1827. Led by a certain man named Elias Hicks, who came out against the atonement of our Lord, and declared that his blood was

2   (13)

of no more account than that of a bull or ram. He diffused his infidelity through the minds of very many of that most excellent and influential Christian union. All of these, religious, ignorant, a sceptical, followed Elias Hicks in his treason and secession, and formed another association, and called themselves Friends, or Quakers—commonly known as Hicksites. This latter organization are generally Abolitionists of the Garrisonian school, and have formed associations to interfere with the civil and moral rights of others, even against constitutional laws. They have united with associations to form underground railroads, to run off slaves from their masters. Through this sham society called Quakers, the true Quakers, or Foxites, have been compelled to endure much persecution. In all external appearance, the Quakers and secessionists are similar; and the Orthodox or Foxites have been charged with all of their infidelity, for they call themselves the Society of Friends.

But the Hicksite Quakers are not the only class of men and women who have interfered with the legal institutions of other States. But every infidel association that has sprang into existence for the last fifty years has seized upon the negro slavery of the United States as a great and terrible moral evil. Men and women who were guilty of every kind of abomination, would seem to look upon the institution of negro slavery with horror, on account of the magnitude of its moral wickedness, and denounce Christian slaveholders as thieves, murderers, and robbers, and the Christian Church as the centre of all abominations, because slaveholders are admitted to their communions. Infidelity has assumed every shape and form known to skilful invention, through which they could bring the slightest influence to bear against Christianity. But no shape nor form of infidelity has yet been discovered that has answered their purposes so well as antislavery; therefore, all their associations have the antislavery link the most prominent. All, all of whom detest the Constitution, and the union of the United States. It would be impossible to enumerate the shapes and forms infidelity has taken within the last sixty or seventy years; all of which have been antislavery and antiunion in this country. And all the *isms* invented in New England in the last fifty years have placed their antislavery and antiunion principles at the head of the list.

Many associations have been formed within the borders of the Christian Church who affiliate with infidelity in their opposition to negro slavery, and in very many cases in their treason against the Constitution and the union of the United States, whose only object, I believe, has been to overthrow the Union. Therefore they have raised the antislavery standard above all others, and have such standard-bearers as Wendell Phillips, Rev. H. W. Beecher, Rev. Dr. Cheever, Rev. Dr. Thompson, Rev. Dr. Furness, Wm. Lloyd Garrison, Gerrett Smith, and many others who meet, shake hands, and call each other brother; and all unite with one accord in the denunciation of the Constitution and the union of the United States.

English infidelity has also denounced the Constitution and union of the United States with even greater venom than our native infidelity; and in every case the pretext has been a morbid sympathy for the poor slaves; all of which is to enlist the malice of mankind against the revealed will of heaven. Those demon-begotten spirits have in many instances assumed a profession of Christianity, and made their way into the Christian ministry, and become great sensation preachers in the Church of God, when their object was to be only half Christian, and the other half infidel, with a double purpose, one to destroy the union of States, and the other to get the people to support them while they were at it.

Many of those who have this morbid sympathy for the *poor slaves*, have long since renounced and denounced the Bible as an infernal book, simply because they could not twist it far enough from the truth, to make it condemn slavery. Now, without the Bible there is no moral law or guide. It is the only constitutional guide of the Christian Church, and the only revealed will of God to mankind, or that ever will be in this world. Yet these pretenders have become so tender on the sinfulness of slavery, that they justify and recommend the extermination of the whole white population of the slave States, and all others who attempt to defend them in their lawful rights, that the negro slaves may be freed, and placed on a social and civil equality with *We, the people!*

I will now undertake to prove from the only moral law or guide that ever has or ever will be given in this world, that slavery is not a moral evil. The

Bible is Jehovah's only revealed will to mankind; it contains all we ever have or ever shall have or know of the moral law, and he who attempts to teach from any other moral law, guide, or doctrines, "is a thief or robber." I will refer the reader to the *seal* of these truths, that he may be careful how he attempts to interfere with God's moral law and revealed will to mankind.

Rev. xxii. 18-19: "For I testify unto every man that heareth the words of the prophecy of this book, If any man shall add unto these things, God shall add unto him the plagues that are written in this book. And if any man shall take away from the words of the book of this prophecy, God shall take away his part out of the book of life, and out of the holy city, and *from* the things which are written in this book."

I presume no Christian, or even a pretending Christian, will attempt to deny that John, while exiled on the Isle of Patmos, wrote the above awful warning to the churches by inspiration. Yet we find many who profess to be called of God to preach his everlasting Gospel to a fallen world, and have been ordained and set apart for that holy and delicate cause, trying to darken counsel as revealed in the book of God, and preaching doctrines not revealed in that book, and denying others which are as clearly set forth, as that of profane swearing, lying, adultery, fornication, or drunkenness, is forbidden, and thereby thousands of the most ungodly and soul-destroying *isms* have been produced in the world—isms that have destroyed the sanctity of churches, ruined families, destroyed nations, and damned millions of souls. And none has been more delusive, deceptive, and destructive to both church and state in our beloved country, than the doctrine that *slavery is a moral evil, or sin against God.* There is no doctrine more clearly set forth in that book than the lawfulness of human slavery, except those in the Decalogue, and slavery is even set forth in that edict, or in the ten commandments; and the moral question is so clearly revealed, that no man who is fit to enter the sacred desk can possibly make a mistake, and be ignorant of such mistake on the moral question of slavery. Some ministers who have been ordained and set apart as expounders of God's holy law, for want of Scripture to condemn slavery as a moral evil, select passages entirely foreign, and apply them to slavery, such as oppression, when it is as clear that the relation of master and slave is not meant as it is that the relation of husband and wife, or parents and children are not meant. All are made precisely the same in morals, so far as the book of God teaches on the subject. But infidelity having but the one aim, and that is the overthrow of Christianity, they, like their great exemplar, the devil, are willing to give up this, the greatest boon ever bestowed on any nation (our independence) for the sake of overthrowing the book of God.

I will now proceed with my proofs.

Genesis ix. 20 to 27 inclusive: "And Noah began to be an husbandman, and he planted a vineyard. And he drank of the wine, and was drunken; and he was uncovered within his tent. And Ham, the father of Canaan, saw the nakedness of his father, and told his two brethren without. And Shem and Japheth took a garment, and laid *it* upon both their shoulders, and went backward, and covered the nakedness of their father; and their faces *were* backward, and they saw not their father's nakedness. And Noah awoke from his wine, and knew what his younger son had done unto him. And he said, Cursed *be* Canaan; a servant of servants shall he be unto his brethren. And he said, Blessed *be* the Lord God of Shem; and Canaan shall be his servant. God shall enlarge Japheth and he shall dwell in the tents of Shem; and Canaan shall be his servant."

Here we have the first introduction of slavery into our world, after the flood, at least. Abolitionists say that the Bible reading is servant, and not slave, and therefore Canaan was only made a hired servant. That servant merely meant a hireling, but we are told by the best linguists who have ever blessed society, that the original meant slave or bondservant, and ought to have been so translated. But as the word servant is accommodating and will represent a hired, or a bondservant, or slave, therefore the word servant was used by the translator. But it is too clear for cavil, in both the Old and New Testament Scriptures, that bondservant and hired servant were two distinct conditions of labor, and the former was the curse that was put upon Canaan for bad treatment to his old grandfather while in an unfortunate condition. It is said that Noah "planted a vineyard, and he drank of the wine, and was drunken;" it is believed that this was the first wine ever made, and Noah not knowing its intoxicating properties made himself drunken. It is the only account given of his ever being drunk. Some people ask, What power there could have been in the words of Noah as above quoted, upon Canaan and his posterity through all future time? I will answer, that what Noah said was merely prophetic, and that it was *God* who imposed the curse upon that unfortunate race. *Therefore slavery is a divine institution,* which I think I shall make clear to every sincere truth seeker.

Some ask why God should have been so cruel to that race of mankind. If I had lived before the Supreme Being, and above him, and could have looked forward to the end of all things like he did, I could, perhaps, tell why he did it; as it is, I cannot. But no doubt it was done for the good of man. I will offer a few ideas on this point. Adam disobeyed God in one single (and it would seem an almost innocent) matter; but yet he was expelled from Eden, he and his entire posterity cursed with a thousand times more sickening and terrible curse than was Canaan and his posterity. Yet every true man will see that Ham's crime was a thousand times more flagitious. It is believed by most commentators that Ham's son Canaan was with him when he discovered his old and respected father in such an unfortunate condition, and joined him in telling it to all they met; and, perhaps, that while Ham felt a deep vindictive contempt towards his old father, when he, as a dutiful son, should have pitied the good old patriarch, and hastened to have covered him from the public gaze, and cautioned his son Canaan not to tell it even to his best friend, that his father might not be disgraced before the public, and that future generations might not feel justified in drunkenness, because the old patriarch got drunk through *ignorance*, he run off and published it to his brethren.

I am asked why Canaan was cursed instead of his father Ham? I will say that, perhaps, if Ham had been cursed, all his posterity would have felt the weight of the displeasure of Almighty God, and the innocent would have suffered for the guilty. The whole human family have suffered from the foundation of the world, because of Adam's disobedience, and will suffer through all time, and unless they are saved through the atonement of our Lord, they will have to suffer through all eternity. The reason for believing that Canaan was with his father Ham, when he discovered his father Noah lying uncovered in his tent, we read from the 22d verse: "And Ham the father of Canaan saw," &c. If Canaan was not with his father, why should his name have been mentioned in that connection? Japheth and Shem had sons, no doubt, but no allusion was made to them whatever. I cannot see how any sincere truth seeker can doubt that idea, when taken in connection with the fact that the terrible sentence was passed upon Canaan, instead of his father. As I have already said, if Ham had been cursed, his whole posterity would have been slaves through all time, and that would have been unjust. And when we remember that God could not do an unjust act, and will not punish the innocent, we must believe that Canaan had something to do with that great disrespect to the old patriarch.

"And Ham, the father of Canaan, saw the nakedness of his father and told his two brethren without."

22d verse clearly demonstrates the duty of children to parents under every circumstance of this life, which moral law has never been revoked by any decree of heaven. Shem and Japheth had the blessing of their father bestowed upon them both, while Ham was left out in the cold, without the warming influence of his father's blessing to cheer his drooping spirits at the grave of his sire. But Canaan was thus cursed with the most obnoxious judgment of any other physical stain ever inflicted upon man since the fall from Eden. A curse that is and will be unchangeable this side of the grave. No, "no Jewish type or sprinkling priest can ever wash the stain away." By the disobedience of Adam to his heavenly Father, all wickedness, all hardness, and all that afflicts the soul, body, or spirit, entered into the world, and fell upon the whole human family, yea, every unpleasant sensation, and all that disturbs union, peace, harmony, and tranquillity; even slavery and abolitionism are all, all the consequences of his disobedience to his Great Sire. Had he been obedient he would now live among us in all the vigor of youth and beauty that he possessed before the fall. So also if Ham and his son Canaan had been true to their father and grand-father, there would have been no slaves nor negroes in this world of ours.

24th verse says, "Noah awoke from his wine, and knew what his younger son had done unto him," and pronounced the unchangeable judgment recorded in the 25th verse, which sentence was divine, as I shall show. How "Noah knew what Ham had done unto him," we are not informed by the inspired penman. Some commentators suppose he was informed by his two eldest sons. And others suppose he knew it by inspiration. How he got the facts, is immaterial; he knew it in some way; therefore the terrible sentence fell upon the right one. Ham was not exempt from the effects of divine displeasure, nor was any of his family, or their posterity. But none was made slaves except Canaan and his descendants; "a servant of servants." The reader will see that Canaan was not only a servant to his brethren, *but a servant of their servants.* It is, therefore, evident that he was placed far below hired servants. Dr. Hales says, "Ham signifies burnt, or black." Therefore his name was significant. Ham, nor his son was not cursed, because Noah pronounced those words against them. But because of the magnitude of their crime. The words of Noah being prophetic only, therefore what he said had no influence whatever upon the physical appearance, or character of those culprits, or their posterity. It was the just judgment of God for their crime against the old patriarch, who was their temporal parent. But Shem and Japheth took a garment, and covered the nakedness of their father, without looking upon him, as every good child would. Therefore a blessing was pronounced upon them. Now the declaration of Noah had no influence whatever upon the lives and characters of his two elder sons, or their posterity, but simply a prophecy, and just as sure as the prophecy was fulfilled in the latter, so it has been in the former, and will continue to be until the end of time.

I do not say that the curse was a spiritual one pronounced against Canaan, for it was not; but was to affect his civil liberty, and his physical appearance, and that of his posterity for ever. None of the descendants of Ham had any permanent abiding place in this world, but were driven about at the pleasure of their brethren, the descendants of Shem and Japheth. Neither does it appear that Canaan was directly enslaved to his brethren; but the process of preparation for bondage was commenced immediately on the pronunciation of the sentence for bondage, and went on through successive generations until they were completely prepared for the yoke. And then to be bond-servants was the greatest blessing that man could bestow upon them, and is so until this day, and will be so through all time to come. This bondage does not interfere with their spiritual liberty and salvation through the atonement, and no doubt millions of that race have embraced it. But that will not alter their relations in this world. There seems to be some hope for them in the Liberian Colony on the coast of Africa. Yet I fear it will prove a failure, though the climate is in their favor, as it naturally forbids the residence of the whites there, by a prohibitory law that is insurmountable, and perhaps unchangeable. But when the influence of the Anglo-saxon races shall be entirely withdrawn from the colonies, the great probability is they will sink into their original heathenism and barbarism. They are the only tribes on the earth that can be easily reduced to slavery, and who prosper and improve best under the yoke of bondage. But I do not wish to discourage the experiment being fully tried in Liberia, for if there is any degree of freedom for them in this world, it is there, and only there.

The Chinese are made slaves in the tropical regions, or the West India Islands, but two-thirds of them die off prematurely. The Cooleys are being brought in large numbers and sold into bondage on all those Islands for a term of about eight years, and perhaps the half of them die off before they are free, and those who live the eight years have not life enough left in them to enable them to procure a livelihood. But the Africans are greatly improved by the yoke of bondage in all parts of the world, and especially in the sunny climes of the torrid zones, and they become vigorous, strong, lively, happy, and long lived in the low hot climates. While those climates positively forbid constant labor in the sun by any other tribes or colors on the face of the globe, and as it is evident beyond all cavil, that the Africans are entirely useless in this world in any other capacity but slavery. And they are found to be the only persons among all the tribes of earth, who can labor constantly and improve in their moral and physical health by having good masters who hold them for life in those climes. I say they can toil in those climates without the least inconvenience, and with such great benefit to themselves, and such vast profit and advantage to the whole civilized world. I ask, would it be right

3

under these circumstances for those climates to be abandoned that produce such blessings to the world, and be forever lost, both in Europe and America, as well as in Africa, when they have proved a blessing through African slavery, of such magnitude to the world, and to none more than the African laborer himself. One of the most important points in this matter is, to show us that children must be respectful to their parents in and under ·all circumstances in this life. One of the commandments says, "Honor thy father and thy mother; that thy days may be long upon the land which the Lord thy God giveth thee."—Ex. xx. 12. Disobedience was the crime which produced all the afflictions known in this world since its creation, and turned a glorious paradise of order and beauty into one perpetual heap of corruption, confusion, and ruin. Therefore other laws equally strict become necessary for the government of this fallen world; and the one above stands next in importance, and equal to the preceding ones of the ten commandments. And Ham and his descendants, especially those through the lineage of his son Canaan, are marks of the displeasure of the Divine Being towards the disobedience of children to their parents, and they are this day moving, living, hearing, and talking monuments of his displeasure towards disobedient children to parents. I am asked why I set the Africans down as the descendants of Ham? It is evident from history, both sacred and profane, that they are the true descendants of Ham, through Canaan. I refer the reader to Drs. Clarke, Benson, Watson, and other divine commentators of the highest standing, and all the best authors who have written on the subject. The sacred text is too clear to be misunderstood on that point.

26th verse: "And he said, Blessed *be* the Lord God of Shem; and Canaan shall be his servant." 27th verse: "God shall enlarge Japheth, and he shall dwell in the tents of Shem; and Canaan shall be his servant."

These words are so significant that comments are unnecessary to prove that slavery was divinely authorized, so far as Canaan and his posterity were concerned. He had no part in his father's blessings given before his death, only as an underling or subordinate.

Genesis xvii. 13: "He that is born in thy house, and he that is bought with thy money, must needs be circumcised."

This text shows that the buying and selling of human beings as chattels was justified by law both sacred and civil. This was four hundred and fifty years after Noah pronounced the awful sentence against Canaan. This shows that Abraham did not only hold slaves, but bought them for his own use. And the old patriarch expresses no misgivings on the subject or moral question of slavery.

Genesis xx. 14: "And Abimelech took sheep, and oxen, and men-servants, and women-servants, and gave them unto Abraham."

Abraham did not hesitate to receive slaves as presents at that time, nor at any other time, though presented by a heathen as Abimelech was. He expressed no conscientious scruples whatever about holding

them as property, chattels, whether purchased or presented, *and yet he held converse with angels.* And they
gave him no intimation that it was an infringement
on the moral law. If slavery was sin against God or
man, then angels must have been very remiss in not
informing the old patriarch, out of whose lineage
the Son of God was to appear, when he stood alone
with them in the mountain and in his tent. And
the patriarch was very humble before the sacred
visitors, and obedient to a letter; yet no instruction
was given him on the sin of slavery. Moses, four
hundred and six years subsequent to Abraham's
connection with slavery, held converse with the
Almighty himself, among the thunderings of the
mountains, and there received the whole moral law;
and in the 17th verse of the xx. of Exodus, we have
the following:—

"Thou shalt not covet thy neighbor's wife, nor his man-
servant, nor his maid-servant, nor his ox, nor his ass, nor any
thing that *is* thy neighbor's."

In the ten commandments the whole moral law
was written, and slavery is mentioned, as quoted
above from 17th verse; and it covers the entire
moral ground until this day. And it stands in full
force, for our Lord and his holy apostles brought the
whole Decalogue forward into the Christian Dispensation, and reindorsed the whole Decalogue with the
tenth commandment, as above quoted. And in that
slavery is completely indorsed and sanctioned. And
in all that mighty thundering, lightning, and alarm,
that was to prepare Moses to receive the law, and
bow obedience to every sacred edict that should be

handed over for the government of the world. And yet the Supreme Being did not utter one word against the institution of slavery. What a pity the Rev. H. W. Beecher, Dr. Cheever, Wendell Phillips, or some other apostle of universal freedom and equal rights, had not been there to have reminded the Almighty that his people had enslaved the Canaanites, and that it was an abomination in his sight, and that he must annul the cursed institution! What troubles they would have saved us in the United States! I will refer the reader to Genesis xxiv. the latter part of the 2d and the 3d verses, to show you that Abraham would not associate with the descendants of Canaan, because they were an accursed race, and Abraham knew it. He knew also that it would be inconsistent with prudence and policy, as well as the design of the divine Being, to have united the child of promise to one of a cursed race, though that curse was only a physical and a political one.

"Put, I pray thee, thy hand under my thigh; And I will make thee swear by the Lord, the God of heaven, and the God of the earth, and thou shalt not take a wife unto my son of the daughters of the Canaanites, among whom I dwell." The 4th verse: "But thou shalt go unto my country, and to my kindred, and take a wife unto my son Isaac."

Now, why was Abraham so afraid of the Canaanites? Shem was an own brother of Ham, the father of Canaan. And on what account was he so particular as to swear his servant by one of the most binding oaths, not to take a wife unto his son Isaac from the Canaanites, among whom he was living, and who he refused to acknowledge as his kin, but

sent him away into a far country, to a city called
Nahor, in Mesopotamia, among the descendants of
Shem, to get a wife for his son? Because he knew
the Canaanites were cursed physically and politically,
and destined for slaves forever. Abraham was a
slave-owner at this time. It was slaves he sent in
pursuit of a wife for his son.

Genesis xvii. 23: "And Abraham took Ishmael his son, and
all that were born in his house, and all that were *bought with
his money*, every male among the men of Abraham's house,
and circumcised the flesh of their foreskin in the self-same day,
as God had said unto him."

It seems clear that God commanded Abraham
in this verse to circumcise his slaves (for he had
bought them with his money), and yet that great and
eternal Being expresses no dissatisfaction at the
institution of slavery. The abolitionists say it was
a different kind of slavery then from what it is now.
I would like them tell how different, for they were
bought, sold, and held as chattels just as they are
now. But they say, they were then white men. I
have some doubt about that; and suppose they were,
is it any worse to hold a negro in slavery than it is
a white man? I have not the slightest doubt but
that all the race was white until after the confusion
of tongues, at the building of the Tower of Babel,
which was one hundred and one years after Canaan
was cursed; and, until after the dispersion, I have
little or no doubt that the most of the slaves were
Canaanites. We see from Genesis xxvi. 25, that
Isaac was also a slaveholder. Look again at Genesis xxxii. 22, "And he rose up that night, and took

his two wives, and his two women-servants." So we see that Jacob was a slaveholder also. Pharaoh was a large slaveholder, as we see in many places. Ex. ix. 20th to 34th verses. They seemed to be put on an equality with cattle, as they often were, by even the Israelites. The Israelites were all slaves at this time, except Moses and Aaron. And how came it that such special effort was made to free them from bondage, where they had been for so long a time, and not the slightest counsel given to free the Canaanites at any time, or any part of them? And no prophetic vision alludes to any time or place in which, or at which time, they are to be free.

I will here put forth a little prophecy, and I hope it will not be forgotten. Whenever the abolitionists shall get sufficient power to amend the Constitution of the United States, and abolish slavery, our glory will end as a prosperous nation, and we shall be cursed from that very hour, as the British, French, and Spanish provinces were and are, by the universal emancipation of their slaves. And notwithstanding the mighty and untiring efforts of the British missionaries with the Bible and gold, the slaves have already sunk quite as low as they are in the interior of Africa, and nothing but the sight of a standing army prevents them from becoming as barbarous as they were in their native territory; and a standing army will have ever to be kept on their account. And from the very day they are all freed here, the reign of terror will set in, and a military despotism will have to be established that will of necessity have to be of greater magnitude than any other on the face of the earth.

Look again at Exodus xxi. 2: "If thou buy an Hebrew servant, six years he shall serve; and in the seventh he shall go out free for nothing." This passage is often quoted by antislavery men in great boast, because they say it proves that slaves could not be held over six years under this law. It is true so far as the Hebrew slaves were concerned; and the sacred Legislator is very particular to make this special provision for the Hebrews, and doubtless because they were the heirs of promise, and had not committed an unpardonable national or domestic sin, as Canaan had done; nor had they been condemned and sentenced to everlasting slavery.

Ex. xxi. 3: "If he came in by himself, he shall go out by himself; if he were married, then his wife shall go out with him.

4. If his master have given him a wife, and she have borne him sons or daughters; the wife and her children shall be her master's and he shall go out by himself.

5. And if the servant shall plainly say, I love my master, my wife, and my children; I will not go out free:

6. Then his master shall bring him unto the judges; he shall also bring him to the door, or unto the door-post; and his master shall bore his ear through with an awl; and he shall serve him for ever."

It is clear, from the above passages, that the wife given to a Hebrew slave, was a slave for life, and also her children, and, of course, she was a Canaanitish woman, or she could not have been held for life. If she had not been, she and her children could have gone out with the husband and father. And if Abraham had allowed his servant to have taken a wife to his son Isaac from among the Canaanites, his children by her would have at least been like the Ishmaelites, and the lineage` of Isaac would have been a curse to the world the same as the Ishmaelites, instead of being a blessing. And, no doubt, his servants, who he sent out to seek a wife for Isaac, were all of the heathen around about; in other words, Canaanites. Therefore the necessity for the strong oath which was administered to them, and the positive charge not to take a wife for Isaac from that race, who had been sentenced to perpetual slavery. Had these servants not have been Canaanites, there would have been no need of such binding oaths. But from the above text we learn that a Hebrew slave could be held for life by his own consent, and only by his own free consent and choice. And when his ear was once bored through, according to law, his condition was then fixed for life, and he was then a bond-servant, and was treated as such, and not as a hired servant, as before that act, even if his wife and children died the next day. In Lev. xix. 20, we are told that if any man have carnal intercourse with a bondmaid, who was betrothed, she should be scourged but should not be put to death like the Hebrew women, because she was not free, and had no power to resist; clearly setting forth that she was not her own, and was treated altogether different from the Hebrews, for the same crime. Lev. xxii. 10, hired servants are spoken of, and we are told in the 11th verse, a priest was justified in purchasing slaves with his money, and deal in human beings. Lev. xxv. 38th to the 55th inclusive.

These 17 verses ought to settle the whole question, for it is given as the word of the Lord. I will give the whole passage for the convenience of the reader, and I think it ought to end all cavil among Christians. But if it should be twisted to mean something else, I think the doctrines of salvation by repentance and faith may be twisted into some other meaning, and the moral influence of the whole book of God will turn to nought. Some professing Christians have said to me, if such declarations were in the Bible as I stated to them, they would dash it from their houses, as an infernal book. I pity such professors, but they must suffer the consequences of their own fanatical prejudices. The passage says:—

" 38. I *am* the Lord your God, which brought you forth out of the land of Egypt, to give you the land of Canaan, *and* to be your God.

39. And if thy brother *that dwelleth* by thee be waxen poor, and be sold unto thee, thou shalt not compel him to serve as a bond-servant:

40. *But* as an hired servant, *and* as a sojourner, he shall be with thee, *and* shall serve thee unto the year of jubilee:

41. And *then* shall he depart from thee, *both* he and his children with him, and shall return unto his own family, and unto the possession of his fathers shall he return.

42. For they *are* my servants, which I brought forth out of the land of Egypt: they shall not be sold as bondmen.

43. Thou shalt not rule over him with rigor, but shalt fear thy God.

44. Both thy bondmen, and thy bondmaids, which thou shalt

have, *shall be* of the heathen that are round about you, of them shall ye buy bondmen and bondmaids.

45. Moreover, of the children of the strangers that do sojourn among you, of them shall ye buy, and of their families that *are* with you, which they begat in your land: and they shall be your possession.

46. And ye shall take them as an inheritance for your children after you, to inherit *them for* a possession; they shall be your bondmen for ever: but over your brethren, the children of Israel, ye shall not rule one over another with rigor.

47. And if a sojourner or stranger wax rich by thee, and thy brother *that dwelleth* by him wax poor, and sell himself unto the stranger *or* sojourner by thee, or to the stock of the stranger's family:

48. After that he is sold he may be redeemed again; one of his brethren may redeem him:

49. Either his uncle, or his uncle's son, may redeem him, or *any* that is nigh of kin unto him of his family may redeem him, or, if he be able, he may redeem himself.

50. And he shall reckon with him that bought him from the year that he was sold to him unto the year of jubilee: and the price of his sale shall be according unto the number of years; according to the time of an hired servant shall it be with him.

51. If *there be* yet many years *behind*, according unto them he shall give again the price of his redemption out of the money that he was bought for.

52. And if there remain but few years unto the year of jubilee, then he shall count with him, *and* according unto his years shall he give him again the price of his redemption.

53. *And* as a yearly hired servant shall he be with him: *and the other* shall not rule with rigor over him in thy sight.

54. And if he be not redeemed in these *years*, then he shall go out in the year of jubilee *both* he, and his children with him.

55. For unto me the children of Israel *are* servants; they *are* my servants, whom I brought forth out of Egypt: I *am* the Lord your God."

No sincere seeker of the truth will deny that the above quotations are the words of the Lord. For the 38th says, *I am the Lord your God*, the 39th to the 43d show us that the descendants of Shem cannot be made slaves or bond-servants, *absolutely*, without incurring the displeasure of the Supreme Being. They are in no way adapted for bond-servants. They were not made for slaves, and cannot be enslaved without their own consent, and when they were taken and sold on account of their poverty or any other cause, the master or purchaser is ordered by God himself to treat them as hired servants, and they are forbid to rule over them with rigor; but that they should treat them as their brethren, because they were of the heirs of promise, and the children of Israel, who were their equals in his sight, even if they were poor. And if one should by chance fall into the hands of a stranger or heathen, in other words, a Canaanite, that may be in their midst, every means should be used to free him at once if the money could be raised for that purpose. His kin are called upon to redeem him, but *not* without paying the full cost or amount of purchase to this heathen (I hope the abolitionists will notice this). Although it seemed to disturb even the Almighty for one of his redeemed children to be a slave to one who was of the Canaanites, and a cursed race, and unlawful for them to hold Israelites as bond-servants for any time. Yet the sacred-law giver made it imperative that the whole purchase money should be returned to this heathen master, after deducting the earnings of the Hebrew servants up to the time of his redemption. But in case the money could not be raised to redeem him, he was to go out free at the jubilee; which was every fiftieth year.

There is not a more beautiful lesson in the whole moral code. The Almighty does not sanction the taking of any man's property from him without giving him the value of it. Though it was not lawful for a stranger to hold a Jew in slavery, yet he had got him honestly, and the just law of God would not allow him to be taken away from his master without returning his money to him. (O abolitionist! where wilt thou stand in the great day of God?) These are the laws of God, and any individual, association, or nation, even in this day of our Lord, will be overthrown, who attempts to grapple with them; and any nation that shall sanction the holding of the Caucasians, Celts, or Anglo-Saxons in slavery, without their own free consent and agreement, are grappling with the righteous laws of heaven, and will ever be in trouble, for the just judgments of the Almighty will rest upon them, and a tyrant shall reign over them, and uncertainties shall surround them day and night; for the white people are the descendants of God's people, whom he brought forth out of bondage by a mighty arm. But the holding of slaves is fully sanctioned by the Supreme Lawgiver in the 44th, 45th, and 46th verses. But they were to be of the strangers or heathen, who were the descendants of Canaan, on whom the terrible sentence was pronounced eight hundred and fifty-six years before.

It is evident from God's own words that no part

4

of the sentence had been modified or abated down to that day—neither has it been down to this date. The difference between a hired and a bond-servant is fully set forth in the quotations I have made from this chapter.

This arrangement of God for the government of the world is a just one, and woe be unto the church or nation that shall attempt to revoke the decrees that the great I Am has put his seal to. The Africans are the strangers or descendants of the heathen that were around about; they are the Canaanites who are useful as slaves only. God has so arranged the nature of the Canaanites or Africans, so that there can be no mistakes made. The marks are such that they cannot be mistaken, day or night; and the natural laws that designate them from the descendants of Shem are unchangeable, and God has so made them that no mistakes might occur. Therefore, every attempt to free them and place them on an equality with the people of God, or the whites, must be wilful. And whenever it shall be done in this country, woe be unto us, for our glory will pass from us as soon as it is done; and every step we take towards that achievement is a step towards the complete overthrow of this national government, just so sure as God gave the above laws. No white race has ever yet taken the Africans on an equality who did not sink down to their level.

I shall say enough on the incompetency of the African race for self-government in another chapter, and their level when left to themselves with the power in their hands. In that we can read our doom whenever universal emancipation shall prevail in this whole country; and then our steps cannot be retraced. The 55th verse seems to seal the law, and shows clearly that the whole seventeen verses quoted were especially in accordance with divine wisdom. There was very special pains taken in this chapter to show who was lawfully set apart for bond-servants forever, and who were to be their temporal masters, without limit; for no time for their freedom is mentioned, or even intimated, nor can be inferred.

The reasons are again repeated in the last verse why the children of Israel should be treated as hired servants (when they were unfortunate, and fell victims to the law of slavery), and not as slaves. And they were, because he (the Lord) had redeemed them from perpetual slavery. They (Israel) had been made long before the children of promise, and whose numbers should be great that they might be a blessing to all the nations of the world. But the Canaanites had no promise of a temporal redemption, neither have they ever been redeemed, nor they will not be in this world. And every official effort to redeem them, will only make their condition worse, for God has set his seal against it, and put an irrevocable and a prohibitory mark upon them so that they cannot be redeemed; and if we attempt to do it, we shall be sunk far below the level of our southern slaves, for the Almighty will not allow us to tamper with his laws with impunity.

In this chapter the line is completely drawn between the children of promise and that accursed race. Though the service of the Hebrews was some-

times long to the jubilee when they happened to be
made slaves, but their redemption at the jubilee
was typical of the redemption from the corruptions
of the fall from Eden; by the Son of God, which is
a spiritual redemption, and all who will accept shall
be made spiritually free, whether bond or free; but
their temporal relations will not be changed, yet
both will be greatly improved by it. A heathen
could not be a type of the promised spiritual redemption by the gift of God's only Son. But they
are a type of all who shall reject the offer of spiritual
salvation through Jesus Christ our Lord, whether
bond or free, black or white, and no more changes
will be made in this world by divine sanction, and
just so far as we attempt to grapple with the laws
of nature, and nature's God, we shall be left to ourselves, and we shall be cursed just in proportion to
our interference with the laws of nature. Slavery
did not then bind a man's soul, and does not now.
A real pious slave ought to be the happiest person
on earth, for he has no worldly cares to trouble him.
No matter if he should have a wife and twelve
children, and be sick, he has no concern about them,
for he knows they are fully provided for. And
they have none of the annoyances or perplexities
the free people have, of either color.

Deut. v. 14th: "But the seventh day *is* the sabbath of the
Lord thy God: *in it* thou shalt not do any work, thou, nor
thy son, nor thy daughter, nor thy man-servant, nor thy maid-
servant, nor thine ox, nor thine ass, nor any of thy cattle, nor
thy stranger that *is* within thy gates; that thy man-servant
and thy maid-servant may rest as well as thou."

This command was given forty years later to slave-holders, and none are so especially mentioned in the command or edict as the slaves, showing that the master had the same power over them that he had over all his beasts of burthen, and it seems that the last clause of this article was inserted into the moral law for the protection of the slaves, they having no natural or lawful rights to protect them from over-burden and imposition, and to prevent the welfare of the slaves being lost sight of by their owners, and woe be unto that master or mistress who shall look upon their servants as beasts of burden only, especially under gospel dispensation. If they do, the Almighty will look upon them as traitors to his moral government, and treat them as such in the great day of reckoning. They are reminded in the 15th of the same chapter that they were once slaves in Egypt.

21st. " Neither shalt thou desire thy neighbor's wife, neither shalt thou covet thy neighbor's house, his field, or his man-servant, or his maid-servant, his ox, or his ass, or any *thing* that is thy neighbor's."

This text differs slightly from the tenth command-ment; in that the field is not mentioned, and this al-most complete repetition by the *Sacred Law-giver* forty years after writing the Decalogue, shows clearly that no change had taken place in his mind on the sub-ject of slavery; and eight hundred and ninety-seven years after Canaan had been sentenced to perpetual slavery, so far as moral, and civil law, written by Moses goes, the moral question of slavery was fully

4*

settled. If there had been some Charles Sumner, T. Stevens, H. Beecher, Dr. Furnace, or any one of the apostles of abolitionism, to have translated the words of the Lord to Moses, amid all that thundering and lightning in the mountain, or to have told the King of kings that he was committing a great and fatal error, what a world of trouble they might have saved us if there was any mistake! In the 14th of the xxi. of Deut. it is strongly inferred that the Israelites did buy and sell human slaves as chattels, by forbidding a husband to make merchandise of his own wife, though she was a heathen. Deut. xxiii. 15–16 verses, seem to forbid the return of a slave to his master; but must have been under some peculiar circumstances; and the only circumstance under which slaves were forbid to be delivered up to their master. And I believe the only passage or text we have on record, which in any way forbids an unconditional surrender of slaves to their legal owner. It is the only one at least quoted by the celebrated abolitionist, Mrs. Childs, of Mass., in her long letter to Mrs. Senator Mason, of Virginia, published January 7th, 1860, in the Philadelphia Ledger. She gave about eighteen passages, only two of which had any allusion to slavery, whatever; and among them was this passage, and the precept of our Lord in Matthew: "Do as you would be done by." And seemed to think she had gained a great victory over Mrs. *Senator* Mason. She was careful not to quote any of the many passages so directly to the point. Dr. Adam Clarke says in his comment on those two verses—

"Thou shalt not deliver the servant which is escaped unto thee." "That is, a servant who left an idolatrous master that he might join himself to God and to his people. In any other case, it would have been injustice to have harbored the runaway."

Dr. Adam Clarke was a native of Ireland, and never was in this country, and was looked upon even by the British government as one of the most profound linguists on the earth, and by all as a man of mighty powers of mind, and of the deepest piety, and was esteemed by all good men in both church and state; and, I think, his opinions ought to be respected. Though he said, on a passage in the New Testament, something like the following: The pains of hell are not adequate to the crime of slavery; in this declaration he must have alluded to some special act of slavery; perhaps the slave trade that was being carried on by the British government at that time on an enormous scale. For on all other passages he clearly shows that slavery was fully justified by both the Old and New Testament Scriptures.

The above severe remarks of Dr. Clarke are quoted by abolitionists everywhere; but they are very careful to quote no other passage from his extended commentary on slavery as set forth in the Bible. And the same course is pursued about what the Rev. John Wesley said on the slave trade, or the crimes so often committed in connection with it by cruel and hard-hearted men. Those declarations are quoted everywhere by antislavery men and women; but they are very careful never to allude to his having so frequently after that baptized the children of slaveholders, and even licensed slaveholders to exhort in the church, and admitted them to the sacraments in the West Indies, and never after he visited the United States of America, and saw for himself the condition of master and slave, did he utter one word against receiving slaveholders into the Church of God.

It is evident from the passage above, that the escaped slaves were descendants of Shem, though this text does not say.   But every article in the law written prior and subsequent proves beyond a doubt that it was Israelites, who perhaps had been taken in war by the heathen, and then escaped and returned to their brethren.   Therefore they were not to be delivered up.   I think the above quotations ought and will satisfy every candid and unprejudiced mind, they all being taken from the heads of moral departments.   I will quote a few more passages, however, from the Old Testament, and say something about the Ishmaelites, to show that even those that mix blood with the Canaanites have never done but little or no good in this world; or, in other words, those sections of the globe occupied by them exclusively—I mean, wherever they have the government in their own hands.   It is clear that the African negroes are the true and unadulterated descendants of Canaan, and the children of all those that intermarried or otherwise mixed kin with them are this day to a greater or less extent under the curse that was passed upon Canaan four thousand two hundred and nine years ago, and perhaps are colored just in proportion to that mixture or kin. Benson said: "The Phœnicians and Carthagenians are also included in the curse denounced on Canaan, for they descended from him, and were both subdued by the Greeks and Romans with dreadful destruction, and made tributary to them." This was four hundred and thirty-six years after the curse was denounced on Canaan by his grandfather, Noah, and after Abram and Sarai had left Egypt with all their property, and the presents given them by Pharoah, among which were slaves, and perhaps of both sexes, and, no doubt, Hagar was one of them, for she was an Egyptian slave, and doubtless a Canaanite, for the descendants of Shem and Japheth could not be made slaves at pleasure, and especially those in the lineage of Shem. As we have heretofore shown, the Egyptian slaves were bond slaves, while all others were hired servants, or treated as such, and were not held for life, except by mutual agreement.

Genesis xvi. 1. "Now Sarai, Abram's wife, bare him no children: and she had an handmaid, an Egyptian, whose name was Hagar."

So we see she was an Egyptian slave, and at that time concubinage was tolerated by both civil and moral law. Therefore Sarai would have had a perfect right to have made an agreement with her husband to give her an heir by some other woman. But in this case she was doubting the promise, and even if she had not doubted, she had no right to have an heir through a cursed race, and a heathen; and we see as soon as this thing was agreed upon between Sarai and Abraham, and Hagar had conceived, that trouble set in between Sarai and Hagar, and even between Sarai and Abraham; and the consequence was Hagar was driven off, and she fled to the wilderness.

Gen. xvi. 7. "And the angel of the Lord found her by a fountain of water in the wilderness, by the fountain in the way to Shur.

8. And he said, Hagar, Sarai's maid, whence camest thou? and whither wilt thou go? And she said, I flee from the face of my mistress Sarai.

9. And the angel of the Lord said unto her, Return to thy mistress, and submit thyself under her hands.

10. And the angel of the Lord said unto her, I will multiply thy seed exceedingly, that it shall not be numbered for multitude.

11. And the angel of the Lord said unto her, Behold, thou *art* with child, and shalt bear a son, and shalt call his name Ishmael; because the Lord hath heard thy affliction.

12. And he will be a wild man; his hand *will be* against every man, and every man's hand against him; and he shall dwell in the presence of all his brethren."

In the first place we are taught by the angel of God in these passages, the right of property in men and women as slaves; see 9th verse. Now was this a divine or human law? If slavery be a sin against God, was not this a befitting time to have made it known? Here was a messenger directly from the throne of the eternal God; yet he utters not one word against the institution of slavery. But tells Hagar to return to her mistress, and to submit herself under her hands. The anti-slavery man says this was under the old law, when God winked at sin. But what law of earth has God and holy angels ever been governed by? This is simply preposterous. They say adultery and fornication was then allowed as well as slavery—which are forbidden under the new law. I will show you when I get into the New Testament, that the two former are positively forbidden, and slavery allowed, and not one word uttered against it in any way. In the 12th verse the angel told Hagar her child should be a wild man, "and his hand should be against every man, and every man's hand against him," and that he should "dwell in the presence of his brethren. It has now been thirty-seven hundred and seventy years since the angel talked with Hagar as above; and from thence unto the present day, the descendants of Ishmael have been against every man, and every man has been against them. And what is their present condition and their location? We find them now located in a section of country, a large territory which stretches from Aleppo to the Arabian Sea, and from Egypt to the Persian Gulf; containing about one million six hundred and twenty thousand square miles, where they have dwelt together for thousands of years. God himself has sent them out free, because they were kin to the children of promise, and therefore could not be made slaves of any kind, either bond or hired. They are divided into twelve tribes and are circumcised, and marry among themselves same as the Jews. They are loose from all political restraint. The wilderness is their habitation, and in a land where no other human beings can live, they have their homes, but no fixed habitations. They com-

mit depredations on all the cities and towns near
their borders. They are universally thieves, robbers, and murderers; after committing their depre-
dation, they can retire into the desert with such
precipitancy that they cannot be caught. Their
fleetness is almost equal to the gray hound. The
Abyssinians, Persians, Egyptians, and Turks have
endeavored to subjugate those Bedouin Arabs, and
sometimes they have thought they were going to
have full success, but ultimately all was abortive.
And from the beginning to the present day they
have maintained their independence; and they remain as living and moving monuments of the truth
of the Holy Scriptures, and of the disapprobation
of God to any mixture of blood with the descendant
of Canaan. All, because Ham made fun of his
father Noah, while prostrated in his tent beneath a
misfortune.

I shall speak of the mulattoes of this country in
another chapter, and show you that the curse of
God is still upon any mixture between the true descendants of Shem, and those of Ham through the
lineage of Canaan. I hope the reader will examine
the xvi. chapter of Gen., and read Clarke's views
on it. What use have those wild Arabs been to the
world? Where have they done any good? What
nation, or tribe, or spot, on this earth has been in
any way benefited by them? None, whatever. Yet
they are descendants of Abraham, as well as the
Jews; but, unfortunately, through a Canaanitish
woman and a cursed slave. The only benefit the
Arabs have been, or perhaps ever will be, is as a

warning to all men not to interfere with divine decrees, and the arrangements of his government by which he intended to govern the world. Abraham was severely punished by the trouble he was thrown into with Sarai—through her slave Hagar. The pure descendants of Canaan are very useful to the whole world as slaves, but in no other capacity. And slavery is as great a blessing to the African in the United States as Christianity is to a heathen, and is so in their native Africa, though to a much less extent, and altogether in a temporal way. And whenever we, as a nation, which God has chosen as his agents and guardians to take care of a part of those descendants of Ham, and to make them useful to him in the world, and to teach them Christianity and the way of life here and hereafter, shall set them all at liberty, his curse will be upon us from that day in which it shall be done, and we shall feel the weight of his hand until the end of time, in some way that will destroy our peace and happiness, as a nation and people; and this country and nation that was intended to be as the ante-chamber of heaven, will be thrown into confusion, tumults and ruin. As I have said much on this point in another place, I will now only ask what would become of us, if four or five millions more slaves were turned loose upon us, *and what would become of them?*

There was a striking difference between hired servants and bond servants. To oppress the former was positively forbidden, even if they were poor and needy. See Deut. xxiv. 14, 15. And they were

5

reminded that they were bond-servants in Egypt, see 18th verse, as a warning to them against their withholding the pay from hired servants, and thereby oppressing them. The descendants of Shem, though often made slaves through poverty and otherwise, so far as the law required obedience to the master, was the same as bond-servants, and so far as remaining their time out; but they were to receive wages in some way, and were to be treated as hired servants who went and came at pleasure; but were just as much bound to serve their time out, whatever that was, as the bond-servants were to serve for life; and, live on such as his master saw proper to give him. In the beginning, while under a provisional government, the descendants of Shem or Japheth, were only allowed to serve six years, and go out free on the seventh, as typical of the Sabbath. But under the permanent government, as established by Moses, the time was extended to fifty years; that is, they were all set free at the jubilee which was every fiftieth year; that making the whole time of service for those who should happen to enter on the first day after the jubilee, forty-nine years; and those entering one year after, would have to serve forty-eight years; and those entering on the forty-eighth year, would have to serve only one year to the first morning of the year of jubilee, when all the children of promise went out free. Lev. xxv. 52, 53, 54, 55. Now the reason why they were not to be held forever as bond or hired servants is clearly set forth in the 55th verse. But what is said of the strangers that sojourned among them? Lev. xxv. 45, 46. Who were meant by *strangers?* Were they not heathens, or in other words, the descendants of Ham through Canaan? How different were they treated! They. were to be bought, sold and kept for an inheritance for their children, and to be held as their possessions forever—to be at the beck and call of their masters, and no intimations given that they were ever to be free, and satisfy themselves on whatever their owners gave them, and had no legal claim on them for anything beyond that.

A wealthy gentleman, in whose breast beats as kind a heart as ever moved the pulse of man, said to me last night, while talking on this subject, in reply to my views, that I must not talk that way; that he could not bear it, for it would be cruel; that God was no respecter of persons. I said to the doctor, Why, then, are they black and so repulsive in their appearance to all our senses? therefore God must have been a respecter of persons, so far as the physical nature of man is concerned. And he does respect man according to his obedience to his government, and has done from the foundation of the world, and will do to the end of time. Spiritually, in a general way, he is no respecter of persons, and has opened up a way for the salvation of every man, without respect to color or condition. A great many men do not seem to draw the line between the spiritual and temporal kingdom of God in the world. If he was no respecter of persons, how came Noah and his family to have been admitted into the ark and saved, and all others left out to perish? How came Lot and his family to be taken out of Sodom by an angel of God, and all the Sodomites left to perish in the flames? How came David to be .chosen and anointed, and Jonathan left out? And how came the Africans to be what they are in color and personal appearance, and the Anglo-Saxon so superior in color and personal appearance? To say God is no respecter of persons, physically and temporally, is preposterous. I know he sends the rain on the good and bad alike, that the bad may have no excuse; and all are invited alike to partake of the waters of life, and all can have it alike, without respect to color, tribe, or nation; and if the Hindoo, Chinese, Indian, Arab, African, or southern slave will come unto God through Jesus Christ, and give him their hearts alike, he will free them all alike from the dominion of sin, and they will be free indeed; and if faithful, the devil and sin will have no more dominion over them. But it will make no difference in their temporal or physical relations whatever, only so far as they may be improved in principle and grace. But it will make no change in the color of the skin, the texture of the hair, or the odor of the body.

Thousands of abolitionists speak of the spiritual freedom of the Bible, and twist it into a temporal freedom, and thus preach it from their pulpits, with long, aped faces, and by that try to make the people believe that they have a large store of pity for the poor slave, that is ten times as happy and well off as two-thirds of our white servant-girls in the northern cities; and no sympathy is expressed for them whatever. Thus they have adulterated the

Gospel of God, and converted the sanctuary into a den of corruption, deception, and slander. Many such are ministers of Apollyon, and not of Christ, and are guilty of high treason against the government of God and this country, and deserve the gallows just as much as old John Brown or any other culprit. And we shall never have peace in church or state until they are hung or stopped in some way. Was it any worse for God to curse the Canaanites with perpetual slavery for a sin of such enormity, than it was to curse the whole world, simply because our first parents *bit* a very delicious fruit in the Garden of Eden? Ham (and no doubt his son Canaan joined with him, or he would not have been selected to take the curse) saw his father lying drunk and naked in his tent, and doubtless the first and last time it ever happened, and instead of covering him, and trying to hide his shame from the gaze of the ungodly, ran off and told his brethren, as before described. Every good man will agree that this was a great sin, and would have been, even if Noah had been a stranger to him; and by this curse only a small part of the human family were stained, and not punished with corporeal punishment. But was the curse that took hold upon Adam and the whole human family simply because he ate the fruit? No; certainly not.

Suppose the stress was laid on the mere act of the two, which was the worst? I would say that Ham's was a thousand times more flagitious than Adam's. In Adam's case there was no harm in simply eating the apple, but in Ham's case there

5*

was a flagitiousness that excelled most all other crimes. Yet, for it, the descendants of one branch of his family were made slaves forever. But what was, and is, the immensity of the curse that affected the whole world, without respect to persons? not only to man, but the beast of the field, the fowls of the air, the fish of the sea, and the earth, and all that grows thereon. The seasons, the winds, the seas, and even the atmosphere was poisonous; all fell under this most terrible curse. The extra curse added to Canaan and his family was not a drop to the ocean, compared to it. The descendants of Canaan was not corrupted any more than what they were before, by the disobedience of Adam. They were gradually turned black, and made slaves. But by the transgression of Adam, Ham committed this great sin; the whole antediluvian world was destroyed, and every pain that afflicts man, beast, fowl, or fish, was produced by it. There would have been no winter, no storms, no burning sun, but one perpetual serene and balmy spring. Had it not been for the sin of Adam, there would have been no slaves, labor would not have been toil, there would have been no thorns or thistles, no venomous reptiles, no unclean thing, or contending parties, no misunderstanding, no fevers, no agues, no pains of any kind, no wars, nor rumors of wars, and above all, no death would ever have been known in the whole family of earth, and the presence of Almighty God would have been the perpetual glory of man. But Adam disobeyed God by eating the fruit he was told not to; therefore God has expressed his great displeasure to disobedience by letting this terrible calamity in upon us.

This curse is an eternal one, it reaches beyond this world, and to all eternity, unless we obey the commandments. The special sin of Ham does not, but only reaches to the grave, there it ends. Therefore it is only temporal and physical, and of such small moment that no special or separate atonement has been made for its extirpation in this world; no amendments has been made to the decree that brought it about; it not being necessary for the salvation of the slaves, they hold the same relation to God the white man does. Jesus Christ died to atone for all mankind; but does that screen us from the curse that fell upon us (by the fall) in this world? It does not, though we may embrace the benefits of the atonements, but we shall still have all the bodily afflictions that come into the world by the sin of Adam, and the last one to the Christian will be death, and eternal damnation after death to the disobedient and ungodly.

This life became a probation by the fall, and the slave is included in this probation, with the master; here we all bear the same relation, and all are invited to embrace Christ, without any respect or reference to our temporal relations. It matters not whether we are masters, bond-servants, or hired servants, we may all be free in Christ Jesus. And God has never called man into his work of the ministry to interfere with those relations between master and slave; if he has, he is inconsistent with himself; for he nowhere has taught us any such doctrines, either in the Old or New Testament. Then who has called all those men to the pulpit to preach doctrines in direct opposition to the inspired word of God? If God himself has done it, he has either changed or he did not inspire the writers of the Bible, and the anti-slavery party gospel preachers declare it to be inspired, and go into pulpits and declare slavery to be a sin against God. If that be so, God is the author, and Abraham, Isaac, Jacob, Job, and David, were all sinners unto death, and St. Paul was a great sinner, and we have no account of his repentance; for he encouraged the relation of master and slave throughout his entire ministry, and should have repented. If he did, it was not put on record for our instruction. Then I ask again who called the anti-slavery *gospel* preachers into the pulpit to proclaim against the government of the United States, and the decrees of the eternal God? But the anti-slavery man says that was a decree of an old drunken man in his dotage. If that was so, how came the class of men against whom the decree was made, to be so affected by it, that their skins turned black, and their hair like black curled bristles? Old Noah's declaration did not amount to anything towards affecting the thing decreed; it was only prophetic; God saw the crime of Ham, and determined to place a warning in the world, against a repetition. And he only, had the power to make the effect follow the cause. Noah had no more power to produce such a thing than he had to create a world. Therefore slavery is a divine institution. Then, did God call men and women into the ministry to preach an antislavery gospel? I say he did not, nor could not, without inconsistency, if the Scriptures be true. Then who did call them? None but the Prince of darkness—that same devil who said unto Eve, Thou shalt not surely die. This fiend of darkness determined to make war against God, and prevent the righteousness of man, if possible, and he has seized upon everything that he could appropriate to his use for that purpose; and as soon as God saw fit to take hold of the poor down-trodden African under the heel of debauchery, and bring him into usefulness for their immediate good, and the benefit and glory of all mankind, and as soon as the all-wise Governor of the universe chose his own plan, and began to introduce them into usefulness among his Christian people, Apollyon commenced his attack upon the institution that was ordained of God for the good of his people; but never until the year 1620, when it was introduced into countries where he saw Christianity would be promulgated, and the poor down-trodden African would be Christianized through the instrumentality of slavery. These Canaanites had been used as slaves and as beasts of burthen for over four thousand years, and we have no account of any opposition being made to it.

As long as it existed among heathens, the Prince of darkness was too cunning to make an attack upon it, in the time of the inspired writers, especially those of the New Testament, for it might have been the means of bringing out some strong declarations that might have been recorded. He wanted it for some future use, and perhaps feared the apostles would frustrate all his designs, by warning masters and slaves to be on the lookout for him. The enemy of God and man knows well that circumstances make the slave question more exciting than any other. And he and his numerous followers, who are found mingling in all Christian congregations and pulpits, know that it is their only scheme by which they can break up this glorious and God-like government. If the Scriptures of truth had forbidden the existence of negro slavery, no doubt, those preachers and the devil would have taken a strong stand for slavery, and would have endeavored to establish it in every part of this country. They are opposed to God and righteousness; therefore their opposition to slavery. I have no doubt but the Prince of darkness was opposed to this planet's being peopled at the time we understand to be the creation of the world. It might have been created many millions of years ago, and perhaps was one of the brightest stars in the whole constellation of the heavens; and perhaps the devil was the chief ruling angel, under the great central Power, and, it may be, he had millions of angels under him who might have acted as messengers to other planets, and to the great Creator of them all. And it may be that this ruling angel and great central power of this planet concluded to set up for himself, and made it known to all his contributories, and called them around him to secède from the great constellation of heaven (just as the Governor of South Carolina did last week, with his host of rebels, and withdrew from this great constellation of States); and, perhaps the very moment the bill passed, this planet was banished into outer darkness, far outside of all moral or optic light, and this glorious star was instantly reduced to a chaotic state, and all its inhabitants (who agreed to the ordinance) into devils, Apollyon being king. And it may have floated about in outer darkness in a state of chaos for millions of years. But at a set time it returned from a state of darkness to its place, a heap of ruins, without a speck of light or glory. And at the time of creation, God let in the light upon it from other planets, on which it is still dependent for light; God took it through a process of preparation for six days, and put it into a beautiful shape, no doubt; and when done, *God blessed it, and pronounced it good*, and then created a new set of beings, perhaps somewhat different in nature from those before the rebellion and attempted secession (and for which presumption the sudden transmigration from angels of light to devils took place), to dress, cultivate, and beautify it. But it being the dwelling place of this enemy of God and the Prince of secession, he assailed our first parents, and seduced them from their purity; and therefore all the corruptions of this poor fallen world.

I have no doubt this planet shone as bright and trinkled as much as any other heavenly body. Now it is clear that the Prince of Hell had no access to the hearts of our first parents, as he now has to us, for he was compelled to employ another who could speak in audible words, and in a beautiful and enticing manner. And no doubt it was some animal that was admired by Eve, and he persuaded her to taste the fruit. She found it sweet, and gave to Adam, and induced him to taste. From that moment the devil has had access to the hearts of every living creature; and there is no power that can resist him but the power of the spirit of Almighty God. I know this is not all Bible doctrine, for some of it is a mere speculation of my own, and therefore cannot be relied on, only so far as it is sustained by the Bible. But any part of it is as clearly taught in the Bible, and as much to be relied upon as the doctrine of the immorality of slavery as taught by modern abolition gospel preachers, and fully as reasonable as it is that African slavery as it exists in the United States of North America is in the abstract sinful, and all such preachers are at variance with the decrees of the eternal God, and are endeavoring to set at nought his plan of civilization and evangelizing this world of sin. But notwithstanding their efforts under the direction of their father, the devil, whom they serve, this planet will be redeemed by the grace of God, through the preaching of the gospel of Christ (and not abolition), from the subjugation of the devil, and all the kingdoms of the world will become the kingdoms of God and his Christ. And the time will come when Apollyon with all his motley crew and abolition preachers, will be swept from this planet over which he has ruled so long, and with such tyranny and hatred into outer darkness, where there will be weeping, wailing, and gnashing of teeth. Where is outer darkness? I suppose it is outside, and away beyond all the planets, fixed stars, and systems, where the light of heaven will never strike their optical vision, and the powers of restraining grace will never be heard of, much less felt, to all eternity.

I have long believed that according to the attributes of Jehovah, no spirit can be destroyed, bad or good, *but will exist somewhere forever, yea, forever and ever*, and as this planet could not be at rest as long as it is his habitation, at a fixed time in the mind of God they will be arraigned before the court of heaven, with all his followers and disobedient, whether human or fallen angels, all false teachers, or pretended gospel preachers, who have added doctrines not written in the word of God, and preached them as very truth, or extracted therefrom what is really written, in order to give it a different meaning, whether on slavery or any other question, even of minor importance, will be found guilty of rebellion and treason. All such "will be banished from the presence of Him who sitteth upon the throne, and from the glory of his power," into outer darkness. There can be no darkness within the Kingdom of God after this planet is redeemed. Therefore "outer darkness" must be outside of the everlasting range of the government of God, where the softening sounds and melting appeals of "come unto me, and be saved," will never be heard, but they will be beyond the reach of all good, even beyond the power of God to save. I will add another class to Apollyon's kingdom, and they are those who are everlastingly interfering with a good government like ours, and finding fault with what is done by authority, and never take one step to try to

6

cure the evils they complain of, and see everybody's wrongs except their own, finding fault with their own church and state, as though everybody in it was bad except themselves, in both ecclesiastical and civil administrations. If there should be any place in God's domains for any such, it will be on the borders, where it may only be a little unpleasant. I will compare another principle of abolitionism with divine law.

Deut. xxii. 1. "Thou shalt not see thy brother's ox or his sheep go astray, and hide thyself from them: thou shalt in any case bring them again unto thy brother.

2. And if thy brother *be* not nigh unto thee, or if thou know him not, then thou shalt bring it unto thine own house, and it shall be with thee until thy brother seek after it, and thou shalt restore it to him again.

3. In like manner shalt thou do with his ass; and so shalt thou do with his raiment; and with all lost things of thy brother's, which he hath lost, and thou hast found, shalt thou do likewise: thou mayest not hide thyself."

The first verse teaches us that it is our duty to take care of our neighbor's property if we see it wasting, or inform him where it is, that he may regain it. The 2d teaches us that if the owner should be far away, and an entire stranger, then we shall take his property to our own house, and keep it until he comes for it, and restore it to him. The 3d verse teaches us that we are to do the same thing with any property or anything that belongs to our neighbor or a stranger. The text says, "all lost things of thy brother's which he hath lost." Now was slaves not a possession, or, in other words, property, according to both the civil and moral law? I suppose no one will pretend to say they were not. Then they were included in "all lost things." Some people will see their neighbor's property destroyed under their feet and make no effort to save it, neither will they inform him of the fact. But abolitionists go much further than that, for they hide their neighbor's property that he may lose it, and they endeavor to get it away from him, that he may not find it. Yes, they even box up slaves, in order to steal them from their owners, that they may lose them. One *good* brother told me he had seventeen slaves hid in his garret at a time, that the anti-slavery party had run off from their masters, all of which they conducted on to Canada, into a cold climate not suited to their nature. This villainous practice has been and still is carried on by many northern men and women and pretended preachers of the gospel from nearly every denomination of professing Christians. Now, I ask again, by what spirit are those men guided? Can it be the righte-ous and benevolent spirit that inspired the writing of these three verses? I think every candid man will say no. Then of what spirit are they? There is but two that can inspire men's hearts, to do bad or good; one is of God and the other of the devil. Am I wrong in saying they are of the devil? I will say I am right, or those verses of Scripture are wrong.

I am told by some that this was under the Mo-saic dispensation, and that the Christian era brought up a new state of things. I think I shall be able to show you that the only change made in the relation of masters and slaves, was, the Apostles taught the slaves that they must be obedient to their masters, for in so doing they served God. Some say there was no such thing as the return of fugitive slaves to their masters in those days. That there were no slave catchers and that they were not to be delivered up if they were sought after. This is like many other things said by *anti-slavery gospel* preachers.

I. Kings ii. 39. "And it came to pass, at the·end of three years, that two of the servants of Shimei ran away unto Achish son of Maachah, king of Gath: and they told Shimei, saying, Behold, thy servants *be* in Gath.

40. And Shimei arose, and saddled his ass, and went to Gath, to Achish, to seek his servants: and Shimei went, and brought his servants from Gath."

Here we see the law fully carried out, for "Shimei" was informed (as taught in Deut. xxii. and first three verses) of the whereabouts of his slaves. And he went for them and no one attempted to interfere with his rights to those two slaves, and they were delivered up to him, and he brought them to his home. Now if the anti-slavery *gospel preacher* will show me one word that condemns "Shimei," or those who informed him, in the whole revelation of God, I will give up that slavery is a sin. I could give many other passages from the Old Testament to show that slavery was an institution formed under the providence of Almighty God. But I think I have given enough to satisfy every believer in the inspired word of God, and will now close this chapter by saying that it is as clear to my mind that slavery is the work of Eternal wisdom, and to help make up the machinery by which God will civilize and evangelize this fallen and sin-stricken world.

CHAPTER II.

Does the Gospel Dispensation condemn the relation of Master and Slave?

THE main part of this chapter was written in the fall of 1860, as an article for the New York Methodist, but was rejected by the editor for reasons given at the latter end of the chapter, in the correspondence between the Rev. Mr. Crooks and myself, and was written before the fifth chapter; therefore, I shall leave out most of the quotations from the Old Testament, and the comments thereon, with the introductory remarks made to that paper. The first account we have of the institution of slavery was established two thousand three hundred and forty-eight years before Christ, by Divine decree and acknowledgment, as I think I clearly proved in the previous chapter by quotations from the Old Testament; and I now propose to show from the New Testament that slavery was not abolished under the Gospel Dispensation, nor condemned by Christ or any of his apostles, or their disciples. That every passage on the subject in the latter endorses the institution, if it does not directly sanction it.

(66)

I will say before I enter into the argument, that I am a friend of the negroes, and every principle in me is in favor of freedom and the general good of all mankind. And I desire the happiness of the negro race as much as I do any other race or tribe on the earth. My opposition to emancipation is not from a principle of opposition to the freedom of the black race, but because I know they are *not* capable of self-government, and consequently better off in slavery. And I believe a free republican constitutional government and union could not exist ten years with one-sixth part of the entire population of the country black African negroes, and the other five-sixth pure Anglo-Saxons, and that a national military despotism would have to be established for their government, for two reasons.

First. To prevent their extermination by the white people; for the colored race would push in for a social and political equality, and then we should have a scene of blood such as has never been on the globe; therefore a military government would be necessary to prevent the greatest act of barbarism on which the sun ever shone. And under such a government there would be infinite danger of *"we, the people,"* being reduced to a social and political equality with them, against which equality I now enter my everlasting protest.

Secondly. If neither of the above evils should take place, and they should be allowed to remain with us in peace, they would become entirely useless, and sink down into the lowest degradation and ruin, as they have done in South America, Mexico, and the

British West Indies, where they have never been of any use to themselves, or any body else, since their emancipation. On these grounds, I am personally opposed to the emancipation of any more slaves in the United States, and I believe it would be a far greater deed of charity to the poor unfortunate free persons of color in this country, to reduce the nine-tenths of them to slavery, than it would be to set the slaves all free. Therefore, even without the clearest teachings of the book of God, I am opposed to the emancipation of the slaves in this country, for the good of both races, especially that of the negroes. And, when we come to the moral law, the emancipation of the negro race is so clearly forbidden, that I dare not advocate their freedom; for in that, I believe, I should be acting against the clearest teachings of Divine inspiration; consequently, I should afflict my conscience by doing different from what I now do on the slave question. If I were entirely selfish, and cared nothing for my country, my God, or future generations, I should have taken another course; for I had no doubt, four months before the Presidential election, that all other parties would be enormously in the minority to the republican party. I was well satisfied before the election, what the result would be in case that party succeeded, as I am now of what has taken place. And I had feared from the election of 1856, that the Republican party would succeed in 1860, and that we should have a collision with our southern brethren, and perhaps an eternal overthrow of this great and glorious Union would be the result—*which Union was my greatest earthly admiration,* while, I believe, its overthrow would be my earthly ruin—that with its end ended all my earthly hopes; and I felt that if I had had a thousand lives, I would have given them all rather than the abolitionists should have got the *reins* of the national government in their hands, for I knew what they intended to do; and I as firmly believed that the result would be a total breaking up of the business of the whole country, which I declared to almost all I talked with.

Under these circumstances, I knew my safest plan would be, to secure my bread (while we should be undergoing the greatest revolution yet known to the world), to go in with the republican party, for I knew none who opposed them, and stood up for the union on the only ground that there was any possibility of its being saved, would have any patronage under the government. But I loved this great and glorious government too well to advocate what I believed would be its everlasting overthrow; and it was so strange to me that every body else did not see it just as I did, that I almost lost all confidence in the capabilities of man for self-government. A Christian brother said to me the other day, on Market Street, that he would like to see me hung up by the neck to the nearest lamp-post, and there hang until I rotted, because I believe coercion, or an attempt to force the seven States back that have now seceded, would destroy all hope for a restoration of peace and union. I firmly believe the seven States can be brought back by peace measures. But coercion will drive several others out, and perhaps throw us into universal

anarchy. Therefore, I can not, under these circumstances, advocate coercive measures. Could I do it,
I should be far better off than I am, so far as my
present bread and meat is concerned; but I love
peace and the union of the whole United States too
well to raise my puny arm against them, by advocating
coercive measures. I solemnly declare the above to
be my clearest and most positive convictions, gathered from the teachings of our Saviour and his holy
apostles, and the clearest reasoning from a long study
of the history of the rise and fall of nations and of
human nature. I have placed several pages of the
forepart of this chapter, as it was originally written
for the Methodist, in the forepart of the first chapter.

I will now proceed with my argument on the
question of slavery, as set forth in the New Testament. Modern abolitionists tell us that slavery has
been the cause of a vast amount of evil, therefore it
should be abolished. I say slavery has not produced any of the evils we have had or now have in
our country. Neither did it produce or cause the
John Brown Raid in Virginia; nor has it produced
the ill feeling now existing between the two extremes of our great and glorious country. But the
opposition to slavery has done all the mischief.
No advent since the world was, has been surrounded
with more evils than the advent of our *Lord* and *Saviour Jesus Christ*. It has been made the occasion of
the shedding of more blood, perhaps, than has been
shed by any king or potentate who has lived since
his advent into the world. Now, tell me, was our
Lord the cause of all the evils which have followed

his appearance to redeem a fallen world, or was the trouble produced by an opposition to his mission among men. I say he was just as much the cause of all those evils, as slavery has been the cause of the John Brown Raid in Virginia. And if slavery was the cause of all the trouble that has surrounded or seemed to hang around it, then our Lord must have been the cause of all the wickedness which followed Christianity.

Now it is clear that the evils which have followed the one, has been produced by the same spirit of wickedness that followed the other. Then if we abolish the one, because of the wickedness that was brought out by the opposition to it, through infidelity and wicked men, then we certainly ought to abolish Christianity as well as slavery. But who will venture to say that Christianity ought to be abolished, because bad men and infidelity hate it, and use every kind of wickedness to drive it (if possible) from the world? If the people of the United States was to make a decree, that Christianity should be driven out of the country, because its opponents make trouble, and howl, and fight, would you justify such a decree? I think no man would do so foolish a thing. Marriage is one of the most honorable institutions ever known in the world, and one of the greatest blessings ever bestowed upon mankind. Yet, the most enormous evils has come out of it, perhaps of any other blessing that was ordained unto us by heaven. Now I ask every sincere man and woman if marriage was the cause of the wickedness that seemed to grow out of it? or was it in consequence of the wickedness of bad men? Now must marriage be abolished simply because enormous evils are practiced upon the ceremony, and bad men whip their wives, and often murder them?

There is a large class of people in the United States opposed to marriages, who are divided into several classes, one called the Shaking Quakers, who are otherwise a moral industrious people. Another large class of religious fanatics, who formerly called themselves the Battle Axe Christians. And still another class who openly avow infidelity. Those classes are much larger now than the Garrisonian Abolitionists were in 1840. All of those fanatics denounce the marriage tie, as the "sum of all villainies," and declare it to be more righteous to put a cat and dog in a bag together, than it is to marry a man to a woman. These fanatics have formed associations all over the free States (and are on the increase), in order to abolish the marriage contract. And give as their reason, that it is slavery of one to the other, and therefore should be abolished from among men.

Now according to the doctrine of all who say that slavery must be abolished because a set of men who have no direct interest in the institution, nor have they the most distant right, either civil or moral, to interfere with it in our Southern States, the marriage contract should be abolished simply because those religious fanatics protest against it and say it is a sin, or moral evil. They have just as good a right, and good deal better, for the marriage contract exists in the States in which they live. But slavery does not exist in any of the States in

which its opponents live, therefore the opponents of
marriage have a better right to claim the arm of the
government to aid them to prevent the evils that
follow the marriage ceremony, by sweeping it from
our land. I could name almost every good institution in our country, and show that it is surrounded
with great evils. Therefore should be abolished,
according to abolition notions of the evils of slavery.

I have written the above in the place of the pages
transferred to the previous chapter, and as an answer to thousands of our most excellent men, who
say that slavery should be abolished, because a certain class of men and women in the free States say
it is a moral evil, and produces great tumults, harass
parties and Legislatures, because the poor African
negroes are in slavery, and "we, the people," are
not. When this class of abolition zealots are mainly
made up of men who never saw a slave in slavery,
and who have no more right to interfere with it than
they have to interfere with the serfs of Russia, or
the dark shades on the face of the moon; and yet
these good men, who are among our best citizens,
say slavery must be abolished if, by so doing, we are
compelled to exterminate the entire white population
of the slave States, and say it would be preferable to
having those abolition fanatics everlastingly stirring
up strife and treason here in the free States, and
keeping us ever in dread and fear that some terrible
judgment will befall us, or that we may be compelled to put down servile insurrections in the South.
Now is not this most wicked? Could old Apollyon
take a more unrighteous course—to go to work and

7

rob the slave States of $4,000,000,000 worth of property, and turn five millions of persons loose to starve and die, or prowl about in a state of the lowest degradation, and be a pest to society? What for? Why, because a set of infidels in our midst, who hate God and all who love him, and who make it their business to disturb all peaceful relations between men who have the good of all mankind in view. I wish I had a talent to set this point before the reader that he might see it in its right and true shape. To rob the innocent, righteous, and unoffending, to satisfy a set of traitors like Wendell Phillips, Charles Sumner, and Wm. L. Garrison, and their thousands of dupes, is an enormity of crime of such magnitude, that I shudder when I think of a sin-avenging God; for woe be unto us when we insult His Majesty with impunity.

Is slavery a moral evil according to the teachings of the New Testament, and did Christ or any of his apostles condemn it, or did they endorse and justify it? I say they did both endorse and justify it in all its legitimate forms. When the government of the United States was adopted, and the Union thereby secured, twelve States out of the thirteen were slave States. We then had universal peace and harmony from centre to circumference of the thirteen States. The slave clause in the Constitution was adopted by a very large majority, and also the extension of the slave trade for twenty years, passed by a large majority; though there was a powerful opposition made to the latter by Luther Martin, of Md., and one or two others. The whole country prospered from that day. The blessings of a kind Providence rested upon the whole nation, and the people loved each other, and knew no North nor no South, and church and state prospered alike. The state looked to the church for moral and religious example, and the church looked to the state for the civil protection she might need. And the blessings of an all-merciful Father seemed to rest upon all alike, and we were the happiest nation on whom the sun ever shone. There was a small fragment in the Northern States who commenced an opposition to the government some three or four years after it was formed, and, in a very few years, infidelity brought every kind of "*ism*" to bear against both church and state; but as long as both rejected that form of infidelity called abolition, they done us no harm.

For many years abolitionists could not even get a nomination for any office in the nation, much less be elected to one. Churches interrogated candidates for the ministry on the question, and if they were found to be abolitionists, they were rejected, though in all other points unobjectionable. The New York Conference rejected two candidates in (about) 1840 to 1842, simply because they were suspected of being tainted with abolitionism, when they were in all other points unobjectionable. As long as this was strictly attended to, the church and state prospered unmolested, though abolitionism and infidelity howled against both. Yet both prospered in spite of all the schemes of infidelity and the devil, through their agents, Wm. Lloyd Garrison, Wendell Phillips, and their sub-agents, Charles Sumner, Henry Ward Beecher, Drs. Cheever, Furness, and others. But as long as those schemes of the devil and abolitionists were openly avowed against church and state, their darts fell harmless at our feet. But they finally took it into their heads to change their mode from candor to deception, and by so doing, they got possession of a large part of the church, and a strong hold in the state. And as soon as the church and state give way for the sake of their votes, and yielded, trouble set in, and danger was perceptible. It was not long after this before churches began to quarrel and divide, and statesmen who had always loved each other, became the bitterest enemies, and soon began to be sectional in their feelings and speeches, and in a very few years churches elected the most ultra abolitionists to conduct their journals. They (the churches) having taken the first steps for a dissolution of the Union.

There was not the slightest danger to church or state apparent, when the votes of those devils incarnate was first sought for. As soon as that concession was made, the blessing of prosperity, peace, harmony, and love began to fade away. Just in proportion to the encouragement given to this class of infidelity by the church and state, just in that ratio both have been retarded in their peace and prosperity.

In about 1842 many thousand seceded from the Methodist Episcopal Church in New England, because slaveholders were allowed to commune in the southern branch of the church, whose leaders were Scott, Sunderland & Co. It would not be hard to prove that those leaders were bad men before they left the church, and perhaps joined it for the very purpose of trying to split and ruin it. Very soon after they withdrew, the most of the leaders went to ruin (I mean the preachers), for some of them took to hard drink, and others to fortune telling, some to Spiritualism, and others to Animal Magnetism, Millerism, Mormonism, and every other kind of ism; all this because they had become so holy and pure that they could no longer remain in a communion that slaveholders were admitted to, though a thousand miles from them. Notwithstanding their great conscientious scruples about slavery, they went headlong into all those blackening inventions of the devil for a livelihood, which I think is as near Apollyon's Kingdom as can be reached in this world. So the leaders mostly exposed their cloven feet before they died.

What became of the twenty thousand laymen, I am asked, that followed them? I know not, but it is to be feared they went about the same road. It is only necessary for us to look at the prosperous condition of the whole nation as well as the church before abolitionism became popular in them, and look at them since it succeeded to power, to know what spirit they are of. Look at our condition now, since abolitionism got the ascendency. Look at the divisions, the tumults, the hard words, the curses, and see the blood that has been shed, and the scaffolds that have been erected to hang men and women from, and assassinations in almost every form. See the ruin to business of every grade, and perhaps five hundred million dollars would not pay the loss produced by the opposition to slavery in this country. There is not an infidel association that I know of who are not abolitionist, and who declare the Bible to be an infernal book, because it endorses or sanctions slavery. And they seize upon the slave question to strengthen their opposition to the Christian religion. And now the strong and bitter feelings between the North and the South, that no doubt will result in a clash of arms, and perhaps will be one of the greatest civil strifes ever known on the face of the earth, and perhaps the slaughter of millions of our race, and ultimately the total extermination of the entire black population of this whole country, or the driving of them from among us, who have had no hand in making this trouble. Those of that race who have the name of freedom are in the greatest danger. It is not necessary to go into details, for every man and woman of the slightest observation ought to know the history, and see the catastrophy just before us, and unless God in his mercy shall interfere in behalf of "*We, the people,*" we shall be dashed to pieces as a nation upon the rocks of a universal despotism or anarchy that will make us quail with fear and pain.

I joined the Methodist Episcopal Church in 1827. At that time the slave and free States were a unit in church as well as state; with the exception of a handful of abolitionists in the free States, there was no sectional quarrels, all was love, peace, harmony, and union, between the two extremes of our beloved country. And so it would be now had no concessions ever been made to infidelity through Garrisonian abolitionism. This class of infidelity had gained so fast after its admission into official stations in the church, that in the General Conference of 1844, Bishop Andrews, of Georgia, one of the most respected, and devoted bishops of our (then) great and powerful Christian Church, was suspended, simply for having married a lady who had fell *heir*, or by will, to some two or three little negro children. What has been the result of that fatal act of that most unfortunate conference is now before us, and all can realize it. It was the first step for a dissolution of this great and glorious union. That step divided this great body of Christians nearly on the geographical line, called Mason's and Dixon's. The following year, our Baptist brethren, the next most powerful church, followed the example set by our church, dividing about on the same line as her leaders did. Some time subsequent the New School Presbyterian separated on about the same line. While other congregational churches who had no general form of church government have not ceased to say hard things of our Southern brethren because they allowed slaveholders in their communions, and have done great service in the fatal cause of destruction to the last, and perhaps the only hope of man for liberty and self-government.

The Old School Presbyterian Church has now virtually divided, and the only ligament which has not been officially severed, is the Protestant Episcopal Church, which is now our only hope for liberty and union. If that fails we are without hope in this country. These churches have not only divided, but are being subdivided, and all brotherly intercourse between members of the same church seems to be lost sight of, while they denounce each other like fiends, one asserting that the negro is as good as the white man and ought to be made his equal, and others dissenting. Ministers seem to have entirely forgotten the sword of the Spirit given them by their Great Progenitor, who told them to use it, and no other, which is love to God and to all mankind. And they have now unsheathed a sword of steel, or the temporal sword, and go into pulpits and recommend it to all their members. No prayers are allowed to be offered for our sectional enemies, no love to be tendered them which was the only spirit and foundation of the union. But Sharp's rifles, cannon balls, and the temporal sword contains all the gospel of love they seem to recommend to those we have first made mad. How sweet it would be to find a communion where none but the sword of the Spirit of the living God was used. I well remember when we had such communions; but not since abolitionists were admitted, and called brothers. Then our peace, union, and love, among our Christian brethren was unmitigated. But alas! how is it to-day? How do we now greet each other? With curses, denunciations, and threats. What has done all of this mischief? Opposition to God's own arrangement for the government of the world. But wo be unto us, if we lift our arm against his decrees.

This rebellion has already produced animosities

between brethren who loved each other with Christian forbearance, that is painful. But we have reason to fear that all our happy and peaceful days as a nation and church are past forever. One of our most popular young preachers, preached a sermon the other Sunday morning, in one of our popular churches, against slavery, that produced disputes, quarrels, and bad feelings which may never be erased in this life. Thousands have left the church in consequence of the agitation of negro slavery in them, and perhaps will be forever lost to the church; and it is to be feared they will lose their preparation for the Kingdom above. It is to be feared also, that many ministers and laymen have committed blasphemy against the Throne of heaven; especially since old John Brown and his co-associates were executed at Charlestown, Va. Ministers of the Gospel have proclaimed from the sacred desk, that (*that old murderer and traitor*) John Brown was the second Jesus Christ; others, that the gallows was sanctified and made precious as the cross of our Saviour by his execution thereon; and others have said the horrors of the gallows were entirely removed, and now it was a desirable death to die. At similar declarations made in this city, at one of our large halls, it is said, by good men, that some laymen and ministers responded with a solemn and hearty amen. They were ministers who draw very large crowds to hear them preach treason to the laws of heaven and earth. These are the true and certain effects of ministerial religious and political opposition to lawful negro slavery.

If I were to attempt to enumerate all the evils growing out of the opposition to African slavery in this country, it would make a very large book; and none have suffered more than the poor slaves themselves. There are evils growing out of the system of slavery, I know; but is that any evidence that the system is a moral evil? If it is, then every good thing we have, or ever had, is a moral evil—even Christianity, as I have already shown, for the devil has never ceased to try to bring all the bad out of good he could. And will any one undertake to say that he has not succeeded to an alarming extent? Yet, notwithstanding all the combined efforts of infidelity and the devil, had it not been for the offer and free gift of Christianity, we should now be in a far worse condition than the natives of Africa ever were. And we are indebted to Christianity for all the benefits we ever had, whether civil or moral. And all the civilization that has been since the world was, was the legitimate result of Christianity. Yet infidelity and abolitionists say Christianity must be abolished, because evils have resulted from its advent. Many leading antislavery men have dashed the Bible from their tables because it sanctions slavery.

If slavery be a moral evil, it ought to be abolished, provided it can be done without producing a greater one. But is slavery a moral evil? If so, it was endorsed by all the actors and inspired writers of the Holy Bible, from Noah to St. Paul, the Son of God not excepted. The evidence of this I have already given from the Mosaic dispensation in the previous chapter. But I will refer again to Exodus xx. 17.

"Thou shalt not covet thy neighbor's house, thou shalt not covet thy neighbor's wife, nor his man-servant, nor his maid-servant, nor his ox, nor his ass, nor anything that is thy neighbor's." If property in men and women is not recognized in this, the tenth commandment, and fully sanctioned by the inspired penman, then houses nor cattle cannot be claimed as property, and man has no moral claim to anything he possesses, and he is sinning against light by not discharging it. Let us look at and examine it until we fully understand it, for an awful responsibility rests upon us; for upon our decision may rest our liberties, our peace, and happiness through all time to come. After we have thoroughly investigated it, and find slavery to be a moral evil, then we must blot out the Decalogue or ten commandments, or charge the Supreme Being with the authorship of a moral evil. Slavery may be looked upon as a greater missionary movement to evangelize the heathen than all the missionary movements of the Christian churches. Let no man forbid the holding of slaves until he can prove by holy writ that slavery is a sin against the moral law; fear lest he should oppose one of the great divine schemes of evangelization. Abraham, the friend of God, and the father of the faithful, a great and good man, was commanded by the eternal to "circumcise the servants born in his house, and bought with his money." Genesis xvii. 13. Yet in all this there is not the slightest command or intimation given against the institution of slavery, or that it was a moral evil, or in any way displeasing to the Almighty.

There are many other passages in the Old Testament, and a great many in the New, that fully endorse the holding of men and woman as property (of a particular race), but no others, except for crime, or by their own free consent. The Roman centurian, whose faith Jesus commended as follows: "I have not found so great faith, no, not in Israel," Matt. viii. 5-13, was a large slaveholder. Yet his faith was commended by our Lord, as being superior to any he had found. But not one word uttered against that institution (or that it was a moral evil), or in any way displeasing to God, much less to the centurian being the master of so many slaves, who were accredited to him as his own property. The Roman law invested the master with power of life and death over his servants. And the fact that the centurian held slaves under this law, did not in the least, in the estimation of Jesus of Nazareth, render him unworthy of the high commendation bestowed on him by Christ, *and recorded for our instruction.* If slavery is a sin, then our Lord neglected his duty in this case, and thereby became accessory to the crime. He could so easily have said to him that he was a sinner by owning slaves, instead of bestowing so high a commendation upon him. And it was such a fit time for him to have warned others against this (alleged) crime, by telling him that *no slaveholder should enter the Kingdom of Heaven. But not one word of the kind.*

As the sons of Adam are bound to submit patiently to the decree that binds them to earn their living by the sweat of their brows, so also must the sons of

Ham, through his son Canaan, submit to their fate. The wise and benevolent friends of the African race may learn from the prophetical curse passed by Noah, *that slavery is a part of the mysterious plan, according to which God is governing the world, and they should be careful for fear they should be found opposing God.*

The Scriptures furnish yet another, and even a stronger argument for the lawfulness of slavery. In the fact that they instruct masters how to exercise authority over their slaves.

Eph. vi. 5. "Servants, be obedient to them that are *your* masters according to the flesh, with fear and trembling, in singleness of your heart, as unto Christ.

6. Not with eye-service, as men-pleasers ; but as the servants of Christ, doing the will of God from the heart;

7. With good-will doing service, as to the Lord, and not to men;

· 8. Knowing that whatsoever good thing any man doeth, the same shall he receive of the Lord, whether *he be* bond or free.

9. And ye masters, do the same things unto them, forbearing threatening : knowing that your Master also is in heaven ; · neither is there respect of persons with him."

If the relation of master and slave be unlawful and sinful, then the relation of parents and children must be the same, for both are exhorted alike to obedience. Except Paul said more to slaves, knowing there was more danger of their being neglectful of their duty to masters, and the danger of masters forgetting their duty to slaves, and to impress the minds of the slaves so deeply, that they might not think they had the right to waste their time which

8

belonged exclusively to their masters, and *not* to themselves, and that they should love and respect them.

If slavery be a moral evil, why was Paul so particular in insisting upon those duties to each other, without giving the slightest intimation that slavery was wrong, or in any way objectionable to Christianity? But St. Paul seemed to make so much greater effort to impress his precept upon the minds of the slaves, than any others he named in those verses; there must have been some special reasons for it. Does it not look as though he had his prophetic eye cast forward to the present times? Those precepts stand in as full force to-day as they did when he uttered them. I am told by the anti-slavery party, that Paul was speaking to servants, and not to slaves. ·I have shown already in a former chapter that whenever the hired servants were spoken of, they were speaking of Israelites, and not Canaanites, and whether they were bought for a term of years or for life, their master had the same unconditional control over them. But what does Paul mean in the latter clause of the 8th verse when he says, "whether they be bond or free?" Are not two distinct classes of servants alluded to? Who does he mean by bond-servants? I hope the reader will examine Webster, Walker, Baily, Reid, or any other lexicographer known in the world, on the word bond-servant, bond-slave, bond-man, and bond-maid. And then ask yourself the question, why all the inspired writers were so particular in designating between a hired servant and a bond-

servant. Was it not to instruct us that the relation
of master and slave was lawful in the sight of God?

A gentleman said to me this morning, that servant
always meant a hireling. I refer him, and all others
who thus believe, to the quotations from Lev. xxv.
if Webster and all lexicographers fail to satisfy
them. For to argue such a question would look too
simple for even children to cavil over. The text
needs no comment.

Col. iii. 18. " Wives, submit yourselves unto your own husbands, as it is fit in the Lord.

19. Husbands, love *your* wives, and be not bitter against
them.

20. Children, obey *your* parents in all things : for this is well
pleasing unto the Lord.

21. Fathers, provoke not your children *to anger*, lest they
be discouraged.

22. Servants, obey in all things *your* masters according to
the flesh; not with eye-service, as men-pleasers; but in singleness of heart, fearing God:

23. And whatsoever ye do, do *it* heartily, as to the Lord and
not unto men."

Col. iv. 1. " Masters, give unto *your* servants that which is
just and equal; knowing that ye also have a Master in heaven."

This is nearly a repetition of the Epistle to the
Eph. And therefore adds more strongly to the
testimony that slavery was, to say the least of it,
as just a judgment upon the descendants of Ham
as the afflictions of the whole human family are for
Adam's transgression. If the relation of master
and slave be a moral evil, St. Paul could not have
been an inspired Apostle. For he treats the relation of master and slave, husband and wife, parents
and children, precisely the same, except as I said

before, he was far more impressive in his injunctions
to slaves. If they were not equally lawful in the
sight of God, Paul's name ought to be stricken from
the New Testament, and not stand as an inspired
Apostle. But as I can see nothing criminal or sinful in the decree under Noah, I shall still look up
to the Apostle Paul as God's greatest ambassador
and favored friend, and believe I am just as much
forbid to interfere with the relation of master and
slave, as husband and wife.

I hope every master will read the first verse of
the iv. of. Col. with special attention, for it was
written for him. He must not oppress his slaves
with harshness and bitterness. Their earnings belong to him, for which he is bound by this precept
to give them enough good wholesome food, comfortable clothing, and not to put more on them than
they can comfortably bear. In short, he must do
to them as he would have them do to him, if circumstances between them were completely reversed.
They are held responsible to the moral law, and
if they neglect their duty in this thing, God will
judge them in justice and truth.

But the 22–23d verses of the iii. chapter rivets
the slave's duty to his master so particularly, that it
cannot be misunderstood or misapplied. While
the masters are reminded that they have a Master in
heaven who will render them their just reward for
their conduct to their slaves, the servants are
commanded *in all things to obey their masters*, and
told that they must do it as unto God, "not with eye-

service, as men-pleasers, but in singleness of heart, fearing God."

If slavery be a moral evil, St. Paul was a bad man, and endeavored to deceive the people. But if the Scriptures be the word of God, and written by inspiration, then slavery is as much a divine institution as labor and the cultivation of the soil of the earth. For Noah said, "Cursed be Canaan, a servant of *servants* shall he be to his brethren." God said to Adam, "In the sweat of thy face shalt thou eat bread, till thou return unto the ground," &c. The decree against Adam was pronounced by the great *"I Am,"* and has been executed to the strictest letter, upon all his descendants without one exception; and no one can deny it. Noah was the grand patriarch under God, and the commander-in-chief of the whole human family, who held so near a place to the heart of the great *"I Am,"* that he was selected to pass from the antediluvian to the postdiluvian world, and was made builder and then commander of the mighty ark, which was planned by God himself. He delivered the decree in the case of his grandson Canaan with the same authority (doubtless) that he erected and commanded the great ark until it rested upon the summit of Mount Ararat. And woe be unto that man, party, or nation, who shall set at nought those decrees, by trampling upon the wisdom of heaven, for he knows what is best.

I will refer to 1 Tim. vi.—

1. "Let as many servants as are under the yoke count their own masters worthy of all honor, that the name of God and *his* doctrine be not blasphemed.

thing else, and consequently have made up their minds from what some infidel preacher of *a* gospel, like the Rev. Henry Ward Beecher, Dr. Cheever, Dr. Furness, or Wendell Phillips, has said on the subject to them, and from their own natural feelings. They believe these great preachers are honest; they have not once thought that they are the very class of men prophesied of, or alluded to, in the 3d, 4th, and 5th verses above quoted; just read the 1st and 2d verses with marked attention, and then read the 3d, 4th, and 5th, with the same attention, and see how clear and positively they point to those preachers, and all such who *pretend* to believe as they do. They may be given over to "*believe a lie, that they may be damned.*" Yet it is hard for me to believe that they are so well off as that. I hope the reader will examine Dr. Adam Clarke on those verses, and see how clearly he points out those hypocrites above named, and all such. Those *pretenders* denounce Paul's exhortation or precept, and make him out a hypocrite and a deceiver of the people like themselves, and every slave owner or master as a thief, murderer, and robber, right in the teeth of Paul's teaching. O man, who art thou, that thou shouldest resist God and denounce his own plans for evangelizing the world? Paul's teachings are, that all such preachers

"Are proud, knowing nothing, but doting about questions and strifes of words, whereof cometh envy, strife, railings, evil surmisings, perverse disputings of men of corrupt minds, and destitute of the truth, supposing that gain is godliness: from such withdraw thyself."

In the above verses, St. Paul was not only an apostle, but an inspired prophet, and I think the present circumstances in the United States is enough to convince any infidel in this country that the Apostle Paul was an inspired writer, therefore we are bound as professing Christians to obey his precepts. I quote those passages for those who embrace the Scriptures as the inspired word of God. I know there is no use to quote Scripture to a professed infidel, for it would only be casting pearl before swine, and the worst kind of swine! For if there is anything that is hateful on this earth, and that ought to stink in the nostrils of all good men, it is the man who mocks at the word of God, and denounces it as a book of lies; yet there is a class of men who are even worse than the infidel. They are those who profess to believe the Scriptures to be the inspired truth of God, and are even ordained preachers of the gospel, who are popular speakers and who draw large congregations, and then preach doctrines to them that completely *nullifies* the laws of Moses, and the Spirit, and letter of the Gospel of God our Saviour, as taught by St. Paul. Some preachers of the gospel of all denominations go high up into pulpits, and tell the Christian slaveholder that he is a thief, a murderer, and robber, and exhort the slave to leave his master, to steal his horse, or his money, that he may make sure his escape. Yes, if his *master, or any one else, attempts to impede his flight, to kill him.* Now I ask, in the name of God and all his holy angels, prophets, and apostles, is this right? even if we leave St. Paul's doctrines of the Gospel of God our Saviour, out of the question, would it be right in the name of reason and common sense for preachers of the gospel to encourage the running off of slaves from their masters, and leave the poor creatures in the most terrible state of degradation, ruin, filth, and suffering, among strangers who have no respect for them; in the name of truth is it right? How much more God-like was the preaching of St. Paul, in his letter to Timothy, than these hellish doctrines, that will sooner or later *turn this glorious government into universal anarchy, and saturate its fertile soil with human blood.*

O how I hate the man who scorns at the word of God! But I hate that man still more who pretends to believe the Bible to be the word of God, and takes upon himself the authority to preach the truths of the everlasting Gospel, and go into his pulpit and annul a large portion of it by recommending Sharp's rifles as being the best Gospel for slaveholders, and encouraging murder, robbery, and theft. Who and what has brought us to such a crisis? *Antislavery preachers.* Has God prepared any place for such preachers in the kingdom of Glory? *If he has, I don't know who will not be there.* Old Apollyon will not be far off. How does Henry Ward Beecher's Sharp rifle sermon compare with St. Paul's letter to Timothy on the subject of slaves and slaveholders? St. Paul says :—

" Let as many servants as are under the yoke, count their *own* masters worthy of *all* honor, that the name of God and his doctrine may be not blasphemed."

What could the apostle have said that would have been more convincing and inviting to all candid persons than the above? How much more God-like than Beecher's sermon, or the whole antislavery doctrine! After the above remarks of the apostle, which were spoken to all servants and masters, without respect to their moral standing, he then alludes particularly to believing masters, and declares them to be brethren. Therefore, a more special obedience to them seemed to be enjoined. But the *antislavery gospel* preachers say, the slaveholders are "thieves, murderers, and robbers, and ought to be shot down like sheep-killing dogs," "or smashed like mosquitoes." What could be invented by the devil better calculated to raise the standard of infidelity in all parts of the world, and reduce the Scriptures of truth to be looked upon as heathen fables? "But rather do them service, because they are faithful and beloved partakers of the benefit. These things teach and exhort."

It is evident from these precepts that there were abolitionists in those days, or the apostle had the nineteenth century in full view when he wrote that epistle, or he would not have said so much on the subject in so many places. He declares that there were believing masters who were faithful, and beloved partakers of the truths of the Gospel. Therefore he enjoins this as a greater reason why their servants should obey them, and that the Church should respect them. But the *antislavery preachers* have used every means to expel all slaveholders from all the communions of the different Christian churches, and declare them unworthy of respect right in the face of the apostle's exhortation and doctrines. Now, tell me, how can such men be Christians? Some say they do not see it in this light. If they do not understand such plain teaching, they are not fit for the Gospel ministry, and should be silenced for their ignorance.

But I cannot believe some of them are as ignorant as all that; they know better. I have no doubt but some follow their own sympathies in preference to Paul's teaching; others take that ground because it is more popular, and yields a better livelihood; but many enter the antislavery circle out of prejudice and malice. But much the larger number enter into the arena because they know it to be more exciting than any other question, and produces the greatest amount of bad feelings, bickerings, and sectional hatreds; and last, but not least, because it is entirely sectional, and they can lavish their slanders without personal danger. "If any man teach otherwise," &c. What does St. Paul mean by these words? Does he not condemn all that oppose slavery? Does he not advocate directly the right of property in men, and that it is the will of the Lord? "And all who teach otherwise are proud, doting about words, to try to make the word of God of no effect." Has not the doings in the M. E. Church and others been a complete fulfilment of what St. Paul said in the 4th and 5th verses? What has been the result of the opposition to slavery, or of *antislavery gospel preaching?* Read those verses, and then read the history of the churches prior to 1840, and investigate its troubles since that time, and tell me what did the mischief. Where did all the evil surmisings come from? How all this bitterness in the Church of God? How about all the disputings, splits, and everlasting separations? And what has produced the secession of six States from this Union, and the almost certainty of the separation of five or six more? What has caused the seizing upon government property by ruthless mobs, and what caused the bombardment of Fort Sumter last week? What has been the means of calling 75,000 men out under arms, ready for the battle-field? What has given infidelity the victory over the church? Who has done all this? *Antislavery preaching*, with all the combined powers of the devil and abolitionists, who may soon have the pleasure of hearing of a million of human souls being sent into eternity by the sword, unprepared.

I refer the reader again to the first five verses of the vi. chapter of 1 Timothy, and hope they may read them over and over until they understand them, and look over the present condition of the church and state, and ask themselves the question as standing at the bar of the eternal God, Who has done all this mischief?

· Paul's letter to Titus ii. says—

9. "*Exhort* servants to be obedient unto their own masters, *and* to please *them* well in all *things;* not answering again ;

10. Not purloining, but showing all good fidelity; that they may adorn the doctrine of God our Saviour in all things."

Here the Apostle also tells Titus to "exhort servants to be obedient to their masters in all things;

9

answering not again," that is, they must not hesitate when they hear their masters' command, but obey it to the strictest letter, and not steal their masters' property nor no other, but show all good fidelity, that they might adorn the doctrine of God their Saviour in *all things*. "But," says the abolitionist, "those were all hired servants." I will ask how hired servants came to have masters, and why could they not do as they pleased, and if they did not do their duty, could not their employers have discharged them and hired others that would do their duty? "Servant" was an accommodating term, it means a hired servant or a bond-servant. But slave means a bond-slave only, and could not be made to cover both, therefore the word servant was used by the translators. The thing being so clear to their minds, that no doubt, they thought a dispute could not arise. I think, perhaps, they did not know the devil as well as they did the languages of the ancients. I insert these passages in full for the convenience of the reader, that he may see how much more comprehensive the Apostle was whenever he alludes to the servants. If one of the relations alluded to be wrong and sinful, all of them are morally wrong, but if any of them are right, they are all right.

I would like some good anti-slavery man to explain to me why the Apostle was more comprehensive and particular in his exhortation to the slaves than he was to any others? If they were journeymen and had a right to leave off at pleasure, or if the master had a right to discharge them without loss, why was the extra language used in the 22d verse; look at it, and tell me why, if they were not slaves for life. These passages are so emphatic and clear, that with even casual readers, comment is unnecessary, and not one word was left on record, from the history of the fall of man to the Revelations, that makes comment necessary to the attentive and unprejudiced reader. I feel compelled to say, that every abolitionist who reads the Bible, and says the relation of master and slave is a sin against God, is an infidel, and ought not to be allowed a place in the Christian ministry. Suppose a minister of the gospel should denounce the relation of husband and wife, and parents and children, as a sin against God, and constantly labor to separate them by any means that would produce the effect. Would such a one be tolerated in the Christian church? No, not one month. And society would hold him up to scorn and derision. Why then should abolitionists be tolerated in the Christian church, when the relation of master and slave is even more strongly sustained in the text, than that of husband and wife, and parents and children. Did St. Paul anywhere instruct the people how to be *idolaters*, or to commit *adultery, perjury, theft, extortion, or intoxication?* Does the Scriptures anywhere instruct those who in violation of the matrimonial law, and live in unchaste intercourse with each other, how they must act towards each other in the unlawful relation which they have assumed? But the Scriptures everywhere teach us that if we have stolen, to steal no more. But they nowhere tell us that the relation of master and slave must be broken up. No, not even one single intimation was given that we can draw an inference that it was objected to. I will also refer the reader to Paul's letter to Philemon, which was a private letter, and was not intended for the public, for Philemon was not an Apostle, but had been converted under the preaching of Paul long before Paul went to Rome, where he was a prisoner when he wrote this epistle to Philemon. I will here give the whole letter of Paul to Philemon—

THE EPISTLE OF PAUL TO PHILEMON.—1. "Paul, a prisoner of Jesus Christ, and Timothy *our* brother, unto Philemon our dearly-beloved, and fellow-laborer,

2. And to *our* beloved Apphia, and Archippus our fellow-soldier, and to the church in thy house:

3. Grace to you, and peace, from God our Father and the Lord Jesus Christ.

4. I thank my God, making mention of thee always in my prayers,

5. Hearing of thy love and faith, which thou hast toward the Lord Jesus, and toward all saints;

6. That the communication of thy faith may become effectual by the acknowledging of every good thing which is in you in Christ Jesus.

7. For we have great joy and consolation in thy love, because the bowels of the saints are refreshed by thee, brother.

8. Wherefore, though I might be much bold in Christ to enjoin thee that which is convenient,

9. Yet for love's sake I rather beseech *thee*, being such a one as Paul the aged, and now also a prisoner of Jesus Christ;

10. I beseech thee for my son Onesimus, whom I have begotten in my bonds:

11. Which in time past was to thee unprofitable, but now profitable to thee and to me:

12. Whom I have sent again; thou therefore receive him, that is mine own bowels;

13. Whom I would have retained with me, that in thy stead he might have ministered unto me in the bonds of the gospel:

14. But without thy mind would I do nothing; that thy benefit should not be as it were of necessity, but willingly.

15. For perhaps he therefore departed for a season, that thou shouldest receive him for ever;

16. Not now as a servant, but above a servant, a brother beloved, especially to me, but how much more unto thee, both in the flesh and in the Lord?

17. If thou count me therefore a partner, receive him as myself.

18. If he hath wronged thee, or oweth *thee* aught, put that on mine account;

19. I Paul have written *it* with mine own hand, I will repay *it:* albeit I do not say to thee how thou owest unto me even thine own self besides.

20. Yea, brother, let me have joy of thee in the Lord: refresh my bowels in the Lord.

21. Having confidence in thy obedience, I wrote unto thee, knowing that thou wilt also do more than I say.

32. But withal prepare me also a lodging: for I trust that through your prayers I shall be given unto you.

23. There salute thee Epaphras, my fellow-prisoner in Christ Jesus;

24. Marcus, Aristarchus, Demas, Lucas, my fellow-laborers.

25. The grace of our Lord Jesus Christ *be* with your spirit. Amen.

¶ Written from Rome to Philemon, by Onesimus a servant.

Why did Paul not advise Onesimus to stay away from his master Philemon, when he could have done it without its ever having been known by his master? If Paul had been a timid man, what a chance here was for him to have done right without embarrassment. But it is very clear that he was not a timid man, for he made the very foundations of heathen mythology and society to tremble, by proclaiming the Gospel of Christ everywhere in public, from Jerusalem to Rome, and denounced their idols, their adulteries, fornications, drunkenness, barbarism, dishonesty, and oppressions, and every kind of wickedness, and told them that God could not behold any of those things with the least degree of allowance, and reminded them on the highway, and upon the house-top, and in church, irrespective of prisons and bonds, that God would judge them. If slavery had been wrong, he would not have sent Onesimus home with the above epistle. It is evident he would have denounced the relation of master and slave, and told Philemon he was sinning against God, and, unless he set Onesimus free, he would be sent away with the devil and his angels into outer darkness, where there would be weeping, wailing, and gnashing of teeth. Yet the apostle, with all his courage and boldness in denouncing sin of every kind, tolerates slavery, by sending Onesimus back to his master (although he had become a Christian) with the above epistle; although Philemon was far away from Paul's prison-house, yet he seemed to have no rest after he learned that Onesimus was a fugitive from bondage, and his Christian brother Philemon's legal property.

If slavery be a *moral evil*, why did the apostle send Onesimus back to bondage, from which he had fled, with an epistle to his master Philemon, who had been converted under Paul, without inserting one single sentence against his moral right to Onesimus

as his property? Being now far from his master's
power, just as much so as a slave from Georgia is when
in Canada. "If it had been right for him to have
continued free, why did this inspired apostle of
Christ send him back to bondage? Did he not see
by the wisdom that God had given him, that he
could not be a true apostle of Jesus Christ unless he
did so? That Onesimus could not remain there and
be a righteous man, in the sight of God, while owing
service to his master without his master's consent.
Why was this epistle handed down to us as a part
of the Scriptures of truth, containing Paul's direction
in this case? Was it not for our instruction on the
subject of slavery? Certainly no Christian man
will say it was not. How a professing Christian can
endeavor to give so different a meaning to all the
passages in the Old and New Testaments, I cannot
tell; and when I read the 18th and 19th verses of
the last chapter of Rev., as follows:—

18. "For I testify unto every man that heareth the words
of the prophecy of this book, If any man shall add unto these
things, God shall add unto him the plagues that are written in
this book.

19. And if any man shall take away from the words of the
book of this prophecy, God shall take away his part out of the
book of life, and out of the holy city, and *from* the things which
are written in this book."

I tremble at the thought of even bad men trying
to overthrow the Christian Church, by misconstruing
the Holy Scriptures; but I fear more when men,
professing to be the followers and believers in the
Lord and Saviour Jesus Christ, and declare they are

called of him to preach his own everlasting Gospel
to a fallen, sinful, and dying world—when they enter
the sanctuary under a pretence of administering in
holy things, and expounding the holy Scriptures,
and then condemn and denounce as the "sum of all
villainy" what is so clearly taught throughout divine
revelation by all the inspired writers of that holy
book of God, who mentioned the relation of master
and slave, I say I fear more that some terrible
judgments will be let fall upon us of the nineteenth
century.   When our ministers of the Gospel of
Christ, in the teeth of the warning quoted above
from Revelations—right in opposition to the clearest
teachings of divine revelation, declare the relation
of master and slave to be a sin against God, when it
is their imperative duty to sustain that relation just
as much as it is to sustain the relation of husband
and wife or father and child; for the teachings of
divine inspiration in reference to the relation of
master and servant is more impressively taught, and
made more imperatively the duty of every teacher of
the Holy Bible to sustain the relations of master and
slave, and it is their imperative duty, under the Gospel Dispensation, to use every honorable means to
send fugitives from labor home to their masters,
whenever they come in contact with them.   If they
do not do this, and "teach otherwise," they are ten-
fold more the children of the devil than they were
before the Bishop laid his hands on their heads, because they refuse to declare the whole gospel truth,
not only by withholding such parts of it as do not
suit their taste, but they denounce those certain

portions as being from the devil, and in league with hell.

St. Paul everywhere exhorts the slaves to be obedient to their masters in all things, not to neglect their work, not to serve with eye service—that is, they were required to be just as faithful in the performance of their duty in the absence of their masters as when they were present with them—not to steal nor waste anything that belong to their masters, but to perform every duty as to God, and they should have a reward in heaven, whether they be "bond or *free;*" that is, whether they were of the Israelites, who could not be made slaves for life, and had to be treated as hired servants, or whether they were of the heathen, for whom there was no liberty or freedom in this world promised. They were all alike exhorted to faithfulness to their masters, without which they had no promises of heaven hereafter. And even the return of them to their masters, when they run away, is required of the Church, as St. Paul sent Onesimus directly home to Philemon, his master. "If any man teach otherwise," he is a hypocrite—a child of the devil; and for "teaching otherwise," he shall have his "portion in the lake that burns with fire and brimstone forever, yea, forever and ever." They will not only destroy the Christian Church, which is the only hope of the free government, but they will break up this great and glorious free republican government, if they have not already done it, and placed it almost beyond the hope of recovery, by their unlawful and ungodly opposition to negro slavery, whose condition never can be bettered in this country outside of slavery.

There is no philanthropy so merciful as that of slavery for the poor unfortunate Africans. There is no trade more hated, and that has the appearance of greater wickedness, than the slave trade. My own soul abhors the very idea of the foreign slave trade. The Rev. John Wesley said it was the "sum of all villainies;" Adam Clarke said very strong things against it, though, perhaps, he never saw a negro slave, and but few negroes, if any, as his entire life was spent in Europe; therefore he had no personal knowledge of the relation of master and slave. Yet he fully justified the moral right to hold slaves for life, throughout his Commentary on the Bible. After Mr. Wesley made use of that very strong denunciation, he visited the United States and the West India Islands, and saw the condition of master and slave. He received masters and slaves both into the church, and administered the sacraments to them, baptized the children of slaveholders, and, I believe, if I recollect right, licensed slaveholders to preach the Gospel of God our Saviour. He was not heard to utter a word against the institution of slavery, or tell any slaveholder that he was a thief, murderer, and robber, because he was a slaveholder, or that slavery was a moral evil, as it existed in the United States or the West Indies; and, if I am not mistaken in my recollection of facts, he admonished the missionaries coming to the United States not to interfere with the relation of master and slave, but to preach the Gospel to both alike. Yet with all the abhorrence to the foreign slave trade, and Mr. Wesley's denunciation, *it has produced more civilization, and raised more human beings from heathenism and barbarism to Christianity, than all the missionary efforts of the world besides,* 'since the reformation, though they have done much good for civilization and true Christianity. I know I shall be *branded* with the most terrible names for giving utterance to such sentiments; if so, I must bear it the best I can, for if I speak at all on the subject, I must speak what I believe to be the truth, as taught in history. As I have said, I am a true friend of the negro race, and pity them; but human nature, common sense, and reason, philanthropy, Christianity, and my great love and admiration of this great and glorious Union, and the fear of the judgments of Almighty God, binds me to these opinions.

Does it not look as if my fears were about to be realized? Look at the condition of our great country—are we not on the very verge of a bloody civil war? Where will it end when once inaugurated? Can it be restored by any compromises, after hostilities once set it? Can we have Union without love and harmony between the slave and free States? Will the taking of their slaves from them produce love and harmony between the two extremes? *For that is the only object of the anti-slavery party.* Opposition to slavery has brought us to this awful crisis. With an army behind us so terrible that it is resistless, while we are on the brink of an endless gulf of the eternal overthrow of the best government on which the sun has ever shone (I don't mean the present administration), and it is only a step before us, which can be averted only by a speedy return to our loyalty, to the Constitution, and laws of the United States, which have been trampled upon by some of the free States for many years, and a speedy return to Christian· forbearance and love, as taught by our Saviour and his holy Apostles.

The free States now have the truly religious means within their reach to save the whole nation from a collision that will engulf us, as a nation, perhaps forever. We *are not* asked.to concede any-thing that belongs to us. If we speedily turn, and do right in the sight of heaven, we shall be saved; if we do not, national ruin, with anarchy or a terri-ble and perpetual despotism may be the result of our folly.

I will give a short extract from a letter I received from the Hon. Edward Everett, of Boston, a short time ago, for those who differ with me about the loyalty of some of the free States. Some of us wanted to get up a large mass meeting, to avert, if possible, the calamities we saw before us. I was requested to write to Mr. Everett, and invite him to come on, and make a speech on the occasion. I wrote, and received an answer, from which I quote the following from recollection, as I have not the letter before me—

"There is no use of making any more speeches for the Union, unless the free States will repeal their unconstitutional personal liberty bills."

Mr. Everett must pardon me if I have erred in the wording, I have given the very sentiment, and it is full of meaning. I have spent about twenty-six years of my time in the slave States, and twenty-nine years in the free. I have been well acquainted in nine or ten of the slave States. And had it not been for my objections to having anything to do with slave labor, I should have settled in the State of Mississippi many years ago. For a finer, more liberal, agreeable, and devout Christian people, I have never seen in this world, of whom I have spoken in full in the first two or three chapters of this book, and to my notion, one of the most pleasant climates in this country, for those who are not com-pelled to labor constantly in the hot sun. I have travelled a good deal, and been a considerable ob-server of the happiness of the people. But I have never seen a class of persons so happy as the negro slaves of that State. I never saw one exception among the slaves of the South, nor one maltreated, and never knew of but one being badly flogged. I did not see that, but if I was to tell what for, you would wonder that he had not been killed on the spot. I knew all the parties well.

The stories about maltreatment to slaves, are the foulest and most unmitigated slanders that were ever hatched up by the devil and his emissaries. If Harriet Beecher Stowe, Mrs. Childs, the Misses Grim-kies, Dred, and a thousand and one more, had been born in the lower regions of the damnation of hell, and had been educated at the feet of old Apollyon, they could not have belched out more foul, infamous slanders, than they have done in the many books they have written against slavery and slaveholders.

10

No one has a better knowledge of the infamous slanders than they have. And thousands of ministers of the gospel join in and help spread those slanders from the desk that has been dedicated to the service of the living God, knowing them to be false in many cases, and if they do not, they ought to be expelled from the ministry for their ignorance. But they cannot be so ignorant, for common sense and reason teaches better things. They are the employees of the King of darkness, who he has commissioned and sent forth to destroy the hopes of mankind. How does their teachings compare with the Apostle Paul in the quotations herein made from the Bible? Henry Ward Beecher says from his pulpit, that Sharp's rifles are the best gospels, and the only one fit to preach to slaveholders. He sent his agents out with Sharp's rifles in their hands, and a Bible in their pockets, to administer to slaveholders with powder and bullets; and I suppose the Bible was for the negroes and followers of the abolition gospel preachers. A celebrated Methodist preacher stationed at one of our finest churches, said in a sermon on the war—

"Brethren, I feel that I cannot restrain myself much longer. I must shoulder my musket, start for the rebels, and the first one I meet, I will discharge the contents of my musket through him, and while the blood is weltering from his veins, I will kneel down by his side, and pray God to pardon his sins." "Great Britain," said he, "is threatening to come and attack us, but" (clasped his thumb to his nose, and spreading his fingers like an ape) "let her come, and she will never try it again."

Now I ask, how much of the mind that was in our

Lord, was in that man? How much of the spirit that moved St. Paul when he was preaching to both masters and slaves? Are such as the above possessed with love? Christ said "we must love our enemies, return good for evil, and by so doing we shall heap up coals of fire on their heads." The sword of the spirit is the only weapon of warfare our Lord bequeathed to those he sent forth to preach his own everlasting gospel. And as soon as we take up the temporal sword, the Holy Spirit takes its flight. Our Lord said to Peter—

Matt. xxvi. 52. "Put up again thy sword into his place: for all they that take the sword shall perish with the sword."

Has all our preachers obeyed this admonition of our Lord. Or did he give his ambassadors licenses that he had not from the great God who sent him to us as his great ambassador. Compare these abolition gospel preachers with our Lord and his Apostles, and where do they stand on the slave question? How did the prophets, the patriarchs, our Lord, and his Apostles, treat upon slavery and slaveholders? Why, our Lord said to his disciples in reference to a large slaveholder, "I have not found so great faith, no not in Israel." Paul said, "slaves, obey your masters in all things." "Yet as many as are under the yoke count their own masters worthy of all honor."

A preacher said to some gentlemen the other day, that he almost desired to be the devil from now throughout all eternity, that he might go down to hell to torture the slaveholders, by piling them up and dashing them to pieces against each other, to increase their torture throughout all eternity: that he feared he, the devil, would be too lenient towards slaveholders. I am glad to say this was not a methodist preacher.

How it is that the masses can be so blinded and led by such devils incarnate, is entirely beyond my comprehension; and how it is that so many good people seem so blind that they do not see the vortex of ruin just before them that these abolition leaders and preachers are leading them into. And if we do not speedily awake from our sleep of blindness and hurl these infidel traitors from our midst, or ever-lastingly silence them, our great and glorious government, that was so heaven-like, will be lost forever, and we shall be placed under a despotism that will end all our liberties, and our happiness of course; or some other diabolical change will take place. War will end all our hopes for future happiness; nothing can now save us but for us to submit to be guided by the teachings found in the gospel of Christ on the subject in dispute.

I was in Mississippi in 1844 while the General Conference of the M. E. Church was in session in New York, which struck the first official and fatal blow at the union of these States. The alarm among the people was beyond description; they thought the people of the free States were determined to drive them out of the Union. They looked upon it as a direct attack upon their rights when Bishop Andrews was deposed because he had married a lady that owned two or three little negro children that had been left her. How must every Christian slaveholder have felt when that most ungodly and unfortunate step was taken. It unlocked the first door to our ecclesiastical and national ruin, and the complete breaking of the glorious systems that God had in his goodness blessed us with. The cotton States then were as the antechamber of Paradise. There were then no distractions, except the howlings of the abolitionists of the north, and the response of a few fire-eaters of the south, who were the legitimate off-spring of the abolitionists of the free States. They were called fire-eaters because they threw back the charges made against them by the anti-slavery party with contemptuous indignation. The abolitionists aimed their blows at their tenderest spots for no other purpose than to break up this great and glorious Union. They made slavery the pretext, and it was only a pretext; for, what can such fellows as the preacher who said he would like to be the devil (for fear the *old* devil would fail in his duty to slave-holders) care for the poor slaves! About as much as the serpent cared about the happiness of our first parents, when he seemed to pity them so much for their ignorance of good and evil, when their ruin was his only object.

So also those devils incarnate pretend to love and pity the poor slaves, and swell out great big words of admiration for the union of States; yet they pretend to love the dear slaves a little better, and by that means they know just as well as the devil did that the tasting of the fruit would curse Adam, that their course would destroy the peace and tranquillity of this nation and our liberties, and ruin the last

10*

hope for poor Africa. All this is aimed at the root of Christianity; it is a hatred towards God, and the peace and happiness of mankind. Theft, slander, persecution, and abuse have been the means used to overthrow this nation, that the Christian Church might be overthrown.

I am met with the reply that it is only a few religious fanatics who do these things. I say that is not so; it is whole communities, counties, and States united with those fanatics. Did not the State of Massachusetts elect Charles Sumner to the United States Senate the second time when they knew just what he was? How many of the free States have passed laws which completely annul the constitutional rights of the slave States. Get the slave laws of Pennsylvania, Massachusetts, Rhode Island, and Connecticut, called personal liberty bills, and read them over until the scales shall fall from your eyes, and you will see that they were framed expressly to embarrass the Constitution and the laws of the United States, and thereby to rob the slaveholders of their own lawful property. These things were done many years ago, and with them the persecutions and slanders have been unceasing. And what has been more insulting than anything else, those terrible denunciations have been made by Christian ministers from the pulpit to large and crowded houses, and now the terrible judgments of Almighty God are upon us, and no man seems to repent of his sin against heaven and earth. May the Lord have mercy upon us, and save us from the judgments which now stare us in the face; for if they are not averted they will soon burst upon us like the raging winds and seas upon the rock-bound mariner. Almost the only passage that the abolition party ever quote from the Bible to condemn slavery is the general rule or precept given by our Lord, Matt. vii. 12.

"Therefore all things whatsoever ye would that men should do to you, do ye even so to them: for this is the law and the prophets."

How this passage can be construed to affect the lawful relations of men, is as puzzling to me as anything else they do. This precept is a general one, and if the anti-slavery party had only just obeyed it, we should now be at peace throughout this entire country. For it compels them to treat the slaveholders just as they would have the slaveholders to treat them. How would they have the slaveholders to treat them? With all candor and respect in all his lawful right. He would not have the slaveholders to interfere with anything which belongs to him without his permission; he would not have them to insult him by calling him hard names, and proclaim to large audiences that he was a thief, murderer, and a robber. Now, under this precept he is bound to treat the slaveholder with the same kindness in all things whatever, which he might desire from the slaveholders. And if he cannot fully realize his duty, let him completely reverse the circumstances between himself and the slaveholder, by supposing himself born and brought up a slaveholder, and suppose he had five hundred slaves on his plantation, how would he have the people of the North to treat him? Would he not have them to treat him with all kindness and respect in all of his lawful rights? Then, by this precept of our Lord, are you not bound to treat the slaveholder with that kindness which you would require if placed where he is? But you say, the relation of masters and slaves is a very different thing. So it is. But does that change the question in the least? Are not slaves bound by the same precept just as much as their masters? Are they not required to render such service and obedience to their masters in all things, that they would have their masters to render unto them full obedience and service, if their circumstances were completely reversed? And the master is only required to treat his slaves as he would be treated by them, if he was their slave; besides, it is his lawful right to hold such persons in slavery.

But no white man who is a true descendant of Shem can be righteously enslaved, except for crime, for the laws of heaven forbid it. But not so with the Africans. An all-merciful God decreed that they should be slaves to the Israelites without limitation. Although it was over twenty-three hundred years before Christ, yet he in his day never uttered a word against the slave law; and he blest men who were large slaveholders, without saying to them that it was sinful. We find St. Paul, some fifty or sixty years after Christ, enjoining the duties of slaves to their masters upon them in the strictest manner, and also the duties of masters to their slaves, and not a word uttered by that great man of God against the slave laws, or a petition for their repeal. But woe be unto every master who shall maltreat slaves by

putting more on them than they are fully able to
bear, or by withholding from them sufficient good
wholesome food and comfortable clothing; for they
have a Master in heaven, who will hold them to a
strict accountability for their treatment to the servants God has allotted to them to care and provide
for.

Suppose we should give to this injunction of our
Lord the one-sided definition that abolitionists do,
and that construction should be agreed upon the
world over. Let us see what the result would be:
A criminal stands before the court for sentence, he
addresses himself to his honor, and says: if your
honor were in my place, and I in yours, your honor
would have me to discharge you without sentence.
Therefore, I demand of your honor to do to me as
you would have me do to you, and let me go free.
The culprit on the platform, under sentence of death,
would say to the sheriff, you know you would not
have me to hang you, if our circumstances were reversed, you know you would have me say to you
go in peace, and sin no more. Therefore, I demand
of you to do as you would be done by, take off
these shackles, and let me go free. This definition
, to this injunction would ruin the world if men
should go by it. While on the other hand, the
injunction with the legitimate construction, and the
only one which can be put on it by true men, if
all should resolve to live by it, wars and rumors of
wars would cease, and the whole world would be at
peace in a very short space of time. There would
be no quarrelling, no fighting, no cheating, no steal-

ing, and a police force would be useless. It is a most glorious precept. One of its principles seems to be overlooked altogether by the abolitionist. That is, it forbids one man to ask of another what he feels in his soul that he would not do for him if circumstances were reversed. And no honest man will ask another to help him under such circumstances. So much for this precept of our Lord.

But slavery is a sin, or moral evil, says the abolitionist, therefore must and shall be destroyed, even if church and state shall both be destroyed with it. How came slavery or anything else to be a moral evil? There must be some rule by which morals are established, therefore there must be a moral law, or there can be no moral evil. It is conceded by all abolitionists that there is moral evil, therefore they must admit that there is a moral law. If there is a moral law, where did it come from, and by whom was it established? There was a moral law among the antediluvians. But the first written law we have any account of, was written by Moses, and it seems that it was handed down to him by the Almighty in the mountain. And in that very law, slavery was fully recognized. Gen. xvii. 12-13, Ex. xx. 17, Lev. xxv. 38-55. Those passages I have copied in full in the previous chapter. It is enough to show that slavery was fully recognized by Moses, the great Jewish lawgiver, in both the moral and civil law. The decalogue, or ten commandments, was given to Moses at the mouth of the Lord himself. And in that, slavery is fully recognized by the eternal God, and no slave laws in the

United States are more positive than those contained in the xxv. of Lev. There can be no *moral law without divine sanction.*

If none of the laws of Moses have divine sanction upon them, then there could not have been any moral evil. Then if there is any moral evil in the world, God must have directed the passage of the laws of Moses, for there could not have been any morals without his presence, and as slavery is recognized in those laws, it must have been recognized as a *moral right.* The xxv. of Lev., the 38th and 55th verses, ought to be noticed with marked attention, as one immediately precedes, and the other immediately follows the most positive pro-slavery laws ever enacted in the world. Read from the 38th to the end of the chapter, and you must admit divine sanction was given to all those verses, if there is any truth in the declaration, that all Scripture was written by divine inspiration.

There are no passages of Scripture which condemus human slavery as it exists in this country. There is not one line, nor one word, from which an inference can be drawn against the relation of master and slave. The relation of husband and wife has not got such Scriptural protection thrown around it that slavery has. And I suppose the only reason for that was, the inspired writers knew that the relation of husband and wife would not at any age of the world need the amount of support, because it was more natural and congenial to both parties than slavery ever would be. There is great caution given by St. Paul to husbands and wives to love each other, but their obligations were not so particularly and specially enjoined, as that to masters and servants. And doubtless the reasons were, that the spirit which impressed the minds of the inspired writers what to write, saw far in the future the bold opposition that would be made to his arrangements for the good of mankind by abolitionists. Therefore the difference, or extra advice to masters and slaves.

What has been the result of the interference with the moral and civil rights to hold slaves as property? The frightful condition of our great republican empire at this time are its legitimate results; and unless the precept of our Lord shall be speedily and righteously adhered to, our great free republican government will be eternally overthrown, and we shall be reduced to an equality with negro slaves. The just judgments of the Almighty are already upon us; an attempt to save the Union by the force of arms will blast all our hopes as a free and independent nation and people forever, and proclaim to the whole world that man is incapable of self-government. We were a free and independent people, governed by laws made by the people—a general government with a limited central power, conceded by a number of free sovereign States. The adoption of the Constitution by all the people of all the sovereign States, produced a free Republican Constitutional Union of all free citizens of North America. It was a free-will offering or concession of all the people, for the good of the whole. Therefore, if one part interferes with the Constitutional rights of the other, and resolves upon any unconstitutional plans to limit or circumscribe those rights, having the numerical power to do so, the minority or the oppressed are no longer under any obligations to the other, and can withdraw at pleasure. This is common sense, common reason, and common law. This was the opinion of most all good men. The Honorable John Quincy Adams, of Mass., gave it as his opinion in a positive way, a short time before his death. How truly does he say—

"But the *indissoluble link* of the union between the people of the several States of this confederated nation is, *after all*, 'not in the *right*,' 'but in the *heart*.'" And also, "*far better* will it be for the people of the disunited States, to *part in friendship* with each other, than be*held together with constraint !*"

Mr. Adams took the only true ground; that our strength was in the union, and not in the right. Now, this being the case, as every common sense man in the nation must agree, who has given the principles of a free republican constitutional Union like ours only a limited, impartial study, in connection with a slight knowledge of human nature, how it is that so many people seem to think that one part of this great nation has a right to slander, abuse, oppress, and hate the other part, and limit them in their lawful rights, and then force them to live in a union with us, is too ridiculous for sensible men to believe. I hear professing Christian men denouncing our southern brethren as the greatest scoundrels and devils on the face of the earth, and declare they shall not leave us if it cost $10,000,000.000

11

and one million, or even five millions of lives of *white* men to force them to live in the Union with us. That is, they would do all this to make slaves of eight millions of white citizens, of our own race and blood, *who are fully capable of self-government,* to free less than four millions of *black negroes, not of our race or blood, and made totally incapable of self-government by a decree of the Almighty,* and must have guardians, or be miserable through all time, if not throughout eternity. We have just as good a right to suppose King "Dehomi" is fit for President of the United States, as to suppose the slaves of this country are fit for freedom and self-government. And just so sure as we betray our trust, and set them free in this country, God will judge us as not being fit for self-government; and every man who is not a *millionaire,* will be reduced to slavery, and placed on an equality with negroes. How men can take the course they do for the emancipation of that race who are so physically dissimilar, and even obnoxious to the sight and taste of every decent white person, and right in the face of the most positive teachings of inspired truth, is an enigma of which I must decline the solution.

The Gospel tends, in its effects, to abolish imprisonment, capital punishment, war, and even involuntary servitude to a limited extent. When the people are all righteous, sheriffs and police will be of no further use, the penal code will be a dead letter, courts of all kinds will be held as a mere prudential system for the convenience of the people, and perhaps the *Decalogue* or ten commandments

will be the only law on the statute books. What
has broken up our peace and happiness as a Christian society? What has been the greatest disturber
of the peace and happiness of this great nation for
the last forty years? What has separated the Christian churches of this country, and what is now separating this great and mighty Republican Empire?
Who and what is plunging us into a bloody civil or
servile war, and perhaps bloody revolutions, which
may not end in a hundred years, and will end only by
reducing us to slavery under one of the most extreme
despotisms that has ever reigned over any people?
Then the difference between the white man and
negro will not be respected by our rulers. I say,
what has done all this mischief? Abolitionism,
with their unlawful and ungodly opposition to slavery; and all the responsibility, with all the awful
consequences are upon them. There was no room
for a doubt, that if the Chicago Platform was sustained by a vote of the people, our ruin would be
sealed by that act. That we should be whipped
with many stripes was certain. All who had
watched the course of things, and had given human
nature a proper study, had not the slightest doubt
of the fatal result. There never has been an event
in the world that was more certain to follow any
contingencies than the secession of the Cotton States
from the Union on the success of the Chicago Platform, or the success of a candidate who had given
his solemn pledge to sustain it if elected. I was
astonished to find so many good men who accepted it
as their political creed, and who looked upon us as

the greatest fools for seeming to fear any danger. They said, in reply to our warnings, that there was not a man in South Carolina who could be kicked out of the Union.

The prospective result was so clear to me, in case that that most unconstitutional political creed was sustained at the Presidential election of 1860, that I sometimes almost doubted their sincerity, because it was so strange to me that every man of observation did not seem to see it, for it was the very course of nature. Christian men seemed now to rely on the arm of Jehovah, and are now bold in saying that they have no fear while he is on the Throne; that the South are altogether in the wrong, and he will rebuke them by turning their negroes upon them, and they would soon call on us to save them from the savage tribe, and the negroes would all be freed without our striking a blow.

Sayings of this kind are in almost every Republican mouth. If I believed Jehovah is on our side, I should not suffer as I do. But I fear we are not in the right, and I cannot claim divine aid in a war for the emancipation of the negro slaves of the South. I believe the judgments of God are already upon us for our interference with his own arrangements among men; and so sure as we go on to coerce the Southern States, our downfall will be completed.

Every southern leader offered to accept the Crittenden Compromise, which gave us the three-fourths of all the public domain of the United States as free territory, which was more than I thought they would do. If we had accepted that, and removed every unconstitutional obstacle out of the way, including the Chicago Platform, and the South had then seceded, as they have done, I believe God would then have been on our side, and I should feel safe. But as it is, I have no hope, because I believe we are in the wrong; and I fear the sequel will prove it to be so when too late. The avenger of blood is already at our heels, and, unless we speedily repent and concede what is right in the premises, God will hold us to a severe account-ability. We have been interfering with their rights for many years, personally, collectively, and by statute laws. We were the first sinners against the Constitution of the nation, and we have acted as though it was made for the free States, and that the slave States had no part nor lot in it. Therefore, if we do not move first, and concede all their rights to them, and no more—and no more have they ever asked—we shall be ruined forever—ruined as a great nation. Our constitutional government will end now, and God will hold us responsible.

I have no sympathy with secession, for they had no right to do wrong because we did. They are not clear of a fearful responsibility, and God will deal out justice to them in proper measure. I am a citizen of Pennsylvania by choice. All my interests are here, and here I expect to live and die. If this great Union is to be dissolved, I shall be a ruined man. There will be no hope for me on the other side of a dissolution of this great Republican Empire. The sound of the cannon and the bray of the war-horse will never cease to be heard by us, until we go hence. I have nothing to do with the South now.

11*

I might write five hundred pages of abuse and slander upon them; it would please those I am compelled to come in contact with, and make me many strong friends, who now hate me because I cannot see and think as they do. To say what I do not believe, and what I know is not the truth, I will not, not even to save my neck from being stretched on the "*lamp-post*," or incarceration in some desolate Bastile. For to do so I should sin with my eyes wide open against heaven, my country, and my own personal. liberties. If I could believe the word of God was any more certain than the course of the republican party is to destroy this great constitutional government, I should have some hope of a restoration with peace and union while that party is in power. But as it is, I have no hope of ever being a free man in the United States again, because I see such a determination on the part of the dominant party to coerce the seceding States back again, knowing the very attempt is disunion and destruction. For union is peace, love, harmony, tranquillity, and mutual agreements; *but war is its very opposite. How can good make bad, or how can bad make good?* Where does our great Christian chart recommend so hateful a course towards our enemies? The great John Quincy Adams said that the strength, permanency, and safety of our great Union "*was not in the right, but in the heart;*" and as long as it was kept in the *heart*, we were the strongest, the most powerful, and the most glorious government on the face of the earth. But as soon as our power was removed from the *heart* to the *arm*, we at once become the weakest of all great nations; and unless we return to our first love, our liberties and peace will never return to us as a great nation, and we shall be laughed at as fools by the whole civilized world, and our glorious *Stars* and *Stripes* will never be respected again as they have been.

The administration, with all their violent supporters, seem to be as ignorant of where our strength *lay*, as Delilah and the Philistines were of Sampson's. As long as God was his strength he was more than a match for the world. But as soon as he was shorn of his strength, his enemies had no trouble in plucking out his eyes. The abolition Delilah found out where our strength lay as a great and mighty empire, and have been using all foul means to remove our strength from the *heart* to the head, or anywhere else so that it was not in the *"heart."* For while it was there God was our strength, and every civilized nation of the globe trembles at the thought—not at our *rights*, for there was no power in the *"right,"* but in the *"heart."* Therefore, infidelity through the agency of abolitionism have shorn us of our mighty power by producing sectional hatreds, divided by a geographical line, separating the North from the South. And infidelity through a special pretended or morbid philanthropy for the negro slaves of the South (*but none for anybody else*), have labored incessantly for more than forty years to remove our strength from the *"heart"* to the head and arm. Knowing that as soon as the North and South was made to hate each other, their work of ruin was complete.

In order to do that, the most damning slanders
have been originated in the free States, and published
from pulpits, platforms, newspaper offices, books,
and periodicals of every description and shape, and
the man who could say the hardest things against
their Southern brethren from their pulpits was the
most popular preacher of the day. "Uncle Tom's
Cabin," perhaps, was the most fatal of all other
periodicals, because it found its way into all the
Theatres in the free States of this country, and all
European theatres, where our Southern brethren
were held up to ridicule and the foulest slanders
ever heaped upon mankind. No theatricals before
them were ever so popular, all because the falsehoods and slanders excelled all before them, and
were made against as high minded, liberal, noble
hearted and truly Christian-like people as ever lived
in this or any other country.

Now, how was it possible under such circumstances for any truly loyal citizen to have expected anything else than civil war. Nothing could have been
more certain to follow, and yet nothing so wicked,
unholy, and ungodly. O, how I hate the men and
women who have ruined my country, my home, and
all my hopes (as a free citizen) for ever. The Southern people have acted bad towards their friends in
the free States, and no punishment would be adequate to their crime against the Constitution and
Union of these once happy States. That being the
case, what ought to be the punishment of those here
in the free States who have labored so long and
incessantly for no other purpose than to drive them

to do just what they have done, under the belief,
that we could whip them without much trouble or
expense? The great reliance being in the negro
slaves of the South rising up and cutting the throats
of all their owners—what could be more wicked
than such a desire or thought? But how sadly has
been our mistake; and in addition to that, however
soon the war may terminate, we shall be slaves to a
national debt which will bind us down for ever.
When I know all this is the price of an ungodly
opposition to negro slavery; yea, when I see my
brethren and race yoked and forced from their families by thousands, and even hundreds of thousands,
and driven into the field to battle for the negro
slaves, to be set free contrary to divine revelation;
that is, the white race are made slaves, that the
negroes may be freed, and put out of use for ever—
I feel an indignation rising that is hard to suppress,
for God said, they ("*We, the people*") should not be
"ruled over with rigor." I will give one more
quotation and close.

1. Peter ii. 18. "Servants, be subject to your masters with all
fear, not only to the good and gentle, but also to the froward."

Here the servants are charged to be subject to
their masters, not only to the good but also the bad
and hard hearted, "with all fear." If I could find
one word in the whole book of God that gave the
slightest intimation that slavery was a moral evil,
there would be some apology for the course of that
class of preachers and people against it. But as there
is no such passage, which can be sustained by other
Scripture, there can be no apology offered in their

behalf. They have joined themselves to the only class of infidelity that ever could have overthrown the Christian church as it existed in this country, and with it our great Christian-like national government and constitutional union, which, when rightly sustained, was the very counterpart of the Kingdom of Heaven. Yet, in all probability, the very men who profess to have been called by the eternal God to preach his own everlasting gospel to a lost and ruined world has ruined this great Constitutional government and free Republican Union.

It is so strange that men cannot see the difference between a voluntary Union by all the people, and an involuntary one established by force or military power. If voluntary by concessions and agreements of all the people, as this one was formed, then of course it must be sustained as it was formed, or it must go down. This is the only plan of a free Republican Constitutional Union in which the people rule, or are a self-governing people. If any attempt is made to sustain the Union by force or military power, that very day you take the government out of the hands of the people, and we become a *monarchical despotism, and the people are no longer free.* This is what Garrisonian abolition was established for in New England, and all who joined them against negro slavery have aided, and many have aimed at bringing this terrible crisis upon our glorious republic, whether in the church or state, and it is a just judgment of almighty God for our attempt to destroy his own arrangements for the salvation of the human race.

I am now done—I have written this chapter about as long again as the articles I wrote for the "Methodist," which was declined publication, for reasons given in the correspondence between the Rev. Mr. Crooks (the editor) and myself, which I now add as an appendix.

LETTER I.

"OFFICE OF 'THE METHODIST,'
NASSAU BANK BUILDING, No. 7 BEEKMAN STREET,
New York, February 25, 1861.

" MY DEAR BRO. ROBINSON :—

"I confess your article did surprise me not a little. I think you have made the common mistake of rushing to one extreme in order to avoid another. Slavery in the Bible is humanized and tolerated, but not, as far as I can see, sanctioned. I think it a state of society which men outgrow, but which they cannot easily be driven from by *storm* and *bluster*. Your article would call out replies and open controversy, which I wish to avoid. There is so much contending to be done necessarily, that I do not wish to bring on a new discussion on another branch of the subject, if I can help it. I have for this reason made no reference to Van Dyke's sermon, which goes over the ground of your article.

"Yours truly,
"GEORGE R. CROOKS."

Brother Crooks' note surprised me quite as much as mine did him. But he does not say what part of it surprised him so terribly. He mentions several points in my article, but he plainly gives one as his reason for refusing to publish the article, and that was the fear of "controversy on new points of this subject." If that were really his only objection

I should be perfectly satisfied, for I do not wish to do wrong; but he strongly intimates that I copied the Rev. Mr. Van Dyke's sermon, that was preached in New York or Brooklyn some time in December, 1860. I never saw the sermon alluded to, nor heard of it until the morning I mailed my article to the Methodist. A gentleman called at my place just as I was going to mail it, and I asked him to read it. He did so. When he had finished, he remarked that my ideas and Rev. Mr. Van Dyke's were simi-lar on the subject. That was the first intimation I had that a sermon had been preached by any one on these points; and I have not had the pleasure of seeing that celebrated discourse yet. But Bro. Crooks will find similar sentiments expressed in a Philadelphia daily, about the first of last November, in a column and a half over the cognomen of *Wide awake.* Therefore Mr. Van Dyke was not the first that imbibed such sentiments. I do not think Bro. Crooks' insinuation was as respectful as it might have been.

But Bro. Crooks says, the Bible *humanized* and *tole-rated* slavery, but did not *sanction it. Humanize* is to soften, or make susceptible of tenderness, or put in human shape or form, or to be human-like. *Tolerate* is to allow what is not lawful. It would appear from the declaration of the Rev. Crooks, that our Heavenly Father saw fit to add to the beasts of burthen men and women, to be used as such; for I do not see how they could be humanized in any other way, unless cattle and horses could be turned into human beings. This would be contrary to the laws of nature. Therefore, slavery could not be humanized in that way. Then I take the ground that the Bible must fully recognize slavery, or it could not humanize it; for to be a slave is to be under the complete control of a master, the same as horses or cattle. I cannot apply the term to slavery in any other way, and I confess that the application I have made is rather vague to my own clumsy mind. I hope Mr. Crooks will tell us what he means by the Bible's *humanizing* slavery, and how it could be done without sanctioning it; for I confess I am too dumb to see. Tolerate is to allow something that is unlawful. Actions and doings were lawful under the Mosaic dispensation, that were forbidden under the laws of our Saviour. Acts xvii. 30. "And the times of this ignorance God winked at, but now commandeth all men everywhere to repent." I understand this to teach that we are to turn away from all unrighteousness. Therefore, if slavery be unscriptural, it cannot be tolerated by the Bible; and I cannot see how the Bible can tolerate anything that is contrary to divine law. Therefore, if the Bible only tolerates the system of slavery, it must tolerate what is unlawful. If the word means to allow what is contrary to divine law, and all that is contrary to divine law is sinful. Therefore, if slavery be contrary to the law, it would be sinful to tolerate it. Mr. Crooks is very far from being an abolitionist, but I cannot understand his logic.

Mr. Crooks' strongly intimates that my article was full of storm and bluster, and that I attempted to carry my point by "storm and bluster." "Bluster"

12

is to roar, as a storm, to bully, to puff. "Storm" is a little different—it is a tempest, a commotion of the elements, assault on a fortified place, tumult, violence, vehemence, tumultuous force. I do not think there is anything of that kind in the article; if there is, I did not mean it. If I had had the advantages of an education like my friend Rev. Mr. Crooks, perhaps I should be able to write without making any impression on my readers. But as I never went to school but a very few months, therefore I am not sufficiently acquainted with language to be able to combat with an opponent without making him feel what I say. Webster's Speller, the Primer, the English Reader, and Bennett's Arithmetic, were almost the only books used in those days where I was educated; and the teachers, perhaps, could not pronounce twenty words correctly in the whole English language. The general impression among the old folks was, that any knowledge of books beyond being able barely to read and cipher to the single rule of three, would be certain ruin to the scholars. Therefore, I must be excused for stating things plain and pointed, so as to be understood. If I was well versed in etymology and English grammar I might become so *"humanized"* that I could find sufficient language, and roll my words up so finely, softly, and beautifully, that the reader would be so struck with my language, so exquisitely beautiful, that my hearers or readers would never know what I was talking or writing about. St. Paul was very pointed and plain. And our Lord was even more so. Matt. xxiii. 33. "Ye

serpents, ye generation of vipers! how can ye escape
the damnation of hell." Bro. Crooks, I don't think
I have said anything in the article I sent you for
publication more severe than the above. Why did
he speak so severe to the Scribes and Pharisees?
Because they had become so hardened in iniquity,
that he knew they could not be touched in any
other way. Just so I think of the abolitionist; yea,
they are even worse than the Scribes and Pharisees,
for they made no pretensions of love to our Lord,
but the abolitionists do. They profess to be his disciples, and preachers of his gospel; and yet they
denounce his precepts, and steal their neighbor's
property, and lie to hide it. They are traitors to
the government of God, and of the United States,
and deserve to be called a generation of vipers and
serpents just as much as the Scribes and Pharisees,
and to be hanged as much as old John Brown did.

I will now close this chapter, by saying to Mr.
Crooks, that I will not write another article for publication in the "Methodist" until I am so *humanized*
by the Bible that I can write without "storm" or
"bluster." I could have made many other quotations from the Bible which would prove that slavery
was not only common in the Holy Scriptures, but
as completely endorsed as any other practice, occupation, or ownership, that was foretold and authorized by the prophets, apostles, and believers in them,
and I think I have given enough for any candid man,
and we must not forget, that whatever the prophets
or apostles said or foretold had no more power to
produce or affect what was foretold than we have to

produce such effects. Noah's declaration that Canaan should be a slave did not make him a black heathen. But the power that enabled him to foresee the flood, and foretell it, effected the curse alike in both cases.

Yours, very truly,
JOHN BELL ROBINSON,

Feb. 28, 1861.

LETTER II.

Are the Africans capable of Self-government? Or can they be made so? If not, ought they to be Free?

MESSRS. EDITORS: It is conceded by all men, everywhere, that happiness is the chief object of the human race throughout the earth. Happiness is what every man desires. Ungodly men are selfish, and care not for the pleasures of others, and will extort, by craft or even force, to reduce their neighbors, and rob them even of their natural as well as their lawful rights to increase their own store of happiness. Godly men desire happiness just as much as the avaricious, but they desire to see their neighbors as happy as themselves, and they will use every righteous means to make them so. Their philanthropy reaches not only to their neighbors (though to them first), but to the happiness of their State, their nation, and then to the whole world; and they are ready to give out of their substance, whether it be great or small, a portion to advance the happiness of the human family in every part of the world, beginning at their homes, which are their godly rights, and then those nearest to them, and the next; and so on their philanthropy spreads over the whole world. Philanthropy is very popular; therefore there is a large amount of false philanthropy in the world, and even in the Christian church. Avarice knows no bounds; stops not even at human life. Happiness does *not* consist in the greatest amount a man has, but in the manner in which he uses it. Alexander the Great conquered the world, and then was tormented the balance of his days because there were no more worlds for him to conquer. John Jacob Astor or Stephen Girard was a thousand times more unhappy than the southern slaves; therefore it is not the greater amount that a man has that makes him happy, but the condition he keeps his mind in, and the cultivation of his disposition for enjoyment. Freedom is sought for as a source of happiness; but an unlimited freedom would be death to all human happiness. Fanatics, and bad, avaricious men, desire and seek for unlimited means and unbounded liberty to satisfy their avaricious cravings and their fanatical ideas of freedom. The Garrisonian abolitionists seem to have but one idea of happiness, and that is universal liberty or freedom of the human race. With them that idea swallows up all others without the slightest respect to circumstances, conditions, races, or capability. The only happiness they seem to think of or seek for is the universal freedom of the African negroes in this country and the placing them on an equality with the white man. St. Paul was one of the greatest and most amiable philanthropists that ever lived, and had but one superior in human shape, and that

12*

was our Saviour. Our Lord sanctioned no liberty as being Christian but civil or constitutional liberty, and said that the powers that be are ordained of God. St. Paul adhered strictly to this doctrine with all the other sacred teachers, and exhorted the master and his slave, the husband and his wife, the child and parent, all, in the same language, to respect each other's civil rights, and used the strongest language to impress this sacred duty upon the minds of all his hearers, and was even more impressive to the slave or bond-servant than to the others, and told him that by his obedience to his master he did the will of his heavenly Father. Liberty is one of the most dangerous blessings ever bestowed upon mankind, and yet the sweetest, and therefore it has been limited with all, and trusted to but few, of the human race.

God seemed to have set this country apart for the purpose of showing kings, despots, and monarchs, that the white race are capable of self-government, and that this constitutional liberty was conditionally intrusted even to *"We, the people"* of the United States, and that is, we must respect each other's constitutional rights without condition, or there can be no real civil or constitutional liberty. A libertine is opposed to all restraint by law or otherwise upon himself, and cares nothing for the rights of others. Abolitionists advocate the freedom of all men, without the slightest respect to their capability for self-government or usefulness in the world, or the safety of the rights of others. They declare that the African slave was included in the Declaration of our fathers when they said " *We, the people.*" This brings us up to the question of the competency or safety of the negro race to mingle in the Government of the United States.

I say the African is unfit, and, therefore, would be unsafe, even if admissible, to take any part in this government, either municipal or general. No people are fit for self-government, or to mingle with " *the people*" in government, who are generally inclined to idle, lazy, and dissipated habits. I think I am as well acquainted with the habits and nature of the negro as most men. I have spent about twenty-six years of my time in the slave States, and twenty-eight years in the free States. No man, I presume, feels a greater degree of sympathy for the African race in the United States than I do. They have always been objects of pity to my mind; and I desire here to apologize for a remark I made in my feeble speech, on the 23d ult., at the great mass meeting in the Statehouse Yard, when I spoke of them as " stinking negroes." It was a slip of the tongue under excitement, and it was not said out of any ill will to the negroes. I do not blame them for the troubles we are now in with our southern brethren. They have had no agency in the terrible calamities that now surround us. Hypocrites and infidels have plunged us into this ungodly war with our own race and kinsmen, under a feigned love for the poor, unfortunate Africans, that they may the sooner destroy them; for no man, having a proper Christian sympathy for them, would advocate their freedom in this country. The negro race is not fit for self-government. They are incapable, in this country and all others, to manage a government as a republic, or even partly so. I know we are told that they have been kept down by being made slaves to the white people. This, at a glance, might seem to be so; but when we come to look at the whole black race, here and elsewhere, we shall see that slavery has not degraded the African, but greatly elevated him in the scale of civilization and the domestic and social relations of this life; while, on the other hand, freedom has, as a general thing, degráded and hea-thenized the African race in all parts of the world.

There is an experiment now undergoing a trial on the coast of Africa, called the Liberian Colony, of some promise, which has my warmest sympathies and strongest desires that it may prove a complete success, and redound to the glory of God and the complete freedom and civilization of all the descen-dants of Canaan on the face of the globe, But I confess that this hope is without warrant in sacred prophecy; for there is not the slightest hope of supremacy, or even of temporal freedom, for the Ca-naanites in this world given in the sacred Scriptures. I may discuss the moral question of slavery, if agreeable to you, hereafter; but the fitness of the negro for universal freedom, and his claims for equality with " *We, the people*," are all I propose to discuss under the heading of these articles.

What are the natural habits, disposition, or ambi-tion of the African race in this country?

Their habits are laziness and negligence. They will not work, if they can help it, under any circumstances, except to prevent starvation. They cannot be made to think of any wants beyond the present, and will not provide for the future. When they, by chance, make a dollar, they at once cease work until it is gone. They will not labor for wages, if they can get food without it, and they will undergo any amount of suffering by deprivation rather than engage at constant manual labor for the comforts of this life. I am told this is because they are kept down by the prejudice of color, slavery, and other wickedness of the white people. This I deny as being generally true. There are instances, no doubt, of such oppression. To prove my assertion I will give a single case that I know to be true, with names and location, and will hold myself ready to prove that it is a complete illustration of nineteen-twentieths of all the free negroes in this country.

My father was a farmer in Prime-Hook Neck, Cedar Creek Hundred, Sussex County, Delaware. He owned a negro woman named Mill. She was an excellent slave. David Hazzard, Esq., a merchant and farmer, who lived at Milton, about four miles distant, and still lives there, owned a slave named Jacob. Jacob and Mill got married, and Jacob usually came to see his wife on Saturday afternoon and remained until Monday morning. My father was at Milton one day, when Mr. Hazzard proposed to him that if he would set Mill free, he (Mr. H.) would set Jake free. My father agreed to it on the spot. The arrangement was effected at once, and their freedom lawfully established. They, while slaves, were sober and useful to their masters; but

as soon as the knot was slipped that bound them to
their masters, a change was apparent. Jake at once
left his home, and came to my father's and took a
seat by his beloved companion, and there they
basked in the pleasures of this life—both ceasing to
labor, but not to live. My father finally told them
they must get themselves a house and take care of
themselves, and told Jake that if he would go and
choose a lot near the cedar swamp, by an old apple
orchard, he should have an acre of ground, and he
would lend him tools and teams, and give him the
timber to build himself a good house. The reply
was, "Sank you, Mass John, I do 'em." Jake took
an axe on his shoulder and started for the cedar
swamp, or woods, as he had his choice, to cut enough
for his house complete and to pay for sawing, as the
mills sawed timber on shares, and one less than a
mile distant. Jake spent the day in chopping away
the bushes around the large cedar trees; but that
was all he did that day, except to make up his mind
that it would be labor to fell the trees and get them
to the mill. He came back, and father asked him how
he was getting along. "Oh, good, Mass John." The
next day he took his axe and started off full speed;
but instead of going to cut the timber he went to
John Smith's mills to see about the sawing. There
he found a large pile of oak slabs that were useless
to the owner, and asked Mr. Smith to give them to
him to build his house. His request was granted,
and back he came for the team to haul them. After
that was done he commenced his building operations,
and the first thing he did was the digging of a

trench around the size he wanted his house, which was about twelve feet square, and dug about eighteen inches deep, and cut his slabs off, with an axe, about nine feet long, and sat them in the trench around, leaving them about seven feet and a half high, and leaving an opening for a door, but no window. He peaked them up at the ends for the pitch of the roof. He then put a pole across for the ridge, and laid poles the other way for rafters, and covered them with brush for laths and oak-leaves for shingles, and begged some cullen boards at the mill, out of which he made a door, and cut the soles out of a pair of old shoes for the hinges, and nailed them on with cut nails. He had no chimney or fire-place, but left a hole open in the roof to let the smoke out. He laid slabs in one corner, with the flat side up, on cross pieces, for a bed, which, I believe, never had anything on them but an old ragged quilt to soften the oak slabs. The dining-table was made in about the same style, and out of the same material. They built their fire at one end, on the ground, and piled dirt against the slabs to keep them from taking fire. Oak leaves were plenty in the woods, and he could patch his roof at any time; but when the snow came, with a strong wind, it would be nearly as deep inside as out. His chairs and shelving were all of rough oak slabs; and there they commenced life together. My mother gave them some bed-clothes and a little assortment of the necessary articles for housekeeping, and I believe Governor Hazzard did the same. They at this time were each about twenty-four years of age. That was forty-four years

ago, and there they live until this day, and have
raised several children in that miserable smoke-
house, not half as good as my mother's hen-house for
an in-dwelling for human beings. I suppose there
is scarcely a piece of wood in the house now that
was first put there, the entire house being replaced
time and again with patches. I believe his acre of
ground has never been sufficiently fenced to keep
the cattle and hogs out of the house, as the single
door of the house has had to be kept constanly open,
winter and summer, for light, there being no window
in the establishment.

Jacob had worked at hewing house frames for his
master while a slave; but my father offered him
white oak timber enough to saw him a frame, and
to pay for sawing, if he would cut the trees, and cedar trees enough for siding and shelving, and to pay
for sawing, and his board until he should get it
finished; but he was too lazy to embrace the opportunity to make himself and family comfortable for a
long life; and there they still live in that miserable
hut, not even fit for reptiles of the lowest grade.
The last time I saw them, their eyes looked to be
almost completely smoke-dried out. If they had
built the right kind of a house, their old masters
would have furnished it and made them comfortable;
but, instead of that, they have dragged out a miserable existence, for about forty-five years, in smoke,
filth, and deprivations of the worst kind.

This is a strong figure, but nevertheless true, and
it is an average case of a vast majority of all free
negroes in the world. The only idea of freedom

they have is to live without labor, which I shall undertake to prove in next week's number.

Now, do you not think that Jacob and Mill would have seen a thousand times more pleasure had they remained slaves until this day? Only look at it without prejudice against the only place designed for that race in this world among the white race.

LETTER III.

IN a former article I stated a few facts on the capability or fitness of the African race for freedom and self-government, under a republican form like ours. I now proceed to give further evidence of their unfitness for freedom and equality with "*We, the people.*"

I gave a short history of a single family who were set free by their master, who believed they would do well, from the fact that they were both such superior servants. They could not have been made to believe that the end of their servitude would be the end of their usefulness and happiness in the world; yet, notwithstanding the great confidence that all had in them, it was so. And so it has been with nineteen-twentieths of all that have been or ever will be set free.

The Rev. Mr. ——, of South Carolina, owned a large number of slaves and a large plantation. He became dissatisfied with the business, as he was an itinerating Methodist preacher, and finally made up his mind to give them (the slaves) the plantation, and rid himself of the responsibility and vexation, and

13

give himself entirely up to his holy and favorite calling, the preaching of the Gospel. He was advised of his fatal error, but had such an unlimited confidence in all his slaves that he could not be made to believe that they would prove faithless and betray their trust. As they had been so faithful to him in all things, he consummated the arrangement, and took his leave for an unlimited time, a year being the time of each engagement. He had not been gone long before he received letters from old neighbors, advising him that things about his plantation were changing very fast, and not for the better; but he thought it was a mere prejudice against his scheme of freeing his slaves, it being the only plan by which it could be done, for the master had to appear as their owner at law, or they would be taken up and sold by the sheriff to the highest bidder. He paid no attention to the first letter, nor to the second nor third; but within a year he received such information as fully satisfied him that he was in danger, and made up his mind to repair to his former home; for his neighbors informed him that unless he speedily returned and took charge of his negroes he would have damages enough to pay to take all his negroes and plantation too, several of them being already in prison for plundering their neighbors' plantations. When he arrived he found the plantation completely swept of poultry, hogs, and cattle; even the work oxen and cows had been killed and eaten up, or sold for rum. His fencing and outhouses were demolished and used for firewood, and even the farming utensils were mostly burnt up, and he found himself a ruined man, for he was answerable for all the damages to his neighbors. They started fair in the spring and planted the crops, but that was the end of their ambition and enterprise, their only idea of freedom being to eat, drink, sleep, and nothing else.

Many similar experiments have been tried in all the southern States with similar results.

I am told this was owing to their being under laws that were prejudicial to their freedom: yet nineteen-twentieths, if not the ninety-nine hundredths of all the slaves who have been freed have resulted in evil to the liberated negro, and has brought them into disrepute and to want, and made them a dead weight to society and a clog to the wheels of general prosperity; for the free negroes have never paid their way in this country, nor never will. Their-Maker never intended them for rulers or leaders in this nation, nor in any way to be placed on an equality with *"We, the people;"* and no true Christian who can read the Word of God will ever advocate the universal emancipation of-the negroes in this country, and their equality with the people of the United States; nor will any true Constitutional Union man who has had opportunities to know the nature of the African negro, and made use of them, as it was his duty to do, wish them freed and placed on an equality with the rulers of this land.

Now let us see if the case I gave last week, and the above, was owing to the laws of the slave States in which they occurred.

In 1819, if I forget not, two thousand acres of

land was procured in Brown County, Ohio, on which
four hundred negroes were placed, and made the
legal owners of the property. In a very short time,
says the Cincinnati Gazette, "they became too lazy
to play." Their vicious, lazy, thieving habits was
so apparent that the neighbor's became much
alarmed; and efforts to remove them was strongly
talked of. The depredations and criminal law suits
of that spot, was nearly equal to the whole county
outside of that colony. The farmers for miles
around could, nor cannot, keep any portable valua-
bles unless they put them under lock and key at
night. And these depredations have increased from
the beginning of that colony even more than the
increase of the population of the negroes, and the
whole colony abounds in filth, stench, licentiousness,
laziness, theft, drunkenness, debauchery, rags, and
profanity; and they are of no use in the neighborhood whatever, but a dead weight and a great curse
to all the people for miles around. An Ohio senator
spoke of them as follows:—

"The black settlement in Brown County was
made in 1819, the original number located there
being four hundred and twenty, for whom about
two thousand acres of land were procured. From
the commencement there has been no improvement
in their morals or social habits. Idleness and vice
are the prevailing concomitants. The cost of criminal prosecutions has been very large in proportion
. to the number of inhabitants, and keeps up a pro-
portionate average with their increase. In the
vicinity of this settlement there is not a family

within two miles who are not kept in constant dread of depredations or injury of some sort. Every valuable that can be removed is stolen. They are absolutely compelled to confine themselves to what is merely necessary to support life, for anything beyond from hand to mouth, must inevitably fall a prey to lurking vagrants, who, far worse than a gang of gypsies, are hovering around seeking literally what they may devour. And this state of things is not confined to any section alone; it extends in a greater or less degree wherever this class of the population is permanently located."

Now this is in the great free State of Ohio, where the shackles of slavery has never been known. And I believe Brown County is, or was, a great abolition county. And yet this terrible state of things has been produced by the presence of this small colony of the black race there. I ask, that if four hundred and twenty in a neighborhood has produced such a state of society, what would four thousand do in a neighborhood, all being free. And suppose further; that there was one free negro in that State for every five or six white people, what would be the condition of things in that great State? It cannot be said that they have not an equal chance in Brown County to prosper and be improved. The fact is, the negroes have never made a particle of improvement in a state of freedom. There is not one single spot on the globe that has been in any way improved by them only in a state of slavery. They have never been of any use to the world, or to human society, except as slaves, not even to them-

13*

selves. But as slaves they have been very useful to the whole civilized world, and no people have been more useful of the same number. But that moment you free them, their usefulness ceases. If this is not so, tell me where and when it was not. Show me one spot on the earth where they have been of any benefit to themselves or any body else, except in the Liberian Colony, which I admit produces a slight promise. But did they, through their own enterprise, make the discovery, and try the experiment? You know they did not, nor had they any hand in it. But it was started by white missionaries from other countries. It was soon discovered that white men could not live there long enough to do any good. And black men were taken as an experiment, and it was found that they lived, and had their health as well there, or even better than here.

There seems to be providential reasons for believing that that may be their place, and God may intend to raise them up to some notice or usefulness in the world. But if African slavery had never had an existence in civilized states, the African colony could never have had an existence; and if slavery should now be abolished in all civilized and Christian states in the world, and left free and equal, the whole Liberian colony will glide into barbarism in a short space of time; for you may depend, they will cease to immigrate to that country if freed and placed on an equality with "*We, the people,*" here, and elsewhere. And when fresh accessions cease to arrive there from civilized and Christian states, that colony will be doomed to barbarism. I will not discuss the present prospects of that colony, only to say it is yet an experiment quite as much as it was at the beginning. I will say here, that whatever my opinions may be about the competency of Africans to govern, I am a friend of that experiment, and want it to go on to the end of time; although God has not given the slightest encouragement on the pages of inspired prophecy for them to expect any honors as rulers, outside of slavery.

But the Scriptures are totally silent on the sub-ject of their emancipation. It is not for me to say there is no hope for them for freedom in their own native Africa; but I will say, there is no hope for them anywhere else in the world, and every attempt to raise them to authority will only make their con-dition incalculably worse than in slavery to southern masters.

But I will say again, the southern slaves are the happiest class of people I have ever seen in all my travels in North or South America or the West In-dies, and I believe they are the happiest people on the face of the globe, except where abolitionists have disturbed their peace, and twenty times more moral, civil, respectful, happy, and well behaved than any colony or state of free negroes I have ever seen.

Now, if the African race in the United States have principles or fitness for self-government, how is it they have not shown it in some shape or form? They have been here over two hundred and forty years, among the best men, and the best examples, and influences the sun has ever shone upon, and yet not the slightest appearance of fitness for rulers, leaders, or teachers has been perceptible among them. If I am wrong, show me how, when, and where, and I will give in. Can any spot be found in the United States that has been improved by the free negroes locating thereupon? Can you tell of a colony of them who have emigrated to the western territories, to clear up the lands, to make themselves permanent and comfortable homes? Or has one ever done so? Where are they to be found, either many or few, taking the lead in any enterprise of worth or hope, that would induce any man, or set of men, of common sense and moral worth to follow in their wake? How many African negroes can there be found, who are free, that have had forethought enough to save up something for a rainy day? Don't point out to me mulattoes and quadroons; I know some few of them have done so— but they are comparatively few and very far between. I know a great many negroes get themselves a house to live in; and what sort of a house is it when got? See the description of Jacob's house I described in my previous article, and you have a description of twenty-nine-thirtieths of all the houses got up by that class of persons. If you will investigate the subject without prejudice or favor, *you will find that just so far as they depart from pure Anglo-Saxon blood, just in that ratio they lose the* principles and qualifications for self-government.

It may be said that I have given a case that was originated while Brown County was a wild forest, and therefore the consequences occurred alluded to above. To show that this was not the case, I will

give one more example that took place under the
direction of the great apostle to negro freedom, Gerret Smith, of New York State: Gerret Smith, Esq.,
is a gentleman of talents, of respectability, and great
wealth and uncommon liberality, and an abolitionist
of the Garrisonian school. He had such an unlimited sympathy and confidence in the poor African
that he determined to set them on their feet, that the
world might see that they were fit to be classed with
We, the people. And he, true to his principles, put
his hand into his pocket to put the negroes where
the world would see that the negroes were honest
men. I am sorry that I cannot lay my hand on the
history of this case, for it tells the story more vividly
than any other. Mr. Smith purchased a large tract
of land in western New York, large enough (if I
forget not) for one thousand small farms (though I
am not sure about the number), and deeded them in
fee to that number of negroes, and gave each one a
nice little start, and no doubt felt that he had done
a good thing. But, to his great disappointment, in
a very few years every farm passed out of their
hands for provisions and rum; and the condition of
society was even worse than in Brown Co. colony,
and Mr. Smith was compelled to concede that he
had done them more hurt than good; for he had
made a selection to take charge of those farms of the
best and safest negroes in the State of New York.

I do not say these things out of any ill will to the
poor unfortunate negroes; I am their friend, and
would defend their civil and moral rights to the
very death: but I must state facts just as they are,

if the sky falls. No man can do them any good by saying what is not true, and in that way place them in a false position before the world; this would, in the end, only degrade them the more. If abolitionists would state facts with their apparent zeal for the poor negroes, they would do them great good; but by stating falsehoods, and placing them in a false light before the ignorant, they have produced all the miseries and woes the poor Africans have ever been subjected to in this country. If all the ministers of the Christian Church had only have followed the example of their great exemplar, St. Paul, of the New Testament Scriptures, this whole nation would now abound in almost paradisiacal glory from one end to the other; and the white people would this day be rejoicing from Maine to Florida, and from the Atlantic to the Pacific, and the slaves would be singing, shouting, and dancing all over the slave States, and brother would not now be at war with brother, and destroying each other worse even than hyenas. You may sum up all of our present calamities, hatreds, malice, and heart-burnings, and *all, all* are traceable to the preaching of abolition sermons in the sacred desk that was dedicated to the preaching of the glorious Gospel of God our Saviour. There is not a fire-eater nor a rebel in the south who is not the legitimate offspring of abolition Gospel preachers. They are the worst enemies the poor slaves ever had in this world.

For an intimation of Egyptian bondage or ancient slavery of the negroes, I will refer the reader to an article in your last Saturday's issue, from the New

York *Journal of Commerce,* 6th page; it will pay for reading. The fact that the African never has made any improvement, or did any good outside of slavery, is to my mind a sufficient reason why he should not be set free. More on the subject next week.

LETTER IV.

In my two last communications I gave a general view of the condition and habits of the freed and free people of color in the United States. I would like now to give a general history of the slaves, but I will only say here, that they are the happiest persons, as a class, that I have ever seen; and the stories of the cruel treatment by their masters, as a general thing, is as false and slanderous as it would be to say the devil is a truthful and good spirit. Such stories have been invented by abolitionists and infidels to break up this great and glorious Christian government, because it had the impress of divine goodness and wisdom upon it. I have no doubt there are cases of bad treatment to slaves by some masters. But they are as few in ratio as such cruelties are in the free States, even to children by parents. And there are but few half so devilish as a large amount of treatment to apprentice and servant girls in our northern cities. But I will proceed with the free negroes.

I was in New Granada, South America, in 1856, where the negroes. have not only their universal freedom, but the reins of government exclusively in their hands. I will give a short account of the

condition of things in that State across the Isthmus
to the ancient city of Panama. I say ancient because it took its start in the early days of the settlement of South America by Spain. There is no
State in the world that excels the State of New
Granada in a fertile and productive soil. They have
no winter frost or chilling winds to impede agricultural pursuits. And it would excel the richest
parts of North America in the super-abundance of
every product except wheat and rye. There is no
country on the globe that would pay the farmer or
planter better than that country. It abounds in all
that is good, even the precious metals. There are no
seasons, but it is one perpetual season. It matters
but little what time of the year planting is done.
Two crops of corn per year could be raised off of
the same ground, and plenty of time between to
clear off the soil. Most of the fruit trees are always
in bloom, and have fruit on them in every stage
from the blossom to the ripe fruit. Sugar cane
grows spontaneously, and wherever it formerly got
a hold, it still holds the soil, and its growth is so
powerful that it overruns everything else, and holds
the soil supreme. And, perhaps, there is not better
cane in the whole world, and stands so thick that a
rabbit would have great trouble to make his way
through it. In short, there is no State on the face
of the globe that offers superior advantages to the
planter or farmer.

And, notwithstanding all this, there is not one
acre of ground in the entire State of New Granada
in any condition of cultivation that I ever saw.

They plant in some places (I know) among the bramble and bushes, but cultivation is not known. I saw but one lot of corn there in all my travels, and I walked over that with the greatest difficulty. The bramble and undergrowth was so great that I could seldom reach ground with my feet. They planted the corn without hoe, spade, or plow; they reached their arms down through the bramble and undergrowth, and scratched the corn under the ground with their fingers without the slightest order, leaving an indefinite number of grains in a hill, say five to ten; and that is the last time they see it until they go to gather the corn. It grows up through the bramble and bushes to an enormous height, with slim stock, not larger than a man's thumb, and each stock bears a nubben of corn two or three inches long. And when they gather the corn, they pull up the stocks, and replant at the same time.

That country was under the government of Spain about three hundred years, and has been in the hands of negroes I believe nearly forty years.

I never saw a road in the State, that a mule could travel safely on, nor a cart road outside of the villages.

The appearance of many abandoned plantations are yet visible all over the State, and everything like industry has disappeared; but not one single vestige is apparent in any part of the State except in the seaport towns, by white men. In fact, everything has sunk to ruin, total ruin, since the negroes were emancipated and took possession of the govern-

14

ment, and that State, with its rich fertile soil, is almost a total loss to the world.

The inhabitants are so low in the moral scale and civilization that their condition is indescribably low. There are some foreign quadroons about the larger seaport towns that do better; but even these have no right to claim a place in civilization. A majority of the inhabitants all over the State are of mixed breed, but in every case the whites have been reduced to the level of the negro, and booth together into the vats of all abominations. There is not one particle of ambition or enterprise among them; they neither marry nor are given in marriage, but are one continual mass of licentiousness and vulgarity. They even all go naked at almost all times, even to church (for they are all professing Christians). The women and men strip themselves together to bathe, and any number can be seen walking and standing together on the rocks, high and dry, in a perfect state of nudity. They are as the beasts of the field, without shame or modesty. They have no sympathy for their offspring.

The few white people that have been born there are as high above them in intelligence and all moral requirements for respectability as it is possible for one set of men to be above another. You will hear them talking about State affairs, and lamenting over the condition of society, the great chances of prosperity, the immense wealth in their soil, and how rich they could be in a short time if they could work in the sun, but they cannot; neither can the mulatto; nor would he if he could. He is more delicate than the white man. But the negro, who is improved and strengthened by labor in the sun in that climate, will not now, nor never did, nor never will work without a master; and unless that great country shall be reduced to negro slavery under the pure white, that rich and alluvial soil is not only now lost, but will be through all time to come, unless God shall change that climate to suit our nature, or the principles, spirits, ambition, and enterprise of the negro to that of the white man, without changing his nature, that is now suited to the torrid zone of the world only.

I know the quadroons or mixed breeds are a much better people than the negroes, but they are altogether inadequate to successfully maintain a republican form of government, and hardly a government of any kind. They are nearly all very treacherous, and not worthy of trust. I wish some of our abolitionists would go down to that country and spend six months among the negroes; I think they would hesitate some time, if they had a trust to give out, to decide which they would bestow it upon, the monkeys or the negroes. Let them see the Jamaica negroes at Aspinwall, who have gone there to get clear of wholesome, lawful restraint, and I think they will never want to behold another free negro, much less to have them on an equality with "*We, the people*" of the United States.

Now those were raised on the Island of Jamaica; they were born free, and some of them can read, write, and speak English, Spanish, and some French.

I will close this article with a short account of

what I saw of free negroes at and about Kingston, Jamaica, from where many of the pure negroes have gone to New Granada, South America. I have often been referred by abolitionists to the glorious effects of emancipation in the Island of Jamaica, and even told by some that the emancipated slaves soon became the ruling spirits of the island, and that they were at the head of all good. It is true, they are lawfully on an equality with the white people, but in appearance, and all, all of the requisites for prosperity and government, are as far beneath the white people as the earth is beneath the heavens. Were it not for the standing army and the British bayonets that glitter in that sunny clime at all times, the whites, ere this, would have been exterminated, if it had been in the power of the negroes to have done so. The negroes are somewhat better there than in South America, but it is owing entirely to the strict wholesome laws and the British soldiers that can be seen at all times patrolling.

Since the negroes were set free by an act of Parliament, in 1833, they have sunk down to the lowest depths of degradation that is possible under good restraining laws. They will not work for wages; in consequence of which a great many of the best plantations on the island have been abandoned, or turned into grazing farms. The stories of any improvement whatever there, by the emancipation act, is as false as the declaration of the serpent to Eve, when he said "Thou shalt not surely die." If the English government could have it to do over again, the negroes would never be made free by the laws of that nation. Many of the leading journals of Great Britain have been warning us for years to be careful how we take any further steps towards the emancipation of the slaves of this country, and refer us to the ruined condition of that island by emancipation, and the complete degradation and entire ruin of the negroes there.

Some of the quadroons do better than the negroes, and a few of them own small plantations; but no such thing is to be found among the negroes; they are a dead weight to progress. It was an experiment when the emancipation bill passed. The English people thought they would work for wages, and therefore it would be altogether better for the planter to hire his labor than to own it; but the sequel proved the sad mistake when too late.

It would have been a thousand times better for us if there never had been a free negro in this (that was a) glorious land. The whole civilized world have been paying the penalty of British emancipation ever since it took place, in high prices of the products of the British West India Islands, and the partial emancipation of the slaves in this country. If universal emancipation should be effected here, woe be unto us, and the slaves too.

LETTER V.

In my first two articles I portrayed the principles, disposition, nature, pride, and ambition of the negro race in this country. In my third, that of the same race in South America and the Island of Jamaica.

14*

The facts I have given ought not to require any application by me, and will not by those who are truly constitutional union men, and do not value the emancipation (and, by that, the degradation and ruin of the entire black race in this country), more than the liberties and prosperity of "*We, the people.*" I say I have given the true character of the free negroes wherever they may be found on the face of this globe. Taking this in comparison with the great usefulness of that race while slaves, ought to satisfy every good man that they were destined for slaves or bond-servants, and nothing else.

Though God has not declared anywhere in his revelation that they never are to be free, yet in Lev. xxv. 46, he says to their masters that they shall be their inheritance, and their children's forever; which I have shown in the two chapters on the moral question of slavery. As I have said, there seems to be some encouragement for them in Liberia, on the coast of Africa. And if they ever are to have freedom, it will be there and nowhere else. But while they remain among white people, they are to be slaves, or they will be in a far worse condition; and any nation who shall attempt to free them, and place them on an equality with the "*people,*" will be made to suffer just to the extent they shall do that wicked act. See the effect on Mexico, Central America, New Granada, and all the British, French, and Spanish provinces. While the two or three former have suffered by constant revolutions and civil commotions for allowing an equality with that race, the latter have suffered the loss of three-fourths of the products of those provinces, and, in addition to that, they have been compelled to keep a stronger standing army to keep the negroes in their place, and have had to pay double price for all the products of those islands that require constant agricultural labor to bring them forth, because the negroes will not engage in useful pursuits and manual labor when free, and therefore they are of no use in the world, but a dead weight upon the prosperity and happiness of any nation which shall venture in such a forbidden path.

Look at the present condition of the free people of color all over this country. See them in this city, where we have about thirty thousand. If you have never looked into the question, I think you will be perfectly satisfied that they would be better off in slavery, even if the institution is as bad as Wendell Phillips says it is. You will not find two thousand out of the thirty doing anything for a livelihood. And even most of these are engaged in pursuits that are of no use to the general prosperity of the city whatever, and the balance are far worse than no account.

What are we as a nation and "the people" now suffering for attempting to lay violent hands upon the institution of slavery? I will say again (and hope it may never be forgotten by the reader), that whenever universal freedom to the negroes shall be established in this country, our Constitutional Union with our liberties will end, and the judgments of God will rest upon us, perhaps through all time to come. You may laugh me to scorn for this idea. No doubt Adam thought it a very small matter to taste a delicious fruit from a tree that he had to prune and dress that he was forbidden to eat by his Creator, yet see the effect upon the whole human family. If Adam had kept that simple little command, we should now all be one race and one people, and there would have been no negroes, nor abolitionists, or any other pest on the face of the globe, not even death. Be careful; "God will not" always "be mocked."

But some men tell me that slavery is wrong, and must be abolished, irrespective of consequences to either race. That it is our duty to free them, and allow them to become our equals in all the relations of this life. For, say they, we were all *"created equal,"* and therefore are all one flesh and blood. And we must loose their bonds, and let them go free. When the dangers of emancipation are pointed out some of those saints say, let them go to the devil, we have nothing to do with that; others say, we will drive them all out of the country, and if they attempt to resist, we will exterminate them all. Now those are some of the men who have such great conscientious scruples about slavery; even so great, that they say, rather than it shall not be destroyed, let our great government be broken up, and a monarchy established or anarchy reign through all time. Now, we are all equally interested in this matter, whether we were born and live in a free or slave State. Our destinies for all time are at stake alike. The people of Maine and Florida will suffer the same. We are all one people, and are equally responsible for whatever may come upon us. Therefore let us reason together, and look this matter fair in the face. If we stick to our fanaticism, and refuse to weigh the facts that can be seen and understood by every man, just so sure as we do not do this, just so sure we shall be overthrown, and our glory will be taken from us and given to some other land.

God has given us that unfortunate race, that they might be made useful to the whole civilized world. They were first brought to this country while we belonged to Great Britain, and there is no room to doubt that God designed it, for every circumstance proves this idea. And it was done to bring that race into usefulness, in the only way it could be done. It is wonderful that any man who has read their history, both sacred and profane, cannot see this, for our *Creator* commanded that every man should live by the sweat of his brow. The meaning of this is, no one will doubt, that every man should toil in some form for the fruits of life, and without it, no man was entitled to the "penny."

I have shown unmistakably, that the African race are a dead weight on society, and a nuisance in the world, in a state of freedom. If this is not so, everywhere (outside of Liberia, which is yet barely an exception, if an exception at all), then I hope some one will show us where it is, and in what part of the world, and how. I know there are some individuals who do better than others, where they are surrounded by influences so powerful that they cannot resist them. But show us a community of colored people away from the powerful influences of the watchful perseverance of the enterprising whites, who have set one single example, that would be safe for us to imitate. What have they done in the world that has been of any benefit to mankind? Where and when have they by companies, formed colonies to clear up the land in our western wilds, or even on the frontier of any State, and made themselves comfortable homes, and by that produced anything beyond their own wants, or even half that amount? Now take a survey from Maine to Florida, and from the Atlantic to the Pacific, and show us the group or colony who have done any good for mankind, or have exhibited the slightest enterprise? Where are their inventions of useful implements, of husbandry, or any of the mechanical arts? Where are they found leading their hosts of workmen in any of the trades, or manufacturing operations of this life, or any of the useful arts and sciences? Now, without one circumstance to show their fitness for self-government, or to mingle with our rulers, or even to take care of themselves under the most wholesome laws that mankind ever was blessed with, where all their rights are fully protected, they having equal access for that purpose, with us, to all the courts of justice, ought we to set them free, or ought they to be free, while they are so exceedingly useful in a state of slavery? Was it not madness* in us to plunge ourselves headlong in this the most ungodly of all wars which have preceded it since the foundation of the world was laid? No, none has been more terrible, more heart rending, or more wicked, and all, all because of an opposition to the just and wise arrangements of the great *Jehovah* to govern his people, as seemeth him good. I know some will laugh at this idea, especially some of those who, it was intended by the Great Spirit, should unite all hearts, and cement them by diffusing his own ever-lasting love among the people. But, alas! they have forgotten the pit from which they were taken, and by whom, and for what purpose, and let false sympathy and fanaticism take possession of their hearts, instead of that unadulterated love that makes a man justified in whatever position of usefulness he may be called to in this life. And instead of preaching Jesus Christ and him crucified, they recommend their hearers to go forth and exterminate eight millions of white people to change or destroy the relation of master and slave (that it is in the order of God), that the negro may be the white man's equal, which is clearly forbidden in his Great Book, which I have already proven.

I wrote this and the three previous articles for the Press, but concluded to withhold them for this book. I have written these mostly on my own knowledge of the facts given. I shall now publish a chapter in which I have given an array of testimony to show that the negro or African race ought not to be freed, and that they are physically and mentally incompe-tent for self-government. My testimony will be from national and municipal records, and official reports from abolition missionaries, travellers, and others. They will clearly show to what an alarming extent designing men have deceived the people on this question.

CHAPTER III.

I FEEL it to be my duty to write a few pages on imports and exports, and illustrate them by statistical facts, which more than sustain me in all I have said about the unproductiveness of the free and the freed negroes, and the productiveness of negro slaves. These statistics will astonish the reader more than anything I have said in this book. The first freed people of color were the negroes of St. Domingo, who ultimately freed themselves of the white population by an indiscriminate massacre of all the white people on that island. In that way they became the sole occupants of that immensely rich soil.

It has been about seventy years since universal freedom was proclaimed on that alluvial island, which I think was in 1793; therefore I will begin with the exports of Hayti in 1790, three years before negro freedom was obtained. In that year the exports of that island were $27,828,000, the main productions being as follows:—

Sugar .	.	.	.	.	.	163,405,000 lbs.
Coffee .	.	.	.	.	.	68,151,000 "
Cotton	.	.	.	.	.	6,286,000 "
Indigo .	.	.	.	.	.	930,000 "

(168)

About thirty years after freedom, the products of that rich island were as follows :—

Sugar	.	.	32,800 lbs.,	less	163,373,000 lbs.
Coffee	.	.	32,189,700 "	"	35,961,300 "
Cotton		.	620,900 "	"	5,664,100 "
Indigo	.	.	000,000 "	"	930,000 "

I will here remind the reader that coffee grows without labor, it being an 'article of spontaneous growth, which accounts for its having fallen off only a little over one-half. Now sugar and indigo have entirely disappeared, and cotton not much better. Logwood, mahogany, and other articles of spontaneous growth, which require no labor to produce them, are the only articles of exportation now. Coffee grows wild (though it has been transplanted there), and therefore requires labor to gather it only, which is made a sporting operation or frolic, like huckleberrying parties retire to the swamps in this country sometimes. See about sixty years after emancipation on that island, which was in such a high state of cultivation in 1790, as far as settled, and then ruled entirely by white masters. In 1849 we have the latest statistics that are reliable from that *fallen star:*—

	1849.	1790.
Sugar	000 lbs.	163,405,000
Coffee	30,608,343 "	68,151,000
Cotton	544,516 "	6,286,000
Indigo	000 "	930,000

It seems to me this ought to be enough to satisfy an abolitionist, even of the Garrisonian stripe, much more Christian men, that the emancipation of the

15

negro race is not only wrong, but a *great moral, social, and political evil.* In or prior to *impartial* freedom on this island, it supplied at least the half of Europe with sugar. It was originally a French colony, and if that island, with the negroes, had remained in the possession of the French people until this day, it would now be the garden spot of the earth, instead of being a lost and desolated state. The negroes were not to blame for this change.

The French people themselves, in France, had become wild on the subject of *"impartial"* freedom, among themselves not including negro slaves, for they were not considered fit for anything else than slaves. But the French people became fanatical about the word *"slave,"* and desired to strike it from the statute book. The quadroons and mulattoes took hold of it, and determined that all who were possessed of their blood should be included among the *"impartial"* freed people. Therefore the destruction caused by the blast of *"impartial"* emancipation.

Just so in our glorious nation and country. When the Convention met in 1787 to form a Constitution, that we might have a more perfect Union as sovereign States, there was not an abolitionist in that Convention—no one thought of freeing the slaves, or desired to free the negroes in the southern States—yet many of them were strongly prejudiced against the foreign slave trade, produced, no doubt, by the cruelties practised by hard-hearted, bad men going into that trade, that should have been carried on by Christian men only. Therefore the fanatical notions about the word slave being placed in our great national chart, the Constitution of the United States. "*We, the people,*" had been a subordinate people, held by a tyrant king, and of whom God said, "should not be ruled over with rigor." Therefore the prejudice that prevailed in the Convention against the word slave or servant being embodied in the national chart of the United States. That prejudice was perhaps the beginning of our downfall as a great nation; for, "What therefore God hath joined together, let no man put asunder." Matt. xix. 6. That national Convention did not intend to abolish slavery at any time, but were thrown a little on the other extreme, by having been treated like slaves by Great Britain, and thinking the Constitution could be formed so as to secure the rights of the people to their slave property without naming slavery in it. They forgot for what a small thing Moses was deprived of the honor and pleasure of marching before the Israelites into the promised land. He was commanded to speak, that the water might come forth; but instead of that, he smote the rock twice. Num. xx. Therefore he was not allowed to enter the land that "flowed with milk and honey," but was buried in "Mount Nebo," on the borders of the promised land.

No doubt France, England, and Spain thought, or mistook the omission of the word slave in our chart, for some future intention of abolishing slavery in all the States, at the same time thinking it would not do to let the United States, who had just emerged into being, take the lead in so great a work. In less than six years France was wild on the subject of freedom, not of the negroes, but of their own race, and half or mixed breed. Those nations did not know at that time, that the end of slavery was the end of labor with the African race. But the French see how it is now, when to late. If the French had that Island now, and owned all the negroes, instead of exporting about $28,000,000, as they did in 1790, they would now export at least $100,000,000 worth annually. But, alas! what is it now? The nearest that it can be got at, at this time, is about $1,200,000. The French had it up to $28,000,000 when the negroes took possession. The demand for the different kinds of wood is twenty times as much now as it was in 1790. Emancipationists, look at this before you go any further in your mad career.

But is this all? Let us look at the Island of Jamaica, which is yet held by the power of British bayonets in the hands of white men.

(I will say here, the statistics I have quoted are from the "United States Commercial Relations," vol. i. pp. 561–2, officially reported to Congress.)

This Island is nearly equal in fertility to Hayti. There have been falsehoods enough told about it by abolitionists to sink a world into oblivion. I will give one statement made by an English missionary in the Five Points mission chapel at New York in the fall of 1856, about three months after I was at Kingston, Jamaica, where he said he had been laboring for many years as a missionary sent there by the Congregationalists of England, if I remember right.

His sermon consisted in *an* alleged history of

the great benefit emancipation had been to that Island, and to the negro race there. I thought if he was a sample of all foreign missionaries, they had all better be called home and put to hard labor in the coal pits of England.

He said the negroes had become leading men in every good enterprise of that Island. That the productions had gradually increased every year since 1833, when the slaves were freed. That they were the leading business men of that Island, that they were nearly all property holders, and many of them largely. That nearly the whole Island was in a state of dilapidation and ruin in 1833, but now everything was in a most prosperous condition. That the city of Kingston had so revived and increased in beauty, style, and wealth, that it did not now look like the same place. That the negroes were commouly consulted by English Lords, on plans of government for the Island. And that many of them lived in palaces of beauty and comfort. In short, he made them out as being far superior to any other persons on the face of the earth. This seems to be the common declaration of nearly all abolitionists, and it would appear to be the faith of the Republican party.

The island of Jamaica contains about 4,000,000 of acres, and was prior to 1833 in a high state of cultivation, as far as occupied, at which time the slaves were all reduced to apprentices for five years, to be freed in 1838, by an act of Parliament.

I will now give a few statistics and reports that will satisfy every reader that that missionary knew he did not tell the truth. I will quote from the Cyclopædia of Commerce, published by Harper & Brothers, of New York, before and after emancipatiou.

PRIOR TO FREEDOM.		AFTER FREEDOM.	
Years.	Value of exports.	Years.	Value of exports.
1809,	$15,166,170	1853,	$4,186,380
1810,	11,517,895	1854,	4,661,580

Two successive years of exports before freedom, $26,684,065; two successive years of exports after freedom, $8,847,960, This ought to satisfy every white man in the world that the negroes ought *not* to be free. The deficit, $17,836,105. I have taken the above about twenty years before and twenty years after freedom, so as to be clear of the agitation of the question.

The bulk of products of Jamaica in 1805—

Sugar	.	.	.	.	.	150,352 hhds.
Rum	.	.	.	.	.	ˉ46,837 punch.
Allspice		.	.	.	.	1,041,540 lbs.
Coffee	.	.	.	.	.	17,961,923 "

This was prior to the stoppage of the importation of slaves to the island of Jamaica, at which time agriculture was in a high state of improvement. The sugar was the largest crop ever produced on that Island. So the following table will show the want of labor in the sugar culture in 1834, one year after slavery was abolished, and the negroes converted into apprentices; but they at once ceased to fear their masters, and consequently to labor as they previously did, and sugar requiring an immense amount of labor and care to produce and save ıt, therefore see as follows 'for 1834, just thirty years after the above crop was produced, which was prior to the agitation of the abolition question.

In 1834, exports of Jamaica—

Sugar	84,756 hhds.
Rum	32,111 punch.
Allspice	3,605,400 lbs.
Coffee	17,725,731 "

Remember that coffee and allspice are of spontaneous growth, and therefore labor was only required to gather them, which is very light work, and mostly done by women and children, which accounts for those two articles not falling off proportionably to the others. Coffee ought to have largely increased, for, like the allspice tree, it takes possession of abandoned lands soon after they are deserted, and grows without cultivation.

The next year after emancipation, sugar fell off 10,000 hhds.; coffee fell off 7,000,000 lbs., and this decrease has constantly continued until 1856, when the productions of Jamaica were as follows:—

Sugar	25,920 hhds.
Rum	14,470 punch.
Allspice	6,848,622 lbs.
Coffee	3,328,200 "

I will compare 1856 with 1805, and I wish every abolitionist would look at it with a single eye to his and his own country's true glory.

	1805.	1856.
Rum	46,837 punch.	14,470 punch.
Coffee	17,961,923 lbs.	3,328,150 lbs.
Allspice	1,041,540 "	6,848,600 "
Sugar	150,352 hhds.	25,920 hhds.

This table shows the effect of emancipation on the Island of Jamaica from the year before the importation of slaves was prohibited and 1856, which was twenty-three years of the glories of free labor with 1856 inclusive. Sugar fell off 124,432 hhds., rum 32,367 puncheons, coffee 14,633,773 lbs.; pimenta or allspice gained 5,807,060 lbs.

It seems to me that this ought to be more than enough for every lover of his country. Certainly no Christian man, woman, or minister will ever advocate emancipation after looking over these reports or statistics, which are from the most reliable sources, and I hope they may be thoroughly investigated. In a very short time, at the same rate of decrease, the Island of Jamaica, that while under slave labor was sufficient to supply the whole United States with all they needed of those products, will be forever lost to the world, like Hayti. If slave labor had been allowed to have gone on until this day, under proper safeguards and protection of law, instead of their only producing 26,000 hogsheads of sugar, they would now produce 250,000 hogsheads, or 425,000,000 pounds; and instead of 3,328,150 pounds of coffee, they would now produce 50,000,000 pounds; allspice and rum in the same ratio, with all other products of that island. Sugar would not now be over four cents a pound, and coffee not over six cents, and all other articles in proportion.

I am reminded by my abolition friends (*exultingly*) that I have not given freedom credit for the large increase of pimenta. Well, the increase of that article was, according to the table, above 5,633,773 pounds, I admit; but that fact sustains my position as strongly as any other. Allspice or pimenta grows in the mountains, on bushes or trees; therefore no labor is required to produce it; to gather it is like child's play; it is more of an exercise than manual labor. Thousands, and even hundreds of thousands of idle negroes, men, women, and children, daily resort to the swamps or mountains, for sport, in gathering allspice, which is a darkish red looking berry, similar to currants. They have only to gather them from the trees, and dry them in the sun; (the tree is a native of those islands.) It requires no manual. labor; therefore those lazy idlers do that because it is more of a frolic than labor, and it produces a scant livelihood or subsistence. Nor does it require the slightest ingenuity or calculation to gather and dry them. These are facts that fully account for the increase of that article.

Coffee is not a native of those islands, but has been transplanted there. It produces better by cultivation; but, once introduced into suitable soil and climate, it spreads like the allspice tree. It does not only spread in the mountains, but, with the allspice tree, takes possession of forsaken lands, and grows in a very short time to a producing size, and is considered far more profitable, and pays better for labor than allspice. But, unfortunately for Sambo, it requires ingenuity, labor, and great care, as it grows within a covering, and cannot be got out and cleansed without work; therefore Sambo and his hosts say, "*me no like 'em*," and turn away to the allspice trees.

This is still a stronger evidence that all I have

said in the several chapters I have written on the
nature of the negro race is true beyond successful
contradiction or proof to the contrary, that the negro race is not now, never has been, nor never will
be of any use, in any part of the world, except in
slavery to white men. There they are as useful a
people as is on the face of the earth.

The coffee crop of Jamaica, 1813, before slavery
was abolished, amounted to nearly 35,000,000 pounds.
For the last eight or nine years the average has
been about 5,000,000 pounds, deficit 30,000,000
pounds per annum, and in 1853 the sugar crop was
only 20,000 hhds. So you see I have *not* taken the
two extremes, or erred, in order to sustain my position, for any kind of an error would injure my case.

The English missionary I spoke of above, said a
large number of estates had been abandoned under
slave labor and considered lost to the world, but
now had been bought by the freed negroes, since
emancipation, and brought into use by them, and
that the freed negroes had made them the most productive plantations on the Island. But how does
his story stand by the side of the above official
reports or statistics? He was not the only man that
did not hesitate to say what he knew was false.
But every intelligent abolition preacher does the
same thing. Let us look at the abandoned plantations a little, from the undoubted reports, and we
shall see that that preacher (who, by the way, was a
very talented and an educated man) knew better,
(for he said he had been on the Island twenty years),
and all others who preach the same doctrine. If

they do not, they are not fit to preach the gospel, and ought to be silenced for their ignorance.

I quote from the legislative reports of that Island as follows: " Before emancipation, the assessments of property, real, and personal, was over $250,000,000. In 1850, the assessment was $57,500,000. In 1851, it was reduced to $47,500,000, and Mr. Westmoreland, in the Assembly, said it was believed that the falling off would be $10,000,000 more in 1852. From an official report to the Assembly, of the number and size of the plantations abandoned during the years of 1848, '49, '50, '51, and '52 are as follows:—

Coffee plantations abandoned	.	.	.	.	96
" " partly abandoned	.	.	.	66
Sugar estates abandoned	.	.	.	.	128
" " partly abandoned	.	.	.	71

The number of estates abandoned the five years immediately succeeding emancipation were as follows:—

Sugar estates	.	.	145	168,000 acres.
Coffee plantations	.	.	467	189,000 "
Add to this, those above	.	361	391,000 "
This gives us in ten years	973	748,000 " lost,

for ever lost.

I have not been able to obtain reliable reports or statistics for any time except the ten years, as above. But, rest assured, that the same process of declension has been going on steadily from 1833 to this the 30th of August, 1862, at about the same rate; and now more than one-half of the plantations and sugar estates of the entire Island are abandoned, and grown up in allspice and coffee trees. These plantations employed over 100,000 slaves, who were then moral, sober, civilized, industrious, and very useful. But now are useless, degraded, savage, vagabonds, who lay about in the sun, or lie in the shade in large gangs, many in a state of nudity and filth, like the mosquitoes, and flies that suck the life blood out of those who are their only hope for any state of happiness in this world without permission. They seem to think they have a right to appropriate to their own use whatever they find out of sight of the British soldier. They are the most loathsome beings on the face of the earth. I speak this from personal knowledge of the facts, for I was among them in 1856, and know what I say is very true.

I have been cutting from official reports and statements from travellers who were and still are emancipationists. Some of the latter I will copy, after giving the following tables, computated from statistics and official reports (by a gentleman who is as well posted on the rise and fall of the West India Islands as any other man living, and I hope he will excuse me for taking his table verbatim. I will say to him I have written manuscripts enough on the subject for 600 pages 12mo., and had I published them one year ago when ready, I might have thought he had borrowed of me. But as I still have the work locked up, I know he selected, as I did). It clearly shows the contrast between *free negro labor* and *slave negro labor*, and I hope every man, woman, and child who are now supporters of the republican party will examine these statistics, and official reports before they ever give another vote for universal emancipation in this country.

"SLAVE" NEGRO LABOR.

	Years.	lbs. Sugar.	lbs. Coffee.	lbs. Cotton.
British W. Indies,	1807,	636,025,643	31,610,764	17,000,000
Hayti,	1790,	163,318,810	76,835,219	7,286,126
Total,		809,344,453	108,445,983	24,286,126

"FREE" NEGRO LABOR.

	Years.	lbs. Sugar.	lbs. Coffee.	lbs. Cotton.
British W. Indies,	1848,	313,306,112	6,770,792	427,529
Hayti,	1848,	none to ex.	34,114,717	1,591,454
Total,		313,306,112	40,885,509	2,018,983
Free Negro Labor Deficit,		496,038,341	67,560,474	22,267,143

I think this is proof enough for any honest man, and much more a Christian. The sugar deficit alone is enough to produce a war of extermination on all abolitionists, and bring the Christian Church, which is our only guide and safeguard as a free people, into bad repute with a struggling world; for very many of her strongest and most powerful ministers have taken the lead for this ruin to the world, and burning blast to our peace and happiness, perhaps forever. Look at it, and you will see the deficit in one year of free negro labor is sufficient to supply every man, woman, and child, black and white, each with over sixteen and a half pounds of sugar; 496,038,341 lbs. of sugar, at 10 cts. per lb., is $49,603,834.10. This is only one article of produce. If the West India Islands and if Hayti had gone on by slave labor under good white masters, sugar and coffee would

16

never be over four to six cents per pound, and
all the luxuries of those islands would now be
as accessible and attainable by every poor laboring
man as they are now by the rich.   The whites would
have been exterminated long before this, had it not
been for the British standing army constantly in
sight.

Mr. Underhill, a member of the Jamaica Assembly,
an abolitionist, from whom I have already quoted,
speaks of Cuba, where slavery still exists, and those
islands where it does not exist, as follows.   Of
Havana he says:—

"It is the *busiest and most prosperous of all the
cities of the Antilles.*   Its harbor is one of the finest
in the world, and *is crowded with shipping.   Its
wharves and warehouses are piled with merchandise,*
and the general aspect is one of *great commercial activity.*   Its exports nearly reach the annual value of
nine millions sterling, and the customs furnish an
annual tribute to the mother country over and above
the cost of government and military occupation.
Eight thousand ships annually resort to the harbor
of Cuba."

Is it not strange that Mr. Underhill did not at
once proclaim to the world his great mistake in supposing that the negro was the white man's equal,
and not fit for anything else than a slave?   Mr. U.·
seemed to have been surprised to find that that pro-
slavery island was still what Jamaica was before the
British government, by that insane and diabolical
act of emancipation, had ruined their hopes forever.
To find Cuba still exporting produce to the amount

of $45,000,000 annually, while that of Jamaica had fallen from nearly as large an amount of exportations to $4,500,000 in consequence of emancipation of the slaves on that island, see the following illustration:—

Jamaica in 1809	$15,166,000
Cuba " 1826	13,809,388
Jamaica " 1854	4,500,000
Cuba " 1854	31,683,731

So you see Cuba, under slaveholders and by slave labor, has gradually increased from 1826 to 1854 from $13,809,388, to $31,683,731; while Jamaica gradually fell off, from 1809 to 1854, from $15,166,000, to $4,500,000. This picture certainly will surprise a great many good people who have been deceived and totally blinded by disunionists and traitors of the north, or free States, among whom are the most talented statesmen, many of whom are now in power under the government; preachers of the Gospel, of all denominations, and some of them the most talented and influential, and, like the English missionary alluded to before, they say in their pulpits what they know is false, from beginning to end, with such grace and zeal, with their hands on their hearts and eyes rolled into the heavens, in such way that their hearers believe them sincere and truthful. They in their pulpits speak of Sharp's rifles as being the best gospel for slaveholders, and talk of blowing men's brains out with (apparently) as much relish as they would have for a fine dinner. Where will such wretches stand in the great day of account?

I met a merchant the other day, an old acquaintance, with whom I had been contending at times on the slave question for twenty-eight years. He tackled me on the prospects of universal emancipation in the United States; referred me to Jamaica, and said it was enough to convert any man who was not given over to believe a lie, that he might be damned. I replied that I thought so too. I believe he thought I had become a convert to his *expressed* opinion, and he went on to tell me of the great and astonishing changes that had taken place in the Island of Jamaica since emancipation. I remarked that that was so. He said the island produced at least three times as much now as it did before the negroes were freed; that everything on the island had improved at the same rate. I just looked him in the face at that point and said I was on that island in 1856, and said no more. He was certainly *embarrassed at the remark.*

That gentleman could be trusted on all other subjects of civil or natural jurisprudence, and was as clever a man as this city held. I regret to say he was buried in one week from that day.

Will any one say that that gentleman did not know that what he said was not the truth? Though a member of meeting, yet he was a boasting infidel, and hated Christianity with a perfect and bitter hatred, and became an infidel because the Bible sanctioned slavery.

It will not be long before cultivation will entirely come to an end on that island. The island contains about 4,000,000 acres, and its white inhabitants, in 1844, was 15,776; Africans, 293,128; mixed breed, 63,500. In 1861 the whites were 13,800; Africans, 346,300; mixed breed, 81,000. So you may see by this table, that it will not be long before this island, like its sister, Hayti, will be totally lost to the world. To know this, it is only necessary to look at the rapid increase of the colored race and decrease of the white. The whole number of inhabitants is 441,100 : 80,700 can read, and 50,700 can write (of the 80,700). So you see that 360,400 can neither read nor write.

In Hayti no census can be taken, no figures can be got, because the negroes have got free and full possession. Abolitionist, look at those figures, and think over this interesting subject before you take another step towards the downfall of this great country. Will you draw that awful blight of negro emancipation over this great nation that will fester in the hearts of future generations, and cause them to rise up and look back with bitter curses upon us. For they will know and feel the effects of our infidelity and disgraceful wickedness that we deliberately inaugurated as a blighting curse upon them. While, history will tell them of the glories our fathers inaugurated and handed down to us. But for us, with all those figures before us, and right in the teeth of divine revelation, with all the teachings of that Holy Book to do what is so clearly forbidden by nature, and nature's God, is more than I can account for. What must our condemnation be in the great day of God!'

I will now give a few extracts from prominent men. An English writer, writing from the Capital of Hayti, says:—

" This country has made since its emancipation no
16*

progress whatever. The population partially live upon the produce of the grown wild coffee plantations, remnants of the French dominion. Properly speaking, plantations after the model of the English in Jamaica, or the Spanish in Cuba, do not exist here. Hayti is the most beautiful and most fertile of the Antilles. It has more mountains than Cuba, and more space than Jamaica. Nowhere the coffee tree could better thrive than here, as it especially likes a mountainous soil. But the *indolence of the negro has brought the once splendid plantations to decay.* They now gather coffee *only from the grown wild trees.* The cultivation of the sugar cane has *entirely disappeared,* and the Island that once supplied the *one-half of Europe with sugar, now supplies its own wants from Jamaica and the United States.*"

Mr. E. B. Underhill was sent out to Hayti by the Baptist Missionary Society, of London. He was an abolitionist of the Thompson stripe; after making many excuses for Cuffee, for his having ruined that *Eden* of this world, was compelled to give the following history:—

We passed by many, or *through many abandoned plantations, the buildings in ruins, the sugar mills decayed, and the iron pans strewing the road-side, cracked and broken.* But for the law that forbids, on pain of confiscation, the export of all metals, they would long ago have been sold to foreign merchants. Only once in this long ride did we come upon a mill in use; it was grinding cane, in order to manufacture the syrup from which tafia is made, a kind of inferior rum, the intoxicating drink of the country. The mill was worked by a large over-shot, or water-wheel, the water being brought by an aqueduct from a very considerable distance. With the exception of a few banana gardens or small patches of maze round the cottages, nowhere did this magnificent and fertile plain show signs of cultivation.

"In the time of the French occupation, before the Revolution of 1793, *thousands of hogsheads of sugar were produced; now, not one, all is decay and desolation.* The pastures are deserted, and the prickly pear covers the land once laughing with the bright hues of the sugar cane.

"The hydraulic works, erected at vast expense for irrigation, have crumbled to dust.

"*The plow is an unknown implement of culture,* although so eminently adapted to the great plains and deep soil of Hayti.

"A country so capable of producing for export, and therefore for the enrichment of its people—besides sugar and coffee; cotton, tobacco, the cacao bean, spices, every tropical fruit, and many of the fruits of Europe, lies uncultivated, unoccupied, and desolate.

"Its rich mines are neither explored nor worked, and its beautiful woods rot in the soil where they grow. A little logwood is exported, but ebony, mahogany, and the finest building timber rarely fall before the woodman's axe, and then only for local use. The present inhabitants despise all servile labor, and are for the most part content with the spontaneous productions of the soil and forest."

Mr. Underhill was a resident Baptist missionary,

or something of the same nature, at Hayti, and an abolitionist, and therefore ought to be respected in all he says on the subject. Like many other good men, he has put the most favorable construction on all he saw, that he possibly could without twisting the truth, as you will see above, where he speaks of "cottages." This naturally impresses the mind here with the idea of a nice little house, when they are nothing but the most miserable thatch cabins without glass windows, and they have earthen floors.

Mr. U. published a work in London, entitled "The West Indies; their Moral and Social Condition," in which some of his excuses are laughable for the degradation of the negroes. Yet every abolitionist ought to read it.

"The Vaudoux," says Mr. Underhill, "meet in a retired spot, designated at a previous meeting. On entering, they take off their shoes, and bind about their bodies handkerchiefs, in which a red color predominates. The king is known by the scarlet band around his head, worn like a crown, and a scarf of the same color distinguishes the queen. The object of adoration, the serpent, is placed on a stand. It is then worshipped, after which the box is placed on the ground; the queen mounts upon it, is seized with violent tremblings, and gives utterance to oracles in response to the prayers of the worshippers. A dance closes the ceremony. The king puts his hand on the serpent's box; a tremor seizes him, which is communicated to the circle. A delirious whirl of dance ensues, heightened by the free use of tafia. The weakest fall as if dead upon the spot. The bacchanalian revellers, always dancing and turning about, are borne away into a place near at hand, where sometimes under the triple excitement of promiscuous intercourse, drunkenness, and darkness, scenes are enacted, enough to make the impassible gods of Africa itself gnash their teeth with horror."

I have said in a former chapter that the negro race might be raised to the highest state of civilization and Christianity they are capable of, under the immediate influence of the best Christian white men and women in the world, and then leave them entirely to themselves, with all the advantages of soil and climate, and a full supply to start on equal footing with the best part of all creation, and with both the moral and civil governments in their own hands, then, in less than ten years, they would be on a level with the most degraded and savage men on the earth. God himself has made them for usefulness as slaves, and requires us to employ them as such, and if we betray our trust, and throw them off on their own resources, we reconvert them into barbarians, *and we shall be compelled to atone for our sin towards them through all time.*

I have given enough evidence to satisfy any true seeker after truth, that unconditional freedom to the negro race is not only a great moral and political wrong inflicted upon them, but a great political and financial affliction and curse to the whole civilized world, and a moral evil of greater magnitude than any before introduced among men. The whole civilized world was blessed by Hayti while in the hands of white men; but those blessings stopped short by that rich and beautiful country passing into the hands of the negro race; the rich man's pocket is heavily taxed in high prices, and the poor are left in want. The testimony I have given to sustain my position in reference to Hayti is not the fiftieth part I have in hand; but it seems to me to be enough.

I will now make a few quotations to sustain the statistics I have given, showing the rise and fall of the Island of Jamaica. I have an editorial from the *London Times* that was in my possession before Mr. Lincoln was nominated for the Presidency; so you will see that the civil war now raging in the United States did not influence it either way. See as follows:—

"There is no blinking the truth, years of bitter experience, years of hope deferred, of self-devotion unrequited, of prayers unanswered, of sufferings derided, of insults unresented, of contumely patiently endured, have convinced us of the truth— it must be spoken out loudly and energetically, despite the wild mockings of howling cant; *the freed West India slave will not till the soil for wages;* the free son of the ex-slave is as obstinate as his sire. He will not cultivate lands which he has not bought for his own. Yams, mangoes, and plantains, these satisfy his wants; he cares not for yours. Cotton, sugar, coffee, and tobacco he cares but little for. And what matters it to him that the Englishman has sunk his thousands and tens of thousands on mills, machinery, and plants, which now totter on the languishing estate, that for years has only returned him beggary and debt. He eats his yams, and sniggers at buckra. We know not why this should be, but so it is. The negro has been bought with a price—the price of English *taxation,* and English *toil.* He has been redeemed from bondage *by the sweat and travail of some millions of hard-working Englishmen.* Twenty millions of pounds sterling—one hundred millions of dollars—have been *distilled from the brains and muscles of the free English laborer*, of every degree, to fashion the West India negro into a free, independent laborer. Free and independent enough he has become, God knows, but laborer *he is not;* and, so far as we can see, *never will be.* He will sing hymns and quote texts; but honest, steady, industry he not only detests, but despises." (The italicizing in all these quotations are mine.)

Have I said anything stronger than the above? The *London Times* makes full confession of its errors. It had supposed that the negroes would work better for wages than under masters; *but, Oh, what a sad mistake;* for they never would, nor never will labor without white masters. And, "woe" be unto this great country whenever all the negroes are freed. Besides, freedom is the end of civilization to the negro race, and his perpetual overthrow and ruin; and God will hold us responsible for all the bad which shall grow out of emancipation.

I will make another quotation from an English writer, who was one of the strongest antislavery men. Mr. Anthony Trollope says, in a book he wrote on Jamaica, and from which the following was quoted by a London paper:—

"A servile race, peculiarly fitted by Nature for the hardest physical work in a burning climate. The negro has no desire for property strong enough to induce him to labor with sustained power. He lives from hand to mouth, in order that he may have his dinner, and some small finery, he will work a little, but after that he is content to *lie in the sun.* This, in Jamaica, he can very easily do, for emancipation and free trade have combined to throw enormous tracts of land out of cultivation, and on these the negro squats, getting all that he wants with very little trouble, and sinking in the most resolute fashion, to the savage state. Lying under his cotton-tree he refuses to work after ten o'clock in the morning. No, tankee, massa, me tired now; me no want more money. Or, by the way of variety he may say—no, workee no more; money no nuff; no workee no pay. And so the planter must see his canes foul with weeds, because he cannot prevail on Sambo to earn a second shilling by going into the cane field. He calls him a lazy nigger, and threatens him with starvation. His answer is: No, massa; no starve now; God send plenty yam. These yams, be it observed, *on* which Sambo lives, and on the strength of which he declines to work, are grown on the planter's own ground, and probably planted at his own expense. There lies the shiny, oily, odorous negro under his mango-tree, eating the luscious fruit in the sun. He sends his black urchin up for a bread-fruit, and, behold, the family table is spread. He pierces a cocoa-nut, and lo! there is his beverage. *He lies on the ground surrounded by oranges, bananas, and pine apples. Why should he work; me no workee to-day; me no like workee, just um little moment.*"

This witness more than sustains me in all I have said about the negro in the United States and elsewhere. I have admissions enough made by anti-slavery men to fully satisfy me that I am right on both the moral and civil question of slavery, even if I had never seen any wrong produced by emancipation. I have not given the strongest testimony I have in my possession by a great deal. I have made no quotations from men who were not anti-slavery men. I will give one more from the same source. I quote from the American and Foreign Anti-slavery Society's report for 1853, p. 170. Speaking of the emancipated slaves, see as follows:—

"Their moral condition is very far from being what it ought to be. It is exceedingly dark and distressing. *Licentiousness prevails to a most alarming extent among the people.* * * * The almost universal prevalence of intemperance is another prolific source of the moral darkness, and degradation of the people. The great mass among all classes of the inhabitants, from the governor in his palace to the peasant in his hut, from the bishop in his gown to the beggar in his rags, *are all slaves to their cups.*"

This much for emancipation and abolitionism. Instead of freedom having elevated the negro, it has sunk him into the deepest degradation and ruin. "The end of slavery is the *end of civilization to the negro race.*"

I will give a few more statistical tables to show the great benefits of slave labor to the world, and the great moral benefit to the negroes, without one exception.

The exports and imports in Cuba in 1859 were as follows:—

Exports for 1859	$57,455,000
Imports " "	43,465,000
Surplus over imports	$13,990,000

This table of itself is sufficient to satisfy all candid men, to see how steadily Cuba, with the other Spanish Islands, have advanced under slave labor; while the morals of the slaves there are a hundred times better than the morals of the negroes in Jamaica. If the institution of slavery be immoral, how does it produce so much good? Can moral evil beget moral good and righteousness? If emancipation of the negro be morally right, how is it that it has produced nothing but moral evil and complete ruin and degradation to the negro race, wherever he has been freed, either here or elsewhere?

17

Abolitionist, think of this, or show some good done to either race by the emancipation of negro slaves.

You will see by the above table that the exportations of Cuba amount to $40 for each man, woman, and child, black and white, on the whole island.

But let us look a little at our own exports and imports. I have not got the figures for 1860 and '61· I will give the tables for the fiscal year ending June 30, 1860.

Including specie, our exports were	.	.	$373,167,000
Foreign produce in addition .	.	.	.	27,000,000
In all			$400,167,000
Imports for the year			361,727,299
Surplus over importations . . .			$38,439,791

This gives about $1.26 per head, supposing our population to be 30,000,000. But in Cuba, where it is exclusively slave labor, it is over $9.30 per head. Our whole exports amount (including the $27,000,000 of foreign produce reshipped), to about $12.44 per head, and that of Cuba to $40.00. I hope the reader will look well at these figures, for they fully sustain my position on all points, and rebuke the whole abolition movement. How strange it is that men let a false or morbid sympathy run off with all their brains! A nation whose judgments are led by their sympathies, will sink into ruin in a very short time. God made animals to move by instinct, and white men by judgment. If we allow anything to rise above that judgment, wo be unto us, for God will leave us to follow our idols.

There has so much been said about the slave States having been a great incumbrance to the free States, ever since the adoption of the Constitution, that hundreds of thousands of the people have got to believe it all over the free States. I have heard so many good men say we should be better off without the slave States, and that we have had to carry them on our backs. Abolitionists have declared the falsehood with such zeal that many of the best and most influential men have taken their word for it, and preached the same doctrine with equal zeal, and think they are right.

Let us look at it a little by figures and tables, for they will not lie. We have been importing between three and four hundred millions, say $362,000,000 round numbers, which is $12.66 per head, for 30,000,000 of people. The exports are $400,000,000, including the $27,000,000 of foreign produce reshipped, and the specie, which is $13.33 per head. Now let us see where those exports come from, and to whom we are indebted for this immense exportation, which is the life of the country, while large importations are her death. But who pays for the $362,000,000, which is nearly all imported by the free States? We must deduct the specie, which is $57,000,000, and the foreign produce, 27,000,000, which makes $84,000,000; this leaves $316,000,000 of American produce exported, which is about $10.50 per head. I now propose to show just how much of the $316,000,000 is of the free States, and then we shall know what the slaves have done.

The free States exclusively $5,071,400
The free and slave States which cannot be exactly
credited to the States it is from, is made up of
raw produce, manufactures, products of agriculture, vegetable food, products of the forest,
and manufactured articles, etc., exports . 96,826,300

The slave States exclusively—

Cotton	$191,806,555
Rice	2,566,400
Rosin and turpentine . . .	3,734,500
Tobacco	15,906,517
Tar and pitch	151,100
Brown sugar	103,244
Molasses	44,562
Hemp	8,951
Total of the slave States . .	$214,321,829

Altogether—

Free and slave States . . .	$96,826,300
Free States exclusively . . .	5,071,400
Slave States exclusively	214,321,829
	$316,219,529

Now here is $96,826,300 jointly exported by the
free and slave States. It is made up of produce that
is raised alike in all the States in the United States;
therefore a correct division cannot be made of the
credible amount to each State. But any one having
the slightest familiarity with the slave and free
States would say, at least one-third of the amount is
of slave labor. There is no difficulty about the rest.
For instance, the $5,071,400 set down exclusively for
the free States is ice, coal, and fish.

Then we are compelled to add to the exclusive
exportation of the slave States—

One-third part of the $96,826,300 . . .	$32,275,433
Slave States exclusive	215,321,829
The full amount exported from the South .	$246,597,262
Exclusively from free States	$5,071,431
Add to the two-thirds of the joint exportations, slave and free	64,550,867
Exclusively from the free States . . .	$69,622,298
Exclusively from the South	246,597,262
Exports of the whole United States .	$316,219,560

I am met with a protest against these tables, and told the free States send a vast amount of produce manufactured to the South, and therefore the slave States should not have credit in the above table for one third part of the joint exportation of $96,826,299. I only have to say in reply to this objection, that the South sends vast amounts of produce to the North, that are not included in the above tables, for they do not enter any custom-house whatever, therefore are not included in the United States Reports at Washington, from which the above is taken. They are as follows, and I want every republican and abolitionist to look at them as well as all anti-slavery democrats—

Cotton manufactured in the free States .	$55,500,000
Sugar	25,000,000
Naval stores, lumber, tobacco, rice, and hemp, perhaps	50,000,000
Aggregate	$130,500,000

I have no figures before me by which I can give the value of the latter slave produce, and should not be surprised if I have placed it far below the mark.

17*

This immense amount is consumed in the free States. There is no doubt but we receive a much larger amount of domestic (raw) produce from the slave States than we furnish them; but they have taken from us a vast amount of manufactured goods, and paid a profit on them, which has been the support of legions of our poor in the free States. In these estimates you will find that the free States export $3.41 per head, and the slave States export $24.60 per head. If you disbelieve it, get the United States Reports by a republican administration, and make your own calculations, and let us have them in black and white, and I, for one, will stand by the right, even if my life was required to pay the penalty.

I will now copy a table prepared by Messrs. Van-Evrie, Horton & Co., No. 162 Nassau Street, New York, which every loyal man in the United States ought to get and read. For ten cents, sent with your address, order No. 2 on statistics. It will surprise you to find how you have been deceived. I have a table of my own made out, but this one is easier to be understood—

Returns from the Treasury Department at Washington, showing the value of the exports and imports for forty years, from 1821 to 1861, with the customs paid during the same time to the United States.

Gross value of exports from 1821 to 1861.	$5,556,339,272
Gross value of imports from 1821 to 1861.	5,501,238,157
Customs, duties on imports paid in the United States Treasury Office	1,191,874,443

Total United States exports for forty years—

			Amount of duty.
Cotton	.	$2,574,834,991	
Tobacco	.	425,118,067	
Rice	.	87,854,511	
Naval Stores	.	110,981,296	
Total in forty years		$3,198,788,865	$689,141,805
Food	.	1,006,951,335	216,682,773
Gold	.	458,588,615	95,349,955
Crude articles, manufactures, &c.	.	892,010,457	190,699,910
		$5,556,339,272	$1,191,874,443

Exports from the South, exclusively for forty years—

			Amount of duty paid by the South.
Cotton	.	$2,574,834,991	
Tobacco	.	425,118,067	
Rice	.	87,854,511	
Naval stores	.	110,981,296	$689,141,805
Forty per cent. of the gold	.	183,588,615	72,227,591
1-3d of food	.	335,650,411	38,139,982
Total in forty years		$3,718,027,891	$799,509,378
Amount of duties from the North	.	.	392,365,065

Excess duties paid by the South over the North in forty years . . . $407,144,313

Duties per head on the present population of the free States, the last forty years ending 1861, was $19.61 paid by the South in the same time per head on the present population of the slave States, including slave women and children, was $79.90. I had heard so much of declensions of the slave States, by the blight of slavery, that I had got to believe there was some truth in the assertion,

and, like thousands of others who were anti-aboli-
tionist same as myself, had got to speaking of slavery
as a social, political, and financial evil. But I took
a tour through several of the interior slaves States
some years ago. I made it my business to lose no
spare time in looking into the political, social, and
moral condition of the slaves and their masters. I
found the political, social, and moral standing of the
latter generally equal to any people I have ever
seen, and I believe equal to any on the face of the
globe. And that of the slaves was indescribably
better on the general than any class of free negroes
I had ever seen. I had not then even thought of
slavery as a moral question. Though, I had so
often heard men say it was a great sin against God,
and that no slave owner ever had, or ever could
enter the Kingdom of Glory. Those declarations
had but little effect on my mind, until preachers of
the gospel began to denounce slavery from their
pulpits as an unbounded moral evil, and slaveholders as moral devils. This caused me to look
into the moral question of negro slavery, and the
result was as stated in the first two chapters of this
book. I think I have proved, both by negative and
positive testimony, that slavery is not only not a
moral evil, but a great moral blessing to the whole
civilized world. While the emancipation of the
negro race has always been, and is now, a moral
evil of the greatest magnitude of any other ever
introduced into this sin-stricken world by the Prince
of darkness. I must see more good than evil from
the emancipation of that race, before I change my

mind in one iota, and then I should be compelled to close the Book of God for ever. For if slavery be a moral evil, the Bible is not the inspired word of God.

If slavery be a moral evil, how is it that it has done so much good to both races? And if emancipation be a civil and moral blessing, or either, how is it that it has proved such a terrible curse to both races throughout civilization, but especially to those countries in which they are freed? See how quick any country is blighted and ruined by the freedom of the negro race. Look at Mexico, Central America, and the Tropics of South America, and all the British and French West Indies—how quick they all fell from a high, prosperous state of cultivation and moral worth to the deepest degradation and ruin! How is it the slave States of our great country have done so much more for the glory of the United States with only one-third of the inhabitants than the free States have done with double the people? How is it that the slave States have so steadily increased their exportations from the adoption of the Constitution to 1860? The exportation is the only spring that keeps a country alive. How is it that the exportations of the slave States amount to about $246,-597,262, annually, while that of the free States was only about $69,622,298? See how constant the increase of the great staple of this country was from 1800 to 1860. In 1800 the slave States produced 35,000 bales of cotton only. In 1860, they raised 4,300,000, and they increased double as fast the last ten years, as they had ever done before.

Tell me how this come to be so, if slavery is such

a great moral, political, financial, and social curse? How come it that over 2,500,000 square miles of the best and most productive land in the known world has been almost entirely abandoned, consequent on the emancipation of the negro slaves? Why is it that every tropical country on the globe, where slave labor was necessarily used, has been at once ruined and almost lost to the human family, on the freedom of the negro, and all the black races of those climes at once reverted back into demoralization and barbarism, from a good state of civilization; and the country from a high state of cultivation, wealth, and prosperity to utter ruin, if the freedom of the negro race be such a great blessing to the human family, and especially to the negroes? Examine the few statistics I have given, and the abolition witnesses I have adduced (of which I have enough such to make a volume yet in my possession) and throw off all your party bias, decide quickly, for national ruin is at our doors. The separation of the Union, or the emancipation of slaves in this great country, will be nearly equally ruinous. A dissolution of the Union will damn all the free States, and end our hopes in this world. And the emancipation of all slaves, will blast the whole nation for all time to come, just as sure as God lives and records the acts of men.

Look at Mexico, Central America, New Granada, Venezuela, Ecuador, British Guiana, Dutch Guiana, French Guiana, and all the British and French West India Islands, in which there is now turned out wild nearly 2,600,000 square miles, of the best land in

the world, and many millions of human beings reduced by it from a good degree of civilization, and
a high state of prosperity and usefulness in the world,
to the deepest state of degradation and ruin known
on the globe, of which I have given some account in
former chapters, and have now proved what I said
to be far more true than stated by the best evidence
the world can produce.

Governor Wood of Ohio, who was an anti-slavery
man, visited Jamaica in 1853, and said of the negroes
there—

"Since the blacks have been liberated, they have become
indolent, insolent, degraded, and dishonest. They are a rude,
beastly set of vagabonds, lying naked about the streets, as
filthy as the Hottentots, and I believe worse. On getting to
the wharf of Kingston, the first thing the blacks, of *both sexes*,
perfectly naked, come swarming about the boat, and would
dive for small pieces of coin that were thrown by the passengers.
On entering the city, the stranger is annoyed to death by the
black beggars at every step, and you must often show them
your pistol, or an uplifted cane, to rid yourself of their impor-
tunities."

I clipped the above from a western paper, and have
no doubt of its authenticity. I was at Kingston in
1856, and can testify to the very truth of Governor
Wood's statement. Now, what ought to be our
punishment for the *crime* of attempting the emancipation of the black slaves of this country? If we
advocate their freedom with all this *ruin* to the
human race staring us in the face, with its blighting,
devastating, and diabolical ruinous effects upon the
blacks, it at once casts us loose from the moorings

of civilization and safety, into a lake of idleness, where there is no anchorage for our earthly hopes.

In the struggle between slavery and anti-slavery parties, the church has already lost its *winning and saving powers*, and also the Christian ministry that was ordained in heaven by the Eternal himself, to guide the ship of the Moral Government of God in the world, as set forth in the Scriptures of truth. There is every evidence that is necessary to satisfy any lover of the Union (*Christianity*) that God intended this great country for one universal Union, as a counterpart (in form), of his own everlasting Kingdom, for our good as his chosen people, and for the salvation of as many of the African race as our Heavenly Father might see proper to intrust us with, for our servants, for the good of both races—not only for our good and that of Africa, but that the whole civilized world might see and know his people, through the great blessings of a universal *Union*, were capable of self-government, and that they *could* govern themselves.

The whole civilized world were upon tiptoe of wonderment at our great prosperity and glory—that so great, happy, and prosperous a nation should be governed better than any other on the globe, without kingly or military power. The Hon. John Quincy Adams *told them how it was*, and that the strength of this great nation "was *not in the right*" (*the arm*), "*but in the heart.*" That is, in the affections and love for each other; and that very moment we appealed to the arm instead of the heart, our government was gone, or was no more than burnt flax, as a Constitutional Union, and we at once became a monarchical despotism, and will never be anything else unless we *return to our first love.* As a free nation we are now without a God (and have no right to appeal to him as the source and fountain of all love, and the only source of peace and union), unless we return to our loyalty to his throne, as set forth by Christ and his holy apostles.

Ministers of the Gospel, think of this before you preach any more war sermons from your pulpits, or present any more Sharpe's rifles and military swords before your altars (that were dedicated to Almighty God in love and holiness for his service only), and' exhort your people no more to rush to the field to spill your brothers' blood. I say, think of your legitimate calling, and take no more steps for the destruction of this great government, whose *strength was in the "hearts"* of the people and *not* in their *arms*, until you can show us some precept or example for such a course in the New Testament Scriptures. God will hold you responsible to his moral government for your conduct in this war. You were called, if called 'at all, to deal out love and mercy to all the people, as your great Progenitor did. While he is your example, he will be your God, *and no longer.* War never did nor never can produce a *union of "hearts,"* for war is of the devil, and union is of God. Paul, the great apostle and ambassador of Jesus Christ, never presented any military swords or guns at the altars dedicated to Almighty God, nor recommended them anywhere else, but said—

18

"Therefore if thine enemy hunger, feed him; if he thirst, give him drink; for in so doing thou shalt heap coals of fire on his head."—ROMANS xii. 20.

"Be not overcome with evil, but overcome evil with good." 21.

"Then said Jesus unto him: Put up again thy sword into his place; for all they that take the sword, shall perish with the sword."—MATT. xxvi. 52.

In the above verses we have both example and precept. But in the following we have the denunciation of all such preachers who recommend the sword to spill their brother's blood.

"Ye serpents, ye generation of vipers, how can ye escape the damnation of hell?"—MATT. xxiii. 33.

This is a terrible denunciation, but is it more terrible than this bloody civil war, that this great nation has been plunged into by abolition gospel preachers? Did those Scribes and Pharisees deserve such a denunciation any more than those preachers who have turned away from teaching the way of life, peace, and union; and glory in spilling the blood of their fellow men, and not only their fellow men, but their own race and blood? And yet with all the pretensions of righteousness that the Scribes and Pharisees ever feigned. By this course you have destroyed the fraternal power of love, in this great nation, reduced us from the lofty state of universal union, which is of God, to universal opposition, malice, and civil war, and saturated the soil of this glorious country with rivers of once fraternal blood, by the sword.

"Ye blind guides! which strain at a gnat, and swallow a camel."

"Behold, your house is left unto you desolate."—MATT. xxiii. 24, 38.

Yet, abolition gospel preachers, you have closed your eyes to the truths plainly set forth in the New Testament (see 2d chapter), you have blindfolded yourselves by the god of this world and taught doctrines in direct opposition to the gospel, as taught by the Apostle Paul. You have not only done, and recommended evil for evil, but you have done *evil* for good. "Behold, your house is left unto you desolate." And instead of being a savor of life unto life, you have been a savor of death unto death, and by your doings, ruin, desolation, consternation, and mourning cover our once glorious and happy land. Even now, if the church would return to God, and repent, and forsake their allegiance to the king of darkness, our glorious union may yet be restored, and peace and love be hallowed throughout our land.

APPENDIX.

If the President of the United States has any desire to restore peace and union to our distracted and ruined nation, and intends to gratify that desire, he will have to make up his mind to restore it just as God gave it unto us, or he will not live to see peace and union restored on this great continent. If slavery had been morally wrong, it would never have been here. God himself produced the circumstances, which made slavery not only necessary, but an insurmountable necessity. I have clearly shown from Divine Revelation, that the Supreme Being not only "sanctioned" slavery, but commanded that a particular race should be made slaves for life without limit to time. And the fact that this great country was so blessed under slave labor, prosperity having crowned our every lawful effort and enterprise from end to end, and from side to side, the truth of God run and was glorified. Gospel efforts blazed everywhere, and both races shouted and praised God aloud throughout the land. No people on the globe was ever so blessed as the slaves, for they excelled all others in unmolested happiness. When we see slavery such a great blessing to this whole nation, and even more to the free States than the slave States, and equally so to the whole civilized world. To know this fact, we only have to look at the condition of nearly all Europe at this time, as well as our own; all of which troubles and ruin has been caused by the attack upon slavery in this country. Yea, all civilized Europe is now frowning down upon us for this most ungodly attack upon the divine institution of negro slavery. With all this in view, and pressing upon us on every side; will the President, and so many good people in the free States close their eyes against the enormous facts, and still persevere to glorify infidelity and the devil, and sink this great nation into ruin? For as God lives, we shall reap just what we sow. If we sow union, peace, and love, we shall reap the same. If we go on in this God-forbidden course, and free the slaves of the South by force of arms, I have only to ask you to inquire of Mexico, Central America, Venezuela, New Granada, British and French West Indies, to know what we shall come to soon.

You say there is no danger in this country, for it

is different from all others. That the freedom of the slaves will improve everything in the entire con- federation. So said Great Britain and France, and so thought the planters in the West Indies, and said it would be cheaper and better for them to hire the negroes than it would be to own them; and many of the planters went in for it, believing they could hire them at less cost than it took to support them as slaves, and thought one hired freed or free negro would do as much work as two slaves. But O, what a sad mistake they found they had made when too late. What was their consternation and disap- pointment when they learned that the freed negro would not work at all for wages or love, and that his only idea of freedom was to lie about in the hot sun, and do nothing but sing and eat yams, as a Cincinnati Journal said of the Brown County negro colony, "*too lazy to play.*"

Inquire of England .how many millions pounds sterling annually has been distilled from the brains and muscles of her white people, in consequence of emancipation in her provinces. She will tell you the $100,000,000 to pay for the negro freedom was not much; but the losses since to the government, and the want of the articles produced on those Islands, had doubled the price of almost all the tropical articles, and vastly raised the price of most all other necessaries of life, so that her poor have been oppressed beyond calculation. And what for? has it done anybody any good anywhere on the globe, of any color? Not a single instance can be found; but it has struck a fatal blow to the wants

18*

of all civilized people on this verdant earth. Is that all? If it was we might put up with it. But it has sunk the black race (who had been brought up to a good state of civilization by being taken there from the most degraded land of barbarism on which the sun ever shone and made slaves to white masters) down to the lowest state of their ancestors. Read the history of Dehomi's kingdom in Africa, and you will learn from what a depth of ruin they were taken and civilized by slavery, and the depth of ruin, degradation, and barbarism, they have again been consigned to by emancipation.

Now if President Lincoln, or his host of followers, with all the abolition gospel preachers, who seem to think that the emancipation of the slaves would be the greatest boon ever bestowed upon mankind, will only weigh this negro question in view of all the true concomitant circumstances, without prejudice or favor, except for the general good of all mankind, they will doubtless make up their minds to restore the Union as it was first formed, with slavery unmolested in all the States who may desire it. Thus God blessed us with the Union, and thus he has blessed us with the greatest prosperity ever known on the face of the earth. And unless it is thus restored, no man now living will ever see it restored, or enjoy union, peace, and happiness again on the face of this continent.

Many seem to have little or no respect for the rights and happiness of *white men,* and for the sake of the restoration of the Union, I am willing to admit that " *We, the* (white) *people,*" deserve all the foretold, and untold ruin which is now upon us, for we had become a proud, high-headed, and stiff-necked people; yet the happiest people that ever had a being. But as those ministers and people seem willing to destroy hundreds of thousands of *"the people"* by the sword, for the sake of placing the negro race on an equality with *"the people"* or a little higher, will they not try to restore the Union as it was, for the good of that poor unfortunate race (the negroes), who have been so useful, and have so multiplied the glories of this world, as slaves? Go to Mexico, Central America, the Guianas, New Granada, Ecuador, the West Indies, or any spot on the earth where the negroes have been freed, and made equal to the white man, and you will see that you are a thousand times more cruel to the black race, than any system of slavery ever was; especially that of this country.

I never saw a good slave yet who was not inexpressibly happier than any free negroes I saw in New Granada, and just as far above them in moral standing. Yet the black race there, or in Jamaica, or Hayti, were just as good before emancipation as our slaves are; but look at them now. Now, for the sake, and in the name of the descendants of Africa, stop your mad attack upon that institution of God, devised for the good of both races, that his name may yet again be glorified in this world.

I will say again that, if all those who have been ordained, or licensed to preach the glorious gospel of our Lord and Saviour Jesus Christ, had stuck to their legitimate calling, and followed the example of their great exemplar St. Paul, we should now be at peace, and the Union would not only exist in name, but in fact, and the whole nation would be as a band of brethren held together by the strong bonds of love to God, and each other. Yea our great strength would still be in the "*heart*" and not in the battle-field.

What will future generations think of the church in the middle of the nineteenth century, when history shall hand our past glories down to them, when they shall compare it with their ruined condition? God will hold the church of the present day responsible for the ruin that has overtaken this nation, which he had called into existence, to be as a city set upon a hill, that all the world might see that this people were capable of self-government, and glorify his great name. But alas, we have fallen into the valley.

I have written the last four or five pages as an appendix to this chapter, since I had finished, to try to get the people to see what was going on around them. And how they are being deceived by the ungodly protestations of newspapers, and public speakers. No falsehood seems too monstrous, no slander too malignant and bitter for them to belch forth to an anxious people, and they have done it with such vehemence and boldness, that many thousands of good people have been made to believe that all they have said was very truth.

This publication may end my liberty; if so, I shall have the consolation of knowing that I have used my little talent in trying to expose the true traitors to this great and glorious government, whose power and strength was in the "*hearts*" of the people, and not in the *arm*. That they might not now blind the people by a great hurrah for the Union, while in their very souls they know they have destroyed it. And now they are wasting hundreds of millions, destroying hundreds of thousands of lives, and demoralizing and beggaring the whole nation, to hide their sins, and make the people believe somebody else did it.

I am now done, and doubt not but I have made many errors on unimportant points, as I have written much from memory of history, but on the main question before me I know I am right. I hope the statistics I have given will receive proper attention. Please look over slight and unimportant errors. If you differ with me on the main question, don't slander me by calling me a traitor, for I hold myself second to no one in this whole nation for true love and loyalty to the Constitution and the Union of the whole thirty-four States. God knows I am sincere; therefore let us have your objections in black and white, that I may be able.to compare and weigh the whole matter. If I have misunderstood the quotations I have made from the Bible, I hope some true and faithful divine will show me my error, as Christ taught "Nicodemus," and not denounce me as a traitor. You must not understand me above to include all the preachers of the Gospel, for God knows I don't. I hope and believe that there is yet salt enough in the ministry to save the Church from a complete overthrow. I only mean to include such as Beecher, Cheever, Furness, Thompson, and others.

Before I give this work into the hands of the printer, I must make a little reply to an article in the New York Methodist of the 13th Dec., 1862. I had finished the chapter long since, except some corrections, but as it is not yet published, I will add a few remarks on this article of *Prof.* Cairnes on the slave power. He is an Englishman writing on the American question. The article before me seems to be Mr. Cairnes' second on the subject. The first I did not see. I only wish to call attention to one or two points in the letter before me.

Mr. Cairnes says, since emancipation in the West Indies, "small proprietors have increased an hundred fold." "Within the last fifteen years, notwithstanding the high price of land, and the low rate of wages, the small proprietors of Barbadoes, most of them formerly slaves, have increased from 1100 to 3537." I will say that I have no objection to the above statement, so far as it is true, and I will not say that any part of it is false, but shall ask a few questions on some points before I get through.

Prof. Cairnes seems to be writing in favor of universal emancipation in the United States, evidently trying to make the impression that emancipation has been a great benefit in the West Indies, by inferences, without saying so. His first expression includes the West India Islands, where universal freedom has been granted, and then gives the Island of Barbadoes as an illustration, and says, "the small* proprietors have increased in the last fifteen years from 1100 to 3537, notwithstanding the high price of land and low rate of wages." I regret that I have not the statistics of that island at hand, and therefore can only say that if the land has increased in price on that island, it is very dissimilar from all the rest of the Antilles. It is true that the small proprietorships have increased an hundred-fold on all the West India Islands and in all States, wherever universal emancipation of the negroes have been granted, both in Europe and America. But who have been benefited, or where is the spot of land that has been improved by it, and what has been the result? Just turn back to the statistics I have given in this chapter, and you will see desolation, degradation, demoralization, idleness, laziness, licentiousness, and drunkenness, have been the only results. Why did not Prof. Cairnes tell exactly what he meant, and give some other evidence of good by freedom, besides the great increase of small (negro) proprietorships? All who know much about negroes, are aware of their disposition to have a home of their own, that they may have a spot from which no man can move them, or interfere with their habits. Read the history of Jacob and Mill, commencing on page 141, and you will have a complete illustration of those small proprietorships in Barbadoes, so boastingly chronicled by Prof. Cairnes. A vast majority of those small proprietorships cover from a quarter to about one or one and a half acres of land, all of which has the appearance of laziness, ruin, and desolation. There is not the slightest appearance of industry of any kind, much less enter-

prise, throughout those small proprietorships, and
they look more like habitations for animals of the
reptile order, than for human beings. These small
proprietorships are general from Mexico east,
throughout the countries, wherever emancipation
of the negro race has been effected.

Why did not Professor Cairnes state the good
results of freedom by that immense increase of proprietors? Because he knew of the degradation,
demoralization, and ruin, to the entire negro race
caused by it, and the almost complete stoppage of
every kind of business, and total stoppage of the
exports of every product that requires any labor to
produce it. He says, "notwithstanding the high
price of land, and low rate of wages." This seems
to be said to impress the mind with the idea that
there is industry and drive-ahead enterprise among
the freed negroes. That, notwithstanding, those two
obstacles since emancipation, the proprietors have
increased from 1100 to 3537 on the Island of Barbadoes.

In the first place, it is not true that wages are low.
The planters would pay any price for hands, but
wages, no matter how high, will not bring them.
For they will not engage themselves for seasonable
labor for love nor money. When emancipation was
effected in the West Indies, planting almost entirely
ceased, and was only barely revived by the importation of Coolies from China, who were kidnapped and
forced from their native land and sold as slaves in
Jamaica and other Islands for eight years; nearly
one-half of whom die before the end of the eight

years' service, and but few have life enough in them to enable them to procure a livelihood. Hard labor in the hot sun in the torrid zones is ruinous to their physical health, and nearly all of them are brought to a premature end by the *cruelties of hard-hearted opponents of negro slavery. And all this to allow Sambo to lounge and bask in idleness under the mango-tree, who was greatly improved both physically and morally by slavery, and was incalculably useful to the whole civilized world,* whose usefulness has been totally lost to the human family, and the slaves suddenly reduced to heathenism and barbarism by emancipation from slavery to good white masters, and the world is taxed at least fifty per cent. on all they consume to encourage Sambo's lazy habits. This is abolition righteousness and emancipation consistency. One of the greatest blessings of the human family must be forever lost, and the greatest civilizer yet known to mankind forever abolished and blotted out, whose place cannot now, nor never will be supplied in this world. Methinks, I almost see old Apollyon sitting in his big armed antislavery chair as placid as a Turk smoking opium, while he views his servants accomplishing so much glory for his kingdom by negro emancipation.

Prof. Cairnes speaks of high priced lands. I will only say that if the land has raised, it is contrary to all other West India Islands. All travellers on those Islands whom I have consulted, tell us that the best of lands can be bought for a mere song. In Jamaica two-thirds of all the sugar estates have been totally abandoned, and one-half of the other

19

third partly. Every sugar plantation on the Island of St. Domingo has been long since totally abandoned, from where they exported nearly 200,000,-000 pounds of sugar annually before emancipation. And if slavery had been maintained there, no doubt they would now export 400,000,000 pounds instead of not now one pound. While Cuba, where slavery has been continued, has been constantly advancing in prosperity and civilization.

Prof. Cairnes declares that white and black people are equal, that both alike will only work under compulsion, and this he says after the experiment had been tried for so many long years, and proved a total failure wherever it has been tried.

Rev. Dr. Channing was considered a great man, and he put forth the following prophecy in 1833, while the emancipation bill was before Parliament. I have no doubt he thought he was right, for the experiment had not been made in any of the provinces of Great Britian. The majority of Parliament entertained the same opinions, notwithstanding the total ruin of the Island of St. Domingo, and the complete demoralization and ruin of the whole black race of that island by emancipation some thirty years prior, and was then fully demonstrated. But the Rev. Dr. Channing, like the Rev. Drs. Cheever and Beecher of this day, was disposed to make an apology for the failure in Hayti, and other French Provinces, Haytians having freed themselves by a revolution and complete massacre of the whole population after the emancipation bill had passed, therefore the Rev. Dr. Channing and all the other English abolitionists

thought if they were set free, and placed on an equality, the white population would be greatly benefited.
Therefore Dr. Channing made the following declaration :—

"The planters, in general, would suffer little, if at all, from
emancipation. This change would make them richer rather
than poorer. One would think, indeed, from the common
language on the subject, that the negroes were to be annihi-
lated by being set free; that the whole labor of the South was
to be destroyed by a single blow. But the colored men, when
freed, will not vanish from the soil. He will stand there with
the same muscles as before, only strung anew by liberty; with
the same limbs to toil, and with *stronger* motives to toil than
before. He will work from *hope*, not from fear; will work for
himself, not for others; and, unless all the principles of human
nature are *reversed under a black skin*, he will work *better
than before.* We believe that agriculture will revive, our worn-
out soils will be renewed, and the whole country assume a
brighter aspect under *free labor.*"

Rev. Dr. Channing spoke very lightly, and con-
temptuously of the opinions of those who knew *that
human nature* was totally "reversed under a black
skin," just as all the abolitionists treat us here who
have sufficiently investigated the nature of the white
and black races, to know that human nature is entirely
and completely "reversed *under a black skin.*" The
Rev. Dr. Channing was told what the result would be,
but he and the British House of Lords would not believe it, until they struck the fatal blow upon the interest of that entire nation, and all other civilized
people. And now, if the blow should be struck
here, and the negroes freed, it will throw civilization back five hundred years, and forever end the
hopes of white men for self-government and per-

fect liberty. It is strange that men will not see the ruin that will follow the success of abolitionism in this once happy country. O that I could open the eyes of the blind, who are being led into ruin by designing men!

I don't know with what amount of literary knowledge Prof. Cairnes may have been possessed, but one of two things is evident. He either has no knowledge of negro human nature, or the teachings of *inspired* truth, and the immense disasters to the business of the whole civilized world, with the complete overthrow of the last hope of civilization for the African race, and their everlasting degradation from civilization outside of Africa by emancipation; or he is an infidel or anti-Christian, and is aiming at the destruction of the latter. For it cannot be possible that he is so ignorant of the degradation to the negro race in all the British and French Provinces, or West Indies, the financial, social, and political ruin to all the white inhabitants of those Islands, and great embarrassment to the mother countries by the freedom of the negroes.

The Islands of Barbadoes and Trinidad are constantly brought forward by abolitionists to show the advantages of negro freedom. They don't tell us of the stringent laws of those miniature islands, and the immense number of Coolies whom they have been compelled to import from China, and make them slaves, on the Island of Trinidad, to keep up their producing operations. Nor do they tell of the laws of Barbadoes, that compels the negroes to drag a heavy block, chained to them, for refusing to work when work is offered to them, and thus they are punished worse than their masters ever punished them for idleness.

I will give one more table that will satisfy every reader that what I say about Prof. Cairnes is about true. In 1800 the West Indies exported 17,000,000 lbs. of cotton, and this country exported 17,789,803 lbs. This was after cotton had nearly ceased to be cultivated in St. Domingo and other French colonies, or they would have been ahead of the United States that year. In 1840 all the West Indies exported 866,157 lbs. of cotton; the United States exported 743,941,061. Is this not enough to satisfy every common-sense man that Prof. Cairnes must have known better, and that the American system is the best in the world? Is negro slavery a social, political and moral evil, and negro freedom a blessing?

The abolitionists say that if there never had been any slaves in the United States, we should now be at peace throughout our own land. That may be so; but not so certain as it would have been if we never had had any abolitionists among us. If there never had been any negroes, we should not have had any slaves; if there never had been any money, we should never have had any pickpockets nor highway robbers; if we never have had any marriages, we should never have had any abusing and abandoning of wives. But God made negroes, money, and instituted slavery and the marriage contract—but he did not make the abolitionists. Therefore,

19*

they have been produced by the other great spirit, who is the father of lies and all bloody wars.

I will repeat, that if I had been called upon (by an irrevocable decree) to have destroyed this great moral government *by the people*, and to have raised up in its place the worst despotism ever known on the earth, and if I failed in the first effort death was to have been the penalty, I should have taken the very course the republican party did in 1860 and '61, and should have pursued the very plans they have pursued to this day, and I should have had no fear of death by the decree.

God intended this government to be as near like what he created man for, as it was possible for man to be in his fallen state, and established the Christian churches as safety valves; but many of the Christian ministry, whom he ordained and sent forth as moral teachers and pioneers of civilization, have turned away from that holy calling, and have substituted Sharpe's rifles, the cannon-ball, and the sword for the Gospel of our blessed Lord, and prayed that they might swim in rivers of blood of their own brethren in the Church, to break up and completely destroy an institution established by God himself for the mutual good of the black and white races in the world; and now the consequences are upon us. Will not those preachers do as Judas did, that peace may come to our land?

CHAPTER IV.

Can the White or Anglo-American Race, and the African or Negro Race, live together on a political, social, and domestic equality in the United States of North America, and how? If so, would it be justified by the laws of Nature or of Nature's God?

HUMAN or civil laws are changeable, and can be suited to the majority of a republic, or the whim or caprice of a king or despot. The laws of Nature vary somewhat, but the fundamental principles are unchangeable and entirely beyond the control of man. Wherever the civil laws or human practices in any way interfere with the laws of Nature, they interfere with the laws of Omnipotence, and the penalty is severe and interminable; and woe be unto that government or people who shall attempt to change or interfere with those laws, only to ex-pose, cultivate, dress, and improve them. On these doctrines we have had line upon line, and precept upon precept, and no man or woman can in this day of light and knowledge plead ignorance of them and their penalties. They may plead ignorance of human or civil laws, for they are changed by the caprice of parties, but the laws of Nature have un-dergone no change since the fall of man. Though miraculous additions have been made to the variety, there has been no change in the fundamentals for nearly 6000 years.

I have said enough in former chapters on the origination of the now African race, the descendants of Canaan, the confusion of tongues, and the separation of the human family, from the building of Babel. There was but one family and one tongue prior to that day. From that miraculous event all the different tribes, races, and nations of the earth sprang, except the Canaanites, now the African race, and the Ishmaelites, now the Bedouin Arabs, or the Arabs of the desert of Arabia; and those tribes who sprang from a mixture of blood with them, by the true descendants of Shem and Japheth, all of whom are accursed races to a greater or less extent. Canaan, as I have shown in former chapters, was condemned to perpetual slavery; from that event springs a *decree* or *edict* in the laws of the code of Nature. Abraham trespassed upon that law when he yielded to the overtures of his doubting wife, and took Hagar to his bosom, who was doubtless a descendant of Canaan, whose whole race was accursed to perpetual degradation and slavery. See Gen. ix. 20–27. To show us that any matrimonial intercourse or connection with them was divinely forbidden, we have the Arabs of the desert, as living monuments of the displeasure of Almighty God to any mixture of blood between the pure descendants of Shem and Japheth and the descendants of Canaan, the grandson of Noah, who doubtless was accursed for making fun of his old grandfather, while laboring under a misfortune. The Africans are living monuments of

Jehovah's displeasure towards children who badly treat their parents. They, the Canaanites, may be improved, but will never be capable of self-government; and slavery is their only hope among men. I have said enough on these points in previous chapters. The above is sufficient to show that certain unchangeable laws of human nature on which I now propose to give a few thoughts cannot be broken with impunity. I have said enough to show that all men are *not* created equal.

Then the question arises, Can the black and white man live together on a social, political, and domestic equality? and if they could, would such an association be sanctioned by the divine law or the laws of Nature? Let us look at this without prejudice or favor, and with a single eye to the glory of God and the good of all mankind. It is conceded on all sides that liberty of conscience, peace, popular government, and union, with great physical health and longevity, are the greatest blessings of God to mankind. This being conceded, then it must also be that man's first duty is to cultivate those blessings above all else that is human, and expel every intruder upon those laws that are life guards of our physical and social salvation. The laws of Nature are to some extent protected by both divine and civil law. For instance, the Sabbath day is necessary for the health and longevity of man. Gluttonous and intemperance of every kind is prohibited, with intermarriages between the whites and blacks, rowdyism, and all overt extravagances that overtax the physical strength of man. Human laws inflict corporcal punishments, fines, and imprisonments upon man for transgressing of many of the laws of Nature, but the laws of Nature inflict more terrible punishments for disobedience to her requirements, all of which are imperative and unchangeable. The penalties are bodily afflictions, poverty, degradation, loathsome diseases, premature death, or long sickly lives. I presume all will agree that human ingenuity ought to be exerted to prevent any and all such extravagances, which are so fatal to the good of mankind. No law could be too severe, and no punishment too extreme for that man or set of men who would establish places to promote disobedience to the laws that will entail with certainty ruin to the peace and happiness of mankind.

Now if I should succeed in showing that the emancipation of all the slaves in this country will place the negro race on a political, and an attempt to social equality, and that that system will produce a diseased, sickly, short-lived, and unhappy race of men and women, would it not be our duty to close every avenue in our power that leads to such fatal results? I have already alluded to the mulatto race, in a former chapter, as being very weak, sickly, and short-lived on the general. There is not the slightest danger of a general or universal amalgamation of blood between the Anglo-American and African races in this country, but if the universal emancipation of the slaves should take place, enough would be found among the Saxons to equal the Africans in number, who from various causes would be reduced to a level with Africans, which causes might be dissipation, crime, and lazy habits, and who would feel more at home, perhaps, and happier among the black race than among the whites. The negroes being free and consequently on a civil equality and in competition with the whites, the lower classes of the Saxons would unite their interests with the Africans, in competition with the higher order of the Anglo-Americans, and the result would be intermarriages or mixing of blood in some way between the negroes and lower orders of the whites. This would result mainly from interest or a combination between the two, to try to compete with their superiors. This would produce in a very short space of time an immense population of mulattoes, who are, with, but few exceptions, a very sickly and short-lived race, especially in the northern climes of this country. This population would rapidly increase at first. The antipathies between them and the pure whites would be too great and bitter for them to dwell together, and insurrections would be inevitable between the two races. This would not be a sectional strife, as the strife now is, and a complete extermination of the weaker party would be the inevitable result.

Suppose this should not turn out to be the case; then say the amalgamationists, we should all soon be of one color, and one people; just what they (the abolitionists) have been laboring for so many years, in order to end the prejudice of color, that our great nation might be at peace. This I admit would be a good thing if it was compatible with the righteous laws of nature and nature's God; and a promotion of civilization, and a general genuine physical health and long life should be the result. But if the contrary should be the inevitable consequence, then your whole scheme of peace, union, and happiness falls to the ground. The scheme is so incompatible with all the blessings of union, peace, tranquillity, harmony, and righteousness, that it is surprising that any man or woman could be found in this land of schools and science so led by wild fanaticism, who would embrace such a doctrine for one moment; yet it is even so. Let us examine it and see how it will stand the test of the unchangeable laws of human nature.

It has been two hundred and forty two years since the first cargo of African slaves landed in this country, and legal records show that laws were passed in some of the colonies nearly two hundred years ago to prevent a spurious color being made between the white and black races. I mention this to show that mulattoes must have been produced that far back, or those laws would not have been passed. Now if mulattodom commenced so nearly with the first introduction of negro slavery in this country, how is it that there are so few mulatto families? Is it not strange that they are so much less prolific than either the pure whites or negroes? You may bring together in matrimony two individuals of any two separate nations of the world of the same pure color, and you will find that their children will not only be very healthy and long lived, but exceedingly prolific, generation after generation, through centuries of time; but if you marry the pure white and negro people together, they will be as prolific as any others, but their children will, three to one, be puny, sickly, and short lived, and cease to multiply almost if not altogether by the third generation, and even the first produces very sparingly, with few exceptions, unless those children return directly to the white or black of the pure colors. But that is even more uncommon than breeding between the pure black or white.

The better class of mulattoes are as much preju- diced against the negroes as the whites are, and was it not for circumstances that force them in company with the negro, the antipathies would be far greater. The negroes are very jealous of the mulattoes, because of the improvement they see in their color and general appearance. The whites know they would sink themselves just as much by an inter- course with the mulattoes as with the negroes, there- fore a return by the mulattoes to either of the pure bloods is almost entirely prohibited by a law that cannot be controlled by man unless he falls to a level with the beast.

The amalgamationists say, this prejudice of human colors is very wicked, and ought to be done away with altogether. I say it is not. The prejudice of color is suffered by our great Maker, if not divinely produced, to prevent spurious mixtures of colors or blood; he having in his providence produced the colors and appearances of these two distinct races of men, for the good of the "*people.*" The divine dis- pleasure is so clearly apparent in the mixture of the blood of these two distinct races, that I am at a loss in some cases to understand how Christian men can be found who defend it, and even advocate it; but in others I am not disappointed, for the devil hates all that is good, and it is his business to advocate any and every principle that is in any way calculated to demoralize society, or depopulate this part of the world; therefore infidelity and abolitionism run almost parallel. It is a mistake that there are a greater ratio of mulattoes produced among slaves than there are among free people of color. But the South is more congenial to their health and longevity than the North. Now, these are natural laws that no power under heaven can change. Though all the civil and uncivilized nations and tribes of the earth may unite for that purpose, they could not change one "jot or tittle" of those laws, for they are unchangeable and irrevocable.

Now, it being so clearly proved by circumstances and experience that any interference with those laws is fatal to the peace and happiness of our race, and equally so to the poor unfortunate negro, and to the whole human race, is it not our duty as a Christian and free people, to watch against and close up every avenue that leads to such fatal, corrupt, and demoralizing results? There is no room for a doubt that if there were an equal number of negroes to the white people in this country, and then let them be prohibited by an irrevocable *decree* that there should be no marriages except between the white and black races, and all sexual intercourse was prohibited between the white people, and all emigration to this country stopped, the whole country would become entirely depopulated in one hundred and twenty years. Mulattoes are a forbidden race, and to prohibit a mixture of blood with the negroes by the white people, our great Creator has made these laws of nature to prohibit a new race of men being formed between those two very distinct races of mankind. He gave us the negroes for our benefit, and their good, and if we prove faithless to our trust, we shall be "whipped with many stripes."

Those who deny these doctrines will please show the contrary, by pointing out unchanged mulatto families, who descended from the pure stock of white or black one hundred years ago; I will then agree that there are some exceptions, but you will find them very scarce.

Prof. Adams says, that the "pure mulattoes cease to produce altogether after the third generation, and that it is very common for the first generation of pure mulattoes to be as barren as mules, unless they marry with the pure white or black blood, and even their offsprings are mostly delicate and short-lived." Quarter-bloods are healthier and longer-lived than half-bloods, and, as they near either pure blood, they increase in health and length of life. If these are not evidences of divine prohibition of the mixing of blood between these two races, I don't know how anything on earth could be sustained by circumstantial evidence. The pure white blood is injured by mixing with any red, copper, or yellow tribes on the globe, but as they mix with those who approach nearer to the black or negro race, they reduce or degrade their issue more.

The abolitionists attribute mulattodom to slavery. This is a misrepresentation. The ratio of free mulattoes in the slave States is perhaps five to one of the mulatto slaves. This shows how clearly emancipation increases amalgamation; and just in the ratio that the negroes are freed, amalgamation will increase. The ratio of original mulattoes born in the free States exceeds those born by or from slave women five to one. There are comparatively few mulattoes born from white women; but ten, perhaps, in the free States to one in the slave States. These declarations will astonish many, for disunionists or abolitionists (they are almost synonymous) have been trying to prejudice the South by foul slander so many years, that good people have got to believe the slander. I don't wish to be understood to say that the people of the southern States are generally better than they are in the free States, for that would not be the truth, but I will say that the ratio of anti-constitutional union men, up to the Presidential election of 1860, in the free States were twenty to one of those of the slave States; neither do I mean to say that the people of the free States are more licentious and dishonest than the people of the slave States, for they are not; therefore, the fact of the greater ratio of mulattoes being produced in the free States, is the legitimate consequence of the universal freedom of the negroes in those States, there being more loose bad men in the free States, and perhaps in a little greater ratio, than in the slave States. The city of New York, for instance, might be called the great metropolis of the United States for bad men, and the worst of men, as well as the greatest commercial city of the country; it also contains a very large number of the best and most upright men in the world.

The idea that there is a greater ratio of mulattoes produced in free States than in slave States is very insulting to many, but if they will examine the question for themselves, they will soon see how far they have been misled by designing men and women. We all know there are a great many more mulattoes produced in the slave States than in the free, but you must not forget that there are about twenty negroes in the slave States to one in the free; yet the mulattodom of the slave States is not in half that ratio to the free. It is well known that most of the Northern men who move South become the most ultra pro-slavers very soon after they arrive there, and the stronger their opposition to slavery was before they left here, the stronger their pro-slavery feelings become there. Why is it so? Simply because they see how they have been misled by designing men, who profess to be such great philanthropists. This is common on all subjects in dispute, with all who are honest, when they see they have been misled and deceived by their leaders.

I will now return to the main subject of this chapter, and will give the following statistics gathered by the late Dr. Jesse Chickering:—

" It appears that the blacks die in Massachusetts in a ratio of three to one, as compared with the whites. This state of things is the result of both moral and physical causes. The depressing influence of extreme social hardships, which no philanthropy can alleviate, accounts in a great measure for this unequal mortality, while physical causes operate perhaps still more to the same effect."

Of the latter, we may learn something from a paper read a few years since before the Boston Society of Natural History, by Dr. Samuel Kneeland, from which the following is an extract:—

"The mulatto is often triumphantly appealed to as a proof that hybrid races are prolific without end. Every physician who has seen much practice among the mulattoes knows that in the first place, they are far less prolific than the blacks or whites—the statistics of New York State and city confirm this fact of daily observation; and, in the second place, when they are prolific, the progeny is frail, diseased, short-lived, rarely arriving at robust manhood or maturity. Physicians need not be told of the comparatively enormous amount of scrofulous and deteriorated constitutions found among those hybrids.

"The Colonization Journal furnishes some statistics with regard to the colored population of New York city, which must prove painfully interesting to all reflecting people. The late census showed that, while other classes of our population in all parts of the country were increasing in an enormous ratio, the colored were decreasing. In the State of New York, in 1840, there were fifty thousand; in 1850, only forty-seven thousand. In New York city, in 1840, there were eighteen thousand; in 1850, seventeen thousand. According to the New York City Inspector's report for the four months ending with October, 1853:—

1. The whites present marriages . .   2,230
    The colored   "   "   26
2. The whites   " births . . .   6,780
    The colored   "   "   . . .   70
3. The whites   " deaths about . .   6,000
    (exclusive of 2,152 among 116,000 newly-arrived emigrants, and others unacclimated.)
    The colored exhibit deaths . . .   160

giving a ratio of deaths among acclimated whites to colored persons of thirty-seven to one; while the births are ninety-seven whites to one colored. The ratio of whites to colored is as follows: Marriages, 140 to 1; births, 97 to 1; deaths 37 to 1. According to the ratio of the population, the marriages among the whites, during this time, are three times greater than among the colored; the number of births among the whites is twice as great. In deaths, the colored exceed the white not only according to ratio of population, but show one hundred and sixty-five deaths to seventy-six births, or seven deaths to three births, more than two to one.

"The same is true of Boston, as far as the census returns will enable us to judge. In Shattuck's census of 1845, it appears that in that year there were one hundred and forty-six less colored persons in Boston than in 1840; the total number being 1842. From the same work, the deaths are given for a period of fifty years, from 1725 to 1775, showing the mortality among the blacks to have been twice that among the whites. Of late years, Boston, probably, does not differ from itself in former times, nor from New York at present. In the compendium of the United States census for 1850, p. 64, it is said that the 'declining ratio of the increase of the free colored in every section is notable. In New England the increase is now almost nothing;' in the southwest and the southern States the increase is much reduced; it is only in the northwest that there is any increase, 'indicating a large emigration to that quarter.' What must become of the black population at this rate in a few years? What are the causes of this decay? They do not disregard the laws of social and physical well-being any more than, if they do as much as, the whites. It seems to me one of the necessary consequences of attempts to mix races; the hybrids cease to be prolific; the race must die out as mulatto; it must either keep black unmixed, or become extinct. Nobody doubts that a mixed offspring may be produced by intermarriage of different races—the Griquas, the Papuas, the Cafuses of Brazil, so elaborately numerated by Pritchard, sufficiently prove this. The question is, whether they would be perpetuated if strictly confined to intermarriage among themselves? From the facts in the case of mulattoes, we say unquestionably not. The same is true, as far as has been observed, of the mixture of the white and red races, in Mexico, Central and South America. The well-known infrequency of mixed offspring between the European and Australian races, led the Colonial government to official inquiries, and to the result, that in thirty-one districts, numbering fifteen thousand inhabitants, the half-breeds did not exceed two hundred, though the connection of the two races was very intimate.

"If any one wishes to be convinced of the inferiority and tendency to disease in the mulatto race, even with the assistance of the pure blood of the black and white race, he need only witness what I did recently, viz.: the disembarkation from a steamboat of a colored picnic party, of both sexes, of all ages, from the infant in arms to the aged, of all hues, from the darkest black to a color approaching white. There was no *old mulatto*, though there were several *old negroes;* many fine-looking mulattoes of both sexes, evidently the first offspring from the pure races; then came the youths and children, and here could be read the sad truth at a glance. The little blacks were agile looking; the little mulattoes, youths and young women, farther removed from the pure stock, were sickly, feeble, with frightful scars and skin diseases, and *scrofula* stamped on every feature and every visible part of the body. Here was hybridity of human races, under the most favorable circumstances of worldly condition and social position."

It seems to me the above would be sufficient to satisfy any class of men, even the abolitionists; but the antislavery question being the only question by which this Union, the succor and glory of man, could possibly be destroyed, therefore this powerful testimony is rejected by the hosts of disunionists here in the free States. Pardon me for these out of place remarks, for they come up so strongly and vividly before me, that my pen seems almost involuntarily to write them down. Hybridity in the North is more fatal than in the South. The half breeds and quadroons are not so sickly and puny in the warm climates, therefore not so short lived, but yet fatal enough to be visible to every observing slaveholder, who knows too well the fatal effects to his interest, of having the blood of his negroes mixed with white blood, to encourage it in any way whatever, even if he had no moral objections to such an ungodly business; and yet every slaveholder is accused of encouraging it between his own sons and his negro slaves, and of engaging in it himself. Now let us ask ourselves the question, How would we like to be thus slandered by the Southern people? Just suppose the tables were turned, how would we like it? I have shown already that hybridity is fatal to the human race in this country, and is prohibited by laws altogether out of our control. Then we may despair of ever bringing the two races together on a social equality on that plan. It is wonderful how any white man or woman can sink themselves low enough to desire such a ruinous and hell-begotten scheme.

I will give one more very singular and striking result in hybridity,. which I hope will be noticed with special attention. In the animal, hybridity hardeneth, and increaseth longevity. Take the horse and the ass, and breed them together, and their offspring will be, and is, almost like brass. There are no hardships too great for the mule; although much less in size than the horse, yet he is far more useful for general drudgery, and suited to all climes. Whether in the torrid or frigid zones, the mules are the same long-lived beast of burden, and no hardships seem too much for their grizzly nature in any climes. Take the wild and tame goose, or the wild and tame duck, or the common and Muscova ducks, and breed them together, their offspring (though entirely neutral and unproductive) will be strong and long-lived.

Now, how is it, that hybridity or mixing of blood among the animal creation produces such great strength and longevity, while between the Anglo-Saxon and African it is so fatal to health and life, and almost as unproductive in the propagation of their species as the animal? Is there no Providence in this? Is it all by chance? Has it no meaning? And how is it that the negro is so much healthier and longer lived in the torrid than in the frigid zones? And yet, like the mule, they will not cultivate the soil without a master. Is this not too significant to be without meaning? Then is it not clear that the negroes were originally intended to be used by the white man to do the drudgery in the hot sun of the tropical regions of the world? This being the case, which all experience and history shows the fact, and the demonstrative evidence now manifest by the emancipation of all the slaves in the British, Spanish, and French Provinces, from thirty to forty years ago, without one palliating circumstance having even yet grown out of that scheme of degradation and ruin to the poor African, and the almost incalculable loss to the whole civilized world by that scheme, ought to satisfy every good man.

How, then, are these two distinct races to meet on a social, political, and domestic equality? Would you have a people totally incapable of self-government to hold their proportion of the offices? Would you have the sixth part of our police force to be African negroes, or the sixth part of our lawyers, our legislators, the Congress of the United States, and every sixth President and Vice-President to be of that race? How would you like to go into our Supreme Court in Bank, and there see a black negro the presiding judge? Would you have the sixth part of our courts to be negroes? Even supposing this could be done without a social and domestic equality, which would be impossible, would you be willing to force anything upon us that would be so extremely forbidding? You know all our senses revolt at the thought. Would you change the beauty of the Anglo-American race for the sake of one of the most obnoxious and forbidding races on earth, to all our senses? Would you sink us from the high and noble state God has given us in the world, down to heathen and barbarism? Don't you suppose that if God had willed such a mixture, he would have thus created us? And if it was right for us to be on an equality with African negroes, would he have placed those laws in human nature so disastrous to its perpetuation and domestic happiness? I think the party who advocate these principles are not only lower than the angels, but a little lower than the devil.

Now the question naturally arises, can the negroes all be set free, and allowed to remain with us, without being placed on a political and social equality, at least, or be completely exterminated? Now, if you set them all free, one or more of these events will come up in our history. Our Heavenly Father has made us to *rule*, and the negroes to serve, and if we, through a pretended sympathy, or a false philanthropy, right in the face of all common sense and reason, set aside his holy arrangements for the good of mankind and his own glory, and tamper with his laws, we shall be overthrown and eternally degraded, and perhaps made subjects of some other civilized nation. This will be our doom as sure as God lives. Then, will you persevere in such foolery, right in the face of truth and righteousness, with your heaven-daring schemes of wickedness, that will as assuredly overthrow this great and glorious Union as the scheme shall be adopted, or-bring about the extermination of the whole negro race in this country? The laws of nature and nature's God prohibit the mixing of the two colors into one blood, which ends that plan. Colonization in their native land of all the negroes would be so nearly impracticable, that it will never be done, and no other spot on this green earth will do for them. It would be the height of cruelty and barbarism to send them anywhere else. If they could all be colonized on the coast of Africa, they would fall back into heathenism and barbarism in less than fifty years; for the civilization of Africa will cease as soon, or very soon after, the influx of fresh supplies shall cease to arrive there from a true and complete civilized nation. That being the only way that the civilization of Africa can be successful and perpetual—all other schemes for the safety of the negro in this country, and the civilization of Africa being out of the question, except through African slavery in the United States.

These ideas will be denounced by all the abolitionists in the whole country, whether republicans, democrats, or Union men; but denunciations will not disprove them. Don't understand me to be opposed to colonization, for I am a strong advocate of that scheme, for great good has been effected by it on the coast of Africa. But if all the Africans in the United States should be colonized there, it would mainly end the deep interest that is felt for the success of those colonies, and it is universally admitted that the black race is a lower order of the human family than any other. It is asserted by many of the best and most experienced men on earth that they are not now or ever will be capable of self-government. But as long as we keep them here, and colonize the surplus every year, and those who are willing to go, a government will be kept up there of some sort, that will be better than no government at all.

Every circumstance seems to prove that slavery in the United States was the work of God, for the civilization of the African race, that it produces a greater wonderment in my mind than any other strange thing I have ever seen or heard, that so many sensible men can be found who reject the idea as a wicked one, and denounce all who embrace it as murderers, thieves, and robbers. If all such would only divest themselves of all prejudice, and examine

21

the question as Christian men ought, they would soon see it in a different light, and change their opinion altogether on the question.

Prior to 1620, every scheme was adopted to successfully cultivate the soil of the tropics of the United States. Three-fourths of the whites who attempted to work the soil in the hot sun, soon sickened and died; they then enslaved the Indians, and they died off faster than the whites. When despair had filled every man in the southern colonies, and they were fast coming to the conclusion that they would be compelled to strike their tents and leave those rich and sunny climes to the Indians and wild beasts, and retire in hopeless despair, news came that a vessel had arrived from the Portugal possessions on the coast of Africa, with a small cargo of Africans. The colonies concluded to try the new experiment. They purchased them and set them to work in the fields, looking for the same result as they had from the Indians and white men; but after the experiment had been sufficiently tried, to their agreeable surprise they found them just exactly suited to their wants, and instead of becoming weak, sickly, and to a premature death, as the white men and Indians did, they waxed strong under the yoke of bondage. The hot sun and hard labor were soon found to be more congenial to their health and longevity, than to the beasts of burden, or labor, or idleness in the shade. Another most remarkable fact showed itself very soon. They were altogether unlike the Indians, who hated their masters, and would slay them in secret at every opportunity; the negroes loved their masters, and leaned upon them as a child leans upon its parents, and do to this day, wherever their minds have not been poisoned by designing, wicked white men and women. ⌐They thus continued for two hundred years, contented and happy, loving their masters more than any other earthly object, and still do wherever they have not been deceived by designing disunionists, and haters of a republican form of government.

Now the fact is that negroes are so much happier, healthier, and longer lived in slavery than they are free, and that free negroes have never been of any earthly use to themselves or anybody else, in this country, as I have fully shown in former chapters. No light never could have been thrown, either gospel or any kind of civilization, into that great and benighted country (Africa), had negro slavery never have been introduced into the United States. All the good that has ever come to the African in any shape or form, has been through the institution of slavery; and every attempt to change that relation has proved a great curse to both races in our once happy land. ⌐He who labors to break up the relation of master and slave, is a traitor to heaven's righteous plans of government among men, and an enemy to the true happiness of mankind. ⌐See now what terrible curses have fallen upon the whole country by our interfering with that institution. Who could have believed two years ago that saints could have so soon been turned into devils! The best and most tender hearted liberal Christian men and women, and the greatest

lovers of our national constitution and union of
States, seem now to be wicked spirits, who glory in
murder and the destruction of liberty and property.
Why this sudden change, and who or what has done
it? It is because of an attempt to abolish slavery
in this country. It is because of the determination
in the North never to cease to interfere with the
institution in the States, where God has so completely provided for its existence, that it should be
a necessity. But in his goodness and wisdom in
making this arrangement for the salvation of Africa,
spiritually and temporally, did not forget that the
white race would be burdened with an evil, therefore he designed that man should be paid for his
labor and trouble, and made slavery profitable to all
good and well-managing men, while he created the
necessity that would force man into the ownership
of slaves.

I will repeat, in conclusion, that the two races
cannot, for the reasons herein given, ever live together on a social or political equality, without the
destruction of the peace and happiness of both races,
and a complete overthrow of this great and glorious
government. The emancipation of all the slaves
will produce the same ruin, for as soon as so many
millions of free people (negroes) are thrown upon
the country and not placed on a social and political
equality, the Union is at once gone. To place them
on an equality, would be a perpetual ruin to the
whole nation. To colonize them is impossible.
Then it is as clear as a sunbeam that the only plan
is to keep up the relation of master and slave unmo-

lested, and colonize the surplus in Liberia, but to
send none over forty years old, and them of the best
and most intelligent class. All the free negroes
under forty and over eighteen years old should be
colonized there, for they are no manner of use here,
but stand in the way of a free republican government and Union. There should be no negroes in
this country, but those who are slaves. ✓I have tried
to come to other conclusions, but circumstances
herein alluded to have forced me into these opinions
against my desire, knowing such opinions would be
exceedingly unpopular with nearly all my best
friends, and would not raise me up any with the few
who may not denounce me as a cruel man, I desiring
to have the confidence of all who know' me or may
hear of me. But I cannot after a complete and
thorough unbiased investigation of the subject, both
civil and moral with all its concomitant circumstances, take a different course. I felt that I could better
bear the loss and wrath of my friends and others,
than I could a conscientious sense of having taken
a wrong or false ground. Policy suggested a different
course on this subject, and the temptation was so
great that in the beginning of this work I wrote
several pages, in which I aimed to trim between the
two extremes on the moral question of slavery; but
on an examination of the Bible, authorities of the
question, and reason for the good of mankind, and
the opinions of the most eminent divines who have
ever written on the Scriptural laws of slavery, especially those who wrote before the strife had risen on
the subject in this country, and the more modern

writers who were so prejudiced against the traffic in human beings that they condemned it in strong terms, I became so powerfully convinced that slavery was divinely authorized that I stopped short and threw away, perhaps, twenty pages of manuscript, in which I had attempted to show that slavery in the abstract would be a moral evil. Having then fully made up my mind that I would rather have a sense of being right than to be popular, consequently I have written this book conscientiously, believing I have taken the only true, safe, and righteous ground on all subjects herein noticed. It being my faith, allow that I am honest, and aim at right, if you condemu the faith as heterodox; for I do believe the negro race heterogeneous to white people.

CHAPTER V.

Who are Union Men?

THE larger part of this chapter was written for the Press after the war commenced, but was refused admission. I have since added four or five pages of new matter.

I, as a Constitutional Union man, who love the Constitution and the Union more than anything else under heaven, desire to know who are the Union men, and who the anti-Union men *per se*. I understand that a real Union man must be a real lover of the Constitution, or if he professes to be a Union man and declares hostility to the Constitution, that he is either a gross hypocrite or a fool. If I have misunderstood the meaning of a true Union man, I should like to be set straight by some "lexicographer," for no man hates the wrong and loves the right more than I, especially in matters of such vast importance as the above. It seems to me that the principles of Union and disunion are so plain that a child four years old can comprehend them. Then, how can a man be a real genuine Union man, and hate the Constitution—the only chain of the Union that holds it together? He must either hate both or love both, for every man well knows that one cannot

exist without the other; therefore, the inferences are,
that if he hates one he must hate both, or, if he
loves one he loves both. How is this question to be
solved? I will undertake to do it as briefly as possible, and, if I mistake, please correct me, for there
is nothing affecting the hopes and fears of this country at present more than this. I look upon a disunionist *per se*, as the most abominable monster on
the face of the earth. I can think of nothing under
the heavens so hateful in the eyes of the Almighty,
and in the hearts of all good men. They are the
very excrescence of the bottomless pit.

I meet with men every day who cry loudly for
the Union, and urge the prosecution of the war beyond possibility; and denounce the administration,
Gen. Scott, and Gen. McClellan, for not having
pushed the war on before this, to the total destruction of the whole South, with their entire interest,
without the slightest respect to the helpless women
and children. They seem to be so aggrieved and
mortified at the Southern people for attempting to
destroy this great and glorious Union, that many of
them say that the whole white population of the
seceding States must be exterminated for the crime
they have committed in the attempt to withdraw from
the Union. They most bitterly denounce every man
as a traitor who speaks of trying to save the Union
without the destruction of human life. *Yet they say
they never want to see the Union restored with peace and
harmony, while there is a slave on American soil. No!
rather than have one negro in slavery in the United
States, they would see the Union split into fragments,*

and a monarchical government established with the most extreme despotism ever known. Or rather than yield up one single line of the Chicago Platform, or to allow one single slave to go into the territories of the United States under protection of law. or one sent back to his master who had made his escape into the free States, "let the Constitution slide," let the Union be broken up, let anarchy reign from Maine to Florida, and from the Atlantic to the Pacific. This class of men, and women too, are very large in this city of Brotherly Love, and they allow no man to speak of peace through the medium of olive-branches. If he dare do it, they denounce him as a secessionist, and tell him he ought to be hung upon the lamp-post by the neck, or locked up in a prison cell and kept there until he rots. One of these kind of Union men, a large merchant in this city, said he had two sons in the battle field, and if he had forty, he would send them all to save this glorious Union from destruction, and if one refused to go he would disown him. Yet this great patriot denounces the Constitution as a compromise with the devil and a league with hell. There are thousands upon thousands of these great patriotic Union men, who would rather anything should take place, no matter how devilish, than there should be one single negro slave in the United States.

Now, I cannot conceive of but one way to solve this enigma, and that is as follows: In the first place they are "wolves in sheep's clothing," as set forth in the Bible. Secondly, they are servants of old Apollyon, and hate Christianity, and all that is good in

this world; in short, they are an infidel crew, sent
forth by the father of lies and the hater of God and
all good government, to destroy this model government, simply because it was marked out by the finger
of *Jehovah*, and destined to remodel the whole world,
and usher in the *millenium* spoken of in the Scriptures. It would not be hard to prove that the great
love and sympathy they profess to feel for the poor
slave is a false pretext, feigned for the purpose of
breaking up the Union between the North and South,
and not that they care anything about the poor Africans in slavery, or have the slightest conscientious
scruples on the subject of slavery or slaveholding.
But they hate pure Christianity more than they love
the Constitution, therefore their opposition to Southern slavery. Why? Because they know there is no
other sectional question of interest in the United
States, and they know that to be a vital and exciting
one to the Southern people. If there were no slaves
they would seize upon something else the most exciting in the country. If these people have so much
sympathy for the poor negro, how is it they have
none for any other species of mankind? Every
man or woman who has any knowledge of facts in
the case, knows the slaves to be well off, and a great
deal better off than one-half of the white population
of the free States. They have few or no troubles,
and are the happiest people on earth; they have no
concern beyond the present moment. Then why is
it there is so much concern felt for the poor slaves,
while the free people of color are in so much worse

• condition in every shape and form, and no sympathy felt or expressed for them whatever?

Where are the thousands of Indians who occupied the very ground on which this great city is built? They pre-occupied this soil, and in that way were the rightful owners of every foot of earth now occupied in the United States by the white man. But where are they to-day? Have they not been driven from their rights and rightful homes, to the western wilds and Rocky Mountains, and thousands upon thousands of them murdered and slaughtered in their own homes, simply because they contended for their birthright? Millions of them have been compelled to perish with cold and hunger, under the snow-flakes of the Rocky Mountains, after having been driven from their just rights and happy homes. Who will pretend to say this is not real robbery, theft, and murder? But who has condemned all this wickedness? Where are the long aping and pitiful faces that have been forced or feigned, or those that originated from pure sympathy, to be found among all the sympathizers in this country with the poor slaves, who have every right conceded to them they ever had or now have? They are well clad and fed, cared for and respected, and enjoy all the fruits of their labor, even more than Stephen Girard ever did. They have good homes, the doctor when sick, and are well nursed. There is not one to be found in the United States, who owes one cent, and all who do right are as happy as men can be in this world of sin. Yet this great and glorious Union which has produced such happiness and peace to

the Africans, is to be broken up, and the whole •
white population reduced to slavery, under some
despotic monarch or thrown into a state of anarchy,
rather than one negro should be left in slavery in
the United States, the only condition of peace and
safety they ever will find in this world.

Now tell me how is this, that we must give up all
that is dear to us in this world, and not do the slaves
any good, but reduce them to a far worse condition
than their present one, and not even a complaint
made against the treatment to the poor Indians, who
have been robbed of all their rights, and slain like
blackbirds, and driven back to the very ends of the
earth, and there left to perish! For all this, not one
association formed, or a meeting called, or a tear
dropped, nor no long sympathetic aping faces made
by those who would give up all that is good, rather
than there should be one negro left in slavery in
this great country. I will tell you how it is.
The Indian question cannot be made a sectional
one. The whole country is of the same opinion,
and it would produce no opposition between the
North and South, nor the East and West. It would
rather tend to strengthen the Union, therefore it
would not answer the purpose. But the slave question is a sectional one, it strikes at the very vitals of
the benefits of one-half of the soil of this country,
the dearest rights of the people thereof, and the
Constitution of the United States. It aims a death
blow at all the civil, social, and domestic institutions
of all the States. And all this is aimed at the very
vitals of this great Union. It is done because the

Union encourages Christianity through the Gospel of Christ. If I am wrong I hope some one will set me right. Ask those men what they propose to do with five millions of free negroes suddenly turned loose on the country! Some answer that they will leave that for an after consideration; others say that they have nothing to do with it, that their business is to free them; and some say they may go to the devil for all they care about them; but others say they must be placed on an equality, that our Creator had made us all equal, therefore we are compelled to take them into a political, social, and domestic equality. Mr. G., who is rather a fine-looking man, said to me the other day, in the presence of a number of witnesses, that he was no respecter of persons on account of their color, that he would just as soon take the arm of a black person, or have them take his (*male or female of course*) and walk through the city, or promenade the social circle, *as he would a white person.* Mr. G. is well-known in this city. A large majority of the above named Union men are of this class, according to their declarations.

Now, I don't believe one word of such asseverations, nor do I believe any man of common sense or good judgment does; for such a thing is contrary to human nature and common sense. All such asseverations are for effect, and all such persons would be the first to rebel against any government that would attempt to enforce it, even if it was the government . of *Jehovah himself*, if it was made morally and civilly right to do so. All such declarations are without

22

the slightest foundation in honest truth, and have
an ulterior object in view, and that is the total destruction of this great and glorious Union. They
are the very men who have brought us to this awful
crisis, and now denounce every man as a secessionist
who dares to speak of saving the Union, and restoring peace, tranquillity, and harmony, in any other
way than the one that will eternally destroy it, just
as sure as we have had peace and prosperity through
and by the Constitution and the Union. Yea! as
sure as there is a heaven above and an earth beneath,
our peace and harmony is gone, eternally gone, if
the above class of Union men are allowed to lead or
are listened to. They know well that a free republican Union cannot exist with five millions of inhabitants interspersed among them totally incapable of
self-government or of being made so. And even if
they were, human nature is such that they could
not be admitted on an equality, for which they would
sue in less than five years. Then a scene would
transpire such as the sun has never shone upon. Our
soil would be drenched with human gore from one
end to the other; and our Union that has been the
harbinger of peace, love, tranquillity, and harmony would suddenly be converted into a reign of
anarchy, which would exist as long as there was a
colored person on American soil, or a terrible despotism established by some tyrant of a Nero, who
would seize the reins of government, mount the
throne, and reduce us all to slavery, or to an equality
without the slightest respect to color, and that would
be the end of civil and religious liberty. I look

upon this class of fanatics as being just such as the devil would have them to be.

I will say, in conclusion, that, as long as the slaves are let alone, in the possession of their masters, the free people of color will be safe in this country, and their rights cared for, but no longer. The four and a half millions of slaves in the United States are the only safeguards the free black man has, and none would suffer a greater overthrow by the emancipation of all the slaves, or destruction of the Union, than they. In either case, they will be the greater losers, unless a Nero should seize the reins of government at the same time, with five hundred thousand troops under his control. This would end all controversy, and forever solve the question of the capability of man for self-government.

The course those Union men are pursuing, is the most cruel to the colored race in this country that could be devised. How men can be so cruel and hard-hearted towards so large a class of innocent, unprotected, and, to this day, a useful people, I am unable to decipher, for I tell you now, that whenever they are all emancipated, you will see cruelties heretofore unknown (even under Nero). Human nature is such, that this trouble will come very soon after the emancipation of all the slaves, unless a military despotism be established on the heels of universal emancipation. For a free republican union, where every subject is a king, cannot stand where one sixth of the subjects are marked with such obnoxious distinctness; so much so, that every colored man would almost give his life to be made a pure white

man for one month. I am not willing to give up
the Union for any cause. Union means love, harmony, tranquillity, and peace. Love is the only bond
that will ever restore the Union. We must love the
southern people, and they must love us, or there never
can be a union between the two extremes. I am
ready for any plan that is the most direct to such a
glorious result. To get at the best plan, every bitter
feeling, with all hard sayings, all prejudice, and sectionalism must be suspended, let us get together
and discuss the best plan to save the Union of the
thirty-four States, for I tell you, a great many people
have got to believe that this war is not to save the
Union, but to emancipate all the slaves, and break
it up forever. This feeling has been engendered
altogether by the class of Union men above alluded
to. These men are traitors, and they tremble with
fear that peace will be made with slavery in the
country. They know the emancipation of all the
slaves would make it necessary to change the government from a free republican Union to a military
despotism; for five millions of people set free among
us, totally incapable of self-government, could not be
ruled without it, for as soon as they are all freed,
the prejudice of color will rise to its highest pitch,
and could be restrained only by military power.
These people are the worst enemies of the colored
race, and the union of the States on the face of the
earth. They have been seeking the destruction of
this glorious Union for more than fifty years, and
now exult over their prospects. O! "Ye serpents,

ye generation of vipers! how can ye escape the damnation of hell?"

I will give another sample or two of these pretended Unionists. I stepped into one of our largest newspaper offices the other day, where there were three or four gentlemen, some of whom were reporters, and an assistant editor. I was asked by one of them what my ideas were about the close of the war. I began to tell them how I believed it could now be settled without any further destruction of human life. This was a few days after the Fort Donaldson victory was reported. I had not proceeded far, before I was asked if I supposed peace could be restored with slavery in the country. I answered in the affirmative. I was laughed at as a strange man. They then denounced slavery as the greatest crime known to God or man. I told them I could not see how they could make out such a case, where neither the moral nor civil law forbids its existence—that it was constitutional according to the declarations of both, and the moral constitution and law sustained it in stronger terms than did the civil. Two of those gentlemen simultaneously denounced the Old and New Testaments as books of falsehoods and lies, and were only calculated to ruin men and women by debauchery and degradation. I saw there was no use to quote Scripture, for it was like casting pearl before swine. I then referred them to the fact that the colored races could not be so civilized as to be capable of self-government—that there was not the slightest appearance of any improvement on the globe made by them, except as slaves under the direction of white men. They referred me to the Liberian colony on the coast of Africa. I told them that that was yet an experiment, which I hoped would succeed, that I was a strong and unyielding friend of the enterprise, but there are circumstances already apparent that have produced doubts in the minds of many friends of the experiment. It is certain there is room to fear that idleness will sooner or later prevail, and, if it should, it was to be feared that barbarism would follow, which can be prevented only by a monarchical form of government. They remarked that that was not so; that the negroes were just as capable of self-government as white men, and had just as good a right to govern in this country. I asked them how it was that the Indians of the United States had not been civilized—that they were here when we came, but removed from civilization as chaff before the wind. They remarked that it was because the Indians had too much good sense even to yield to such a humbug as civilization —that it was opposed to life and liberty, and was only calculated to make men work twelve hours in the day, and consequently made slaves of us all. I told them I could not talk with them any longer on that subject, as they had rejected the foundations of all my arguments for the Union, and my hopes for this life and that which is to come. They said they hoped the war would not cease as long as there was a slave in the United States, and, if nothing else would free them, let the entire white population of the slave States be exterminated, and the soil given up to the slaves, to whom it righteously belongs.

These men are in very responsible situations, where they can wield a powerful influence over the minds of both young and old. I meet with so many such men, that my hopes for the restoration of the Union with tranquillity and harmony, are sometimes very faint; and when I am denounced as a traitor by such men, I wonder what kind of government we should have if such as they had the entire control! They seem to think there would be no harm in making white men slaves, provided they were made slaves to negroes. One of their sweeping arguments which they almost invariably use, is, how would you like to be a slave? I know I would not like to be a slave, because it would be degrading to me. I am one of the individual rulers or governers of this country, and was intended by the Supreme Ruler of the world to be a free man. Neither I nor my ancestors were ever heathens or slaves; neither were they black, nor could not be made so, because it was not the will of God. The negroes are greatly elevated by slavery. They are black, and wholly inferior. Their ancestors were black heathens and barbarians. They kill and eat each other with as much relish, as we kill and eat turkeys. Some of the Fejee Islanders never have a feast without a roasted negro, and he an acquaintance or subject. Therefore they are greatly blessed and elevated by being brought here and made slaves. The slaves of the United States are, on the general, so much better off and happier than the so-called free people of color, and are not degraded but elevated by slavery. The morals of the slaves are so incalculably better than that of the free colored people, that it is surprising to any man who has not been ruled by party cliques, or run wild by an exciting hobby, to meet such men. But how would you like to be a slave? say they. I say I would not like to be a slave, especially to my colored brethren.

I will ask those very refined soft fingered ladies and gentlemen how they would like to be cesspool cleaners? Those of the large cities know what and who I mean. How would you like to start with your horses and carts, buckets and hoes, at 10 o'clock at night (instead of retiring to your beautiful downy couch, surrounded with the finest drapery, with a sweet wife and child), and drudge through the streets, and enter some gentleman's back yard, and descend the cesspool to clean it out, and after toiling nearly all night in that filth, return to your mansion and to your bed? Now I ask again, how would you like to be a cesspool cleaner? I know you will answer in the negative, and so will your wife and family. Is that any proof that that business is morally wrong, and should not be followed by any one else, simply because you would not like to do it? According to your own arguments, all such callings should be abolished at once, it being morally wrong and cruel, simply because you would not like the occupation yourself.

Again: How would you like to turn out daily with a gang of hardy, sun-burned, German laborers, with your paving pick and pounder, and pave streets, lay water pipes for your living, and your wife to go out daily and wash, with her tender hands? I know you would not like it any more than I would like to be a slave. Now is it morally wrong and barbarous to employ those German laborers to do that kind of work, simply because you would not like to do it yourself? Must that kind of work be abolished, and our streets left knee-deep in mud? Is it morally wrong to wash clothes, because your wife would not like to retire to the back yard of some lady's house to wash? Must washing be abolished because she would not like the business, and you yourself deeply humiliated by the operation? These arguments can be used against any of the above occupations with just as much force and good sense, as yours can be against slavery.

I will say again that the only temporal salvation on any spot of this verdant earth for the African race, is in being slaves to white men, unless it should turn out to be otherwise on the coast of Africa, which I hope and pray may prove successful. The Supreme Being has so ordained it, and every attempt by us to make it otherwise, will prove a terrible curse to both races. Every national affliction we have had, since the adoption of the Constitution, with one exception, has been produced either directly or indirectly by an inconsiderate opposition to negro slavery. The war with Mexico was the consequence of a constant interference with Southern State rights because of slavery, by the people and legislators of the free States. I believe just as much as I believe I am now writing, that God so directed the convention of 1787 in its deliberations in framing our national Constitution, to grant the independent state rights, that slavery might not be disturbed or interfered with by the abolitionists of the free States. If slavery was a cruel barbarism, and a sin against God, it would have but few opponents among such as are now abolitionists. I will ask those who deny the truth of this assertion how it is that no sympathy has been expressed for the poor Indians, who were the aborigines in all these States? who have been murdered and slaughtered by thousands and driven to the ends of the earth by us, and there left to starve under the snow-flakes of the Rocky Mountains. We have robbed them of their moral and just rights, and driven them from their homes. As inhuman as this seems to be, no abolitionist has ever mourned over the cruelties to this most interesting race. Why is it so? Because the movement would be right in the sight of God, and could not be made a sectional issue, therefore would produce no quarrel between the two extremes of our common country; and our national glory and God-like Union would be in no danger of an eternal overthrow by such a righteous movement and sympathy.

This war with all its horrors and concomitant circumstances, is the direct product of the anti-slavery party. I mean that portion of them who have been unceasingly interfering with Southern rights, and denouncing the slaveholders as devils incarnate, and charging them with the most hideous crimes known to criminal law. Those charges were not against a slave owner who might chance to be a bad man, but they were and are made against all slaveholders indiscriminately, and every one of them charged with the highest crimes known in the whole world, such as murder and robbery, and all their sons with constant cohabitation with their negro female slaves to produce children for the market. I say it is more wonderful to me that this most ungodly and wicked rebellion did not break out many years sooner than it is it has now broken out. When we think of all these things, in connection with the many schemes of interference with Southern rights to this species of property by the free States, and the constant denunciations of Southern slaveholders from a thousand pulpits on each successive Sabbath day, is it not wonderful to all who have given human nature and the jealousy of our lawful rights a proper thought? I will appeal to every honest, thoughtful, unprejudiced man for an answer to this question. Is it not wonderful that this rebellion, as wicked and ungodly as it is, did not come sooner? Remember that this was a free-will, volunteer Constitutional Union, made up by free-will concessions, "for a more perfect Union," and not for one section of the country to hold the other as with a halter; to slander, insult, and persecute them with the foulest defamations known to the vicious.

If it is true that the constant cohabitations take place in the South as alluded to above, how is it that there are any real negroes to be found in the slave States by this time, for they have been thus charged for more than two hundred years; and if the white men of the free States are so much purer in that way than those of the slave States, how is it that the proportion of mulattoes in the free States are so much larger than in the slave States? Now, don't lay this to the white females of the North, for that would be a still greater slander, and would not abate the disgrace, but rather increase it. These things have been stated by designing men and women, with such boldness and assurance, that many of our very best people in the free States have been overcome and made to believe it, and some of them will flare up if you tell them it is false. I want all such to read over what I have written on this point of the subject, with particular care, and examine the statistics of each ten years, and see for yourselves whether the slave States are any worse than the free, on the mulatto question.

I will again say, if the Southern people are as bad as the abolitionists would have them, I don't want to be in the Union with them. I am no little surprised to find so many of those who believe all such foul slanders, so anxious to save and prolong a Union with them. I think, to say the least of it, that it shows a degraded and demoralized taste, just as foul as that with which they charge the slaveholders. The very fact of our sympathies being so often appealed to by abolitionists, in asking how we would like to be slaves, is a proof positive that they are governed entirely by their sympathies and feelings, if anything but wickedness, and not by conviction or judgment. What sort of a country should we have had by this time, if every person was to move and rule according to their sympathies. Suppose Gen. Washington had yielded to his sympathies in the prosecution of the Revolutionary war, should we ever have been an independent nation? Suppose all men and women should govern their children by their sympathies; what sort of children would they have? Suppose a surgeon should act upon the dictation of his sympathies, would he ever do any good to himself, or any unfortunate afflicted person? Feelings or sympathies are the most dangerous guides for church or state to follow, and if followed without the guide of good judgment, they will break up every church and government in the civilized world.

I know all such charges to be mainly false, therefore I am willing to be in the Union with the Southern States. But can this Union be restored by constantly proclaiming such foul slanders against those we have got to reconcile before any Union can be formed with them? Would it not be better to look upon and speak of them as our unfortunate misguided brethren, who have misunderstood the majority of the North, in the late Presidential election? Whose misunderstanding was produced by the wholesale slanders herein alluded to, and by their Constitutional and lawful rights having been constantly interfered with almost from the adoption of the Constitution to the present day, by individuals, associations, and statute laws of the free States. Under these circumstances, have they not ground for great complaint? And if they have such ground, is it not our duty, as a liberal, benevolent, Christian people, to remove every such ground from our escutcheon? Is it not right for him who gives the first insult, to make the first concession?

23

You say the general government of the United States has always allowed and protected them in their Constitutional rights. I say they have not. For Congress has ever refused to protect their rights to all property in all the territories of the United States. The Republican party adopted a platform in 1856, repudiating protection to their property in the territories of the United States, and renewed it again at Chicago in 1860, (and in both instances chose both of their candidates for the Presidency from the free States,) and this directly in the teeth of the Constitution and the decision of the Supreme Court of the United States in 1854. Now, I ask every candid man, if this was not sufficient to impress the mind of the whole South that we intended to crush them with all their peculiar institutions.

I cannot say that I have ever heard the slightest sympathy expressed by any leading republican for the sufferings of our unfortunate southern brethren. I hear them bitterly cursed almost daily; by some, for fleeing from their homes with their wives and children on the approach of our troops, while others seem to exult at every such report, and laugh over it as though "nobody was hurt, and no harm had been done." Among these are some professing Christian ministers and their disciples, whose profession binds them to mercy's side of every question. The examples set in the Scriptures, from Genesis to Revelations, are altogether on the side of mercy, especially those of our Saviour. We are there informed that we must not only forgive seven times, but seventy times seven. The South had borne with our encroaching upon their rights for many years, which caused the rebellion.

If human nature had ever been forced to love, or an example could be found on the pages of Holy Writ for forcing people to love each other, I should have some hope that this war would ultimately restore the Union. But as there has been no successful precedent recorded on the pages of sacred or profane history, I am left without the slightest hope of any forced restoration of harmony and peace between the two extremes of our beloved country. This being the case, would it not be better to propose an amnesty with our southern brethren? I would pardon the whole South, if that would restore peace, harmony, and obedience to the laws throughout the whole country. I believe God would bless the effort, and make it successful. We may conquer the South, but that will not restore the Union, without which there never can be peace and harmony in this great nation. There is only one way to restore the Union, and that must be through love as proposed by our Lord and Saviour Jesus Christ, who said, "Bless them that curse you." The only bond of this Union was love for each other ; therefore sectionalism was started to destroy it, that being the only means by which it could be effectually done. The war will produce horror upon horror, and hatred upon hatred, and the longer it is prosecuted, the further we shall be from harmony and peace. I would submit to any depth of humiliation for the sake of handing a perfect Union down to future generations. I know that if it is not soon settled, it never can be, and we shall go down to our graves, leaving it a terrible despotism or in a state of universal anarchy. May God in his mercy save us from the interminable ruin that seems to be before us, all of which is the legitimate result of opposition to slavery, which was only a pretext of the leaders to destroy the Union. When the taxes come, we shall be made to sweat and atone for our hypocrisy.

The worst troubles are yet to be realized. If the slaves should all be freed, they will become a mass of ruined humanity, that will be an intolerable weight around the neck of society, which will chafe our future hopes, our national pride, and clog the wheels of the onward course of the prosperity of the whole country. God has given them to us for the mutual benefit of both races, but the relation to be master and slave, as decreed about four thousand two hundred and forty-eight years ago. Our only moral right in the matter, as a people and nation, is to see that they are humanely treated. I know my best and most influential business and social friends are bitterly opposed to me in these views, and some of my religious friends say they would be pleased to see me hung up by the neck. They may crucify me, but while I can speak and write, I will state my clearest convictions, and nothing else. In facts I have told the truth; I may have erred a little in some of my inferences, and some of my quotations from history may be a little misplaced, as I have written mostly from memory.

Wherever professing Christians take up the sword

to avenge their enemies, they sin against the holy precepts of the Son of God and his holy apostles.

"Therefore if thine enemy hunger, feed him; if he thirst, give him drink; for in so doing thou shalt heap coals of fire on his head."—Rom. xii. 20.

"Then said Jesus unto him, put up again thy sword into his place; for all they that take the *sword*, shall perish with the sword."—Matt. xxvi. 52.

The very essence of the principles on which this war is waged by professing Christians, fully and completely repudiates Christianity, and all free republican governments and unions. Our general government was wholly begotten and truly Christian in all its articles and clauses, made up by mutual concessions and compromises, without the temporal sword. I know they came to a dead halt while forming it, but was the sword drawn from its scabbard? No, brethren! Did they quarrel and call each other hard names, such as thieves, murderers, and robbers? No; they did no such thing. How, then, did they get unlocked? They unanimously agreed to send for a celebrated clergyman to come into their midst with his Bible, read a chapter, and pray for the Holy Ghost to rest down upon them. The result was, the dam gave way, union of sentiment was at once restored, and the Constitution speedily agreed upon.

This war, and every particle of the malice and hatred between the North and South, has grown out of resisting the constitutional and lawful rights of the slave States of the Union. All those who instituted the sectional antipathies by resisting those rights, and

23*

those who have carried it on to present results, are guilty of murder in every life that has been lost; and all those who persist in urging the war against our southern brethren, without first restoring their fullest Constitutional rights, as agreed upon after the Rev. Mr. White read the chapter, and prayed for the bless· ing of Jehovah to descend into all the hearts of those constituting the Convention, are sinning against God and their own civil and religious liberties. I do not include the soldiers who have obeyed the call of the Chief Magistrate of this nation. The war cannot be justified until every right belonging to the slave States, under the Constitution of the United States, shall be restored to them; then, if they still rebel, I shall have nothing to say. But I am well satisfied that there would not be the slightest necessity of firing another gun or unsheathing another sword, providing the offer should be made in the same spirit that the Rev. gentleman was invited into the National Convention that adopted the Constitution. That is, if the offer should be fully clothed in the spirit of love, the only power that has ever yet conquered the wickedness of the human heart, so that enemies would love each other, without which we never can again have any Union of these United States. The extremes must love each other, or union is impossible. Con· vince me that war will produce love to each other; then I will be for war, or anything that will restore the Union; for union means love, harmony, and tranquillity.

I don't want to be understood to justify this wicked rebellion, for I abhor it more than any event that has taken place since the fall from Eden. I abhor it, not only because it is destructive to human life and morals, and to the happiness and prosperity of the free States, but because it is destructive to our Southern brethren themselves, and still more so to the poor negro race in this whole country. The rebellion is far more than equal to the provocation given by the abolitionists of the free States, and complete extermination would not be more than equal to the crime of such wicked rebellion. But when we think of the cause of their crime, it is enough to cause our hearts to sink with sadness; and when we remember how small a matter would have prevented it, and placed us on terms of harmony and love, it is enough to make the very stones cry out and say, destroy us that we may not see the extent of the wrong we have done ourselves.

But this great and glorious Union cannot be restored by war, for it is its opposite, and the more we fight the further we shall be from a Union. Every step taken by the Son of God and his holy Apostles, so clearly sets forth that he came into the world to do away with all cruelties, and carnal weapons of warfare, and to bring about a new state of things. A state in which Christians should ever stand ready to concede to each other enough of their political opinions to enable them to acquiesce in civil and religious government, that it is so astonishing to me to find so many Christians and Christian ministers, recommending war to the hilt, even to the extermination of the white population of one-half of the territory of the United States, because they will not submit to have their Constitutional rights and liberties trampled upon, instead of offering them a compromise or the least concessions which the slave States have never asked for or desired. They have always been ready, and offered to concede a large portion of their Constitutional rights for the sake of peace and union, until after a number of the cotton States had prepared to secede. Then they offered to stop, and remain contented in the Union with us forever, if we would allow them their full Constitutional rights in said Union; which offer was unanimously and indignantly refused by the anti-slavery party. They were offered by those gentlemen in the latter part of December, 1860, in the Senate Committee of thirteen appointed to compromise the dispute between the extremes. In those offers they asked for nothing but their own, under the Constitution and laws of the United States. If their offer had been accepted by the free States we should have had no war, and our civil peace and Union would now be like a paradise, and the only unpleasant sound that would grate upon our ears, would be the howling of infidelity, caused by the great disappointment in not being able to break up this *heaven-born Union* that was *even* a happy home for African negro slaves.

I repeat that I am greatly discouraged and have fears that I have lived to see the end of a free Republican Constitutional Union, and the only hope of free institutions, and the rights of conscience in this world, and the end of peace. I am asked why I am almost hopeless? I answer, because I find the

Christian church, the anchor and safeguard to all free institutions, advocating the war on our Christian brethren. Yea, they seem to glory and exult in the devastation and consternation of the slave States, produced by the advance of the superior powers of the free States. All this without first conceding to them their just rights in the Union; and when we know we have the superior numerical strength and power, and could afford to do right and be liberal without the slightest humiliation, and still more when we have men of great Christian power and influence, attributing this war to the Supreme Being, and this directly in the teeth of every precept of the New Testament and every principle of a free republican government. I believe the great God of the universe has suffered this outbreak, to teach us that we cannot trample upon the rights of our Christian brethren with impunity.

That we can conquer the slave States, I have not the shadow of a doubt. But will it be any honor to us? Will it give us a glow of pleasure when we look upon the ruin that has followed our superior powers to crush them? When we find all this has not restored peace and union, and we shall be compelled to give them all they asked for previous to the outbreak, and knowing that if we had accepted their offer, this terrible calamity would all have been avoided. When we see that after all this, the great blessings of a perfect Union are gone, perhaps, never to return.

If Christian men still teach that the Holy God instituted this war, just at the right time and in the right place, what will the world think of the Christians' faith or their God? Will it not lead them to believe that the Supreme Being is opposed to republican governments, and enter into extreme infidelity? I fear this will be the result, because I believe God to be a jealous God, and that he has chosen us to take charge of this republican government, to be as a city set upon a hill, that its great brilliancy might dazzle the eyes of the whole world, and teach them that the white man was made for self-government, and competent for it, and to show us that the only plan under existing fallen human nature, was to concede to every man his lawful rights. Therefore, under His blessings of love we were divided into independent State governments, in all the municipal enactments; and each left without the shadow of a right, by the great adopted mother of them all (the Constitution of the United States), to interfere in any manner whatever with the rights of each other. But in spite of the precept to do unto others as we would they should do unto us, we have interfered with the lawful rights of other States; therefore we may look for universal anarchy and confusion, or a perpetual iron-hearted despotism, which will place Anglo-Americans and Africans on a social and political equality, unless we make up our minds (and act it out through all the ramifications of this life) to concede to all others, white or black, all their lawful rights under the Constitution of the United States.

If the Christian church had stuck to her integrity, with a single eye to the glory of God, there would never have been any separation nor civil war in this country. When I read such speeches as were made by the Hon. T. N. Arnold of Ill. in the House of Representatives, on the 17th of February, 1862, my hopes for the Union go down to a low ebb.

We have had no calamity yet, to be compared to the one that universal emancipation of the slaves in this country will entail upon us. Think of 5,000,-000 set at liberty among us, who will by such a national act be placed on a political and social equality with the white man, and in a very short space of time demand it. Then think of the prejudice of color, manners, and style, and of the pride of the human heart. I will leave Mr. Arnold to judge of the consequences; for every sensible unprejudiced man will see the end from the beginning. *May the Lord God of Israel have mercy upon all such men,* and avert such a direful calamity! For if he does not, and the slaves are all freed, we shall be reduced from the highest and most powerful nation on earth to the most degraded.

In conclusion, I will say again that the seceding slave States committed as great a crime as ever was committed against any nation or people since the foundation of the world, except that of Adam; and according to human government and precedents, there is no punishment adequate to their crime short of complete extermination of all the leaders, and banishment of the aiders and abettors. But those who drove them to such desperation are still worse, and deserve double punishment. They did it with their eyes wide open, and knew well what

they were at. They did it without the slightest provocation. They resolved, many years ago, to agitate,
slander, and persecute the slave States, until they
would drive them to commit this desperate act.
*Now the very leaders of those men cry rebellion against
the South louder than all the world besides. They do
all this to turn attention away)from their own treason,
to make the world believe that they are great patriots,
and lovers of the Union of States ; but they never say
a word in)favor of the constitution, the only safeguard
of the Union.* It is so strange to me that so many
people of the free States, are so completely blindfolded by these *northern disunionists and rebels
against the best government ever known in this earth,
since that*in Eden,* nearly 6000 years ago. And this
great and glorious boon is to be destroyed to place
the African negro on a social and political equality
with the white man. Yet hundreds and thousands
of our best citizens follow in their lead, and they
cannot be made to see the diabolical treason of these
leaders; and they seem to look upon all who endeavor to point out to them the deception of these
devils incarnate as the friends of the southern rebellion. Consequently the mouths of the true friends
of the Constitution and Union are locked up, and
they are not allowed to speak out their true convictions, to expose the immense treason in the free
States, and it is feared they will not see until it is
too late; for union is love and war its opposite.

Tell me how it was that Wendell Phillips, Esq.,
after having delivered his soul of a great load of its
anathemas against the Constitution and Union in the

Smithsonian Institute at Washington, D. C., the other day, and told them how long he had been laboring to destroy this, the greatest boon ever given to man, and then was invited to visit the Senate Chamber of the United States, and there received the most cordial congratulations by the majority of that august assembly. If this is not a war on the institutions of the South, and for the destruction of the Constitution, why was this not only suffered, but the fell traitor and rebel invited to sow a fresh batch of *treason* and *sedition* at the capital of the nation? Now if these leaders are fighting to save the Constitution, how came this circumstance to take place? I would like Mr. Sumner, or some such talented member of that majestic body, to explain this enigma, for I confess that I am too shallow to comprehend it (if they are all Constitutional Union men).

And again, after he (Mr. Phillips) had let loose his embittered treason and sedition against the Constitution of the United States in the very citadel thereof, how came he to be invited by the State Senate of Pennsylvania to go to the capital of that State to repeat the same treasonable and seditious doctrines? The majority of the party in power must be in favor of those treasonable doctrines, or this could never have been so. How is it that I and others have been threatened to be hanged to lamp-posts by the neck or locked up in some fort for even desiring peace and union without the shedding of blood? Yet this arch traitor was not only allowed but invited to visit the United States Senate and the Senate of Pennsylvania to convert the few remaining

24

loyal men, in those important bodies, for the safety of' this great Union, to treason and sedition. If those Senators are Constitutional Union loving men, how is this? Tell me, for God's sake, for I am in great trouble on this subject.

A celebrated Garrisonian abolitionist told me this morning that he had been called upon three times by an authorized committee,-to inquire of him if I was not a fit subject for incarceration in Fort Lafayette. I know I have often been threatened not only with a home in some fort, but to be hanged by the neck. Now tell me how is this? Why were such threats made against me? Why did those Republicans denounce me as a secessionist, traitor, and rebel, when I had been opposing abolition movements against the Constitution and the Union for the last twenty-five years? They then denounced me as a negro hunter, thief, murderer, and robber, and why? Because I stood up for the Constitution and Union, and declared them to be the greatest blessings that heaven had ever bestowed upon any nation of this sin-stricken earth. They have reason to believe and know that I have never uttered one word on the subject, that was not in defence of the Constitution and the Union. They also know that I hate a traitor or a rebel against this great heaven-like government, more than anything outside of the kingdom of darkness. There is no class of human beings so sunken in crime, that I hate as I hate the man or woman that would even express a dislike to the great safeguards of this great and glorious government. It has been the object of my earthly admiration from my first understandings of the great and glorious national scheme. No abolitionist or secessionist, no Constitutional Union man or woman, has ever heard me utter a single word against these the greatest earthly blessings ever bestowed upon any people. No man nor any set of men can come forward and say with the slightest semblance of truth, that they have ever uttered a sentence in my hearing against these two great blessings, that I did not raise my voice in their defence, and they had a right to believe that my life was not respected by myself when I heard these great national blessings denounced as a "covenant with the devil, and a league with hell!"

He who charges me with having at any time or under any circumstances, got up any association, or united therewith, or joined any party or association, for any other purpose than to arrest sectionalism in the general elections of this nation, are foul slanderers. I knew just as well fifteen years ago, that if they ever succeeded in a national election, that we should have a civil war in this country, as I now know that it is existing, and the most terrible ever known since the Christian era set it. They thus accuse me because of the strong stand I have always taken in defence of the Constitution and the Union. They do it because of the fearless manner in which I try to expose their treason, and if such a committee ever waited on my Hicksite friend as he said this morning, they must have been base traitors like himself. They could have had no other object in view (fearing I would tell on them, and expose their infidelity to the Constitution and the Union, they knowing that I had a personal knowledge of their treason) than being anxious to put me out of the way.

My Hicksite friend, even in this conversation, denounced me as a traitor, and told me my only object in joining the Constitutional Union party was to encourage the slave trade; and bitterly charged every man who voted for Bell, Breckenridge, or Douglass with being traitors, and in league with the South for keeping up the slave trade. He who charges me with being favorable to the slave trade, either foreign or domestic, is guilty of the basest slander, no matter what his pretension may be. I have always been opposed to the slave trade, because it is unlawful; still I do not believe slavery to be a moral evil. But if those directly interested had not been interfered with by those Northern traitors, slavery would have been the greatest blessing to the slaves that could be bestowed upon them in this world, and a blessing to the whole white population of this country, as much so to the New Englanders as the Southerners, and all other civilized nations of the earth. If they should all be freed, they will at once become the greatest curse to themselves and the whole white population of the United States, that has ever fallen upon any free and happy people. I have said enough on this point in former chapters, therefore I will leave it for the present.

There is not a rebel in the South who is not the legitimate offspring of the abolitionists. These Northern traitors are something like Judas Iscariot, Simon's son, when he said, "Why was not this ointment sold for three hundred pence, and given to the poor? This he said, not that he cared for the poor; but because he was a thief, and had the bag, and bare what was put therein." John xii. 5–6. Now these abolition fanatics care no more for the welfare of the poor slave, than Judas did for the poor, when he had accepted the price and was ready to betray the Son of God. The abolition fanatics, perhaps, have got the bag, and if they succeed in the universal emancipation of the slaves, they of course expect to take charge of the government, and control its purse strings. If we are allowed to judge from what we now see divulged by their near approach to power, what will it be when they are fully installed at the head of this great nation. The poor negroes will lament their emancipation, if they should not be put on an equality with the whites, which every man and woman of common sense knows, will never be in this country; and the attempt to bring about such a state of social and political intercourse, is more devilish, *if possible*, than the Southern rebellion. If successful, it will produce a general rebellion of the white people against the negroes, who are now harmless and innocent, only so far as they are deceived into wrong by their pretended white brethren; a rebellion that will not cease, perhaps, until the American soil is completely saturated with innocent blood, from Maine to Florida, and from the Atlantic to the Pacific. This will assuredly be the result of universal emancipation of the slaves in the United States, unless a universal despotism is established on the heel of emancipation

24*

with an immense standing army under the control of a single monarch. Then our abolition fanatics will have their wish, for in this way we shall be brought down and placed on an equality with Africans.

It is denied by many that one of the objects of the republican party was the emancipation of all the slaves in the United States. If that is so, how came Congress to pass the following into laws by the approval of the President of the United States?

1. "A resolution to induce the States to free their negroes."

2. "An act abolishing slavery in the District of Columbia," without the consent of the people there.

3. "An act empowering the negroes to carry the United States mails."

4. "A new article of war, prohibiting officers in the army and navy, from returning the negroes to their masters, who run into their ranks."

I think these acts need an explanation to make them harmonize with the declarations of said ·party, that they would not interfere with slavery where it already existed. All four of them are unconstitutional, and will go far towards weakening the chances for the restoration of the Union; and every true unconditional Constitutional Union man, who fully understands its eminent glories to man, will think as I do, and who is not willing to jeopardize these great blessings to man (white or black) for the sake of freeing a few slaves, or for any amount of military glory, not even to be Commander-in-chief of the armies of the United States. The thought of losing the Union is more terrible to them than any other earthly calamity that could possibly befall man. If the restoration of the Union, with peace and harmony, was the only and exclusive object sought for by the party in power, there would be no attempt to free the slaves. But it is clear to every thinking man, that emancipation is the main object sought for by many of the leaders, and a vast number of their constituents.

Tell me how can these be purely Union men, and yet trifle with it for matters comparatively of no moment to us for good, but fraught with evil, and even if successful without a complete overthrow of the Union, would throw us back as a prosperous nation at least one hundred years, and make the condition of the poor negro hopeless? Don't tell me again that I sympathize with the Southern rebellion, for if I was capable of hating as bitterly as the devil hates Christianity, I could not satisfy myself with hatred to any party who favors the destruction of this great and glorious Union, or denies that white men are capable of self-government; therefore I hate the war and the means used, and the men who produced it. Abolitionism is the progenitor of this rebellion, and will be thus held in history. They are responsible for its origination, for all the sectional hatred between the North and South, and for all the destruction of life, limb, and the horrors of this most ungodly rebellion, for all the devastation and consternation broadcast over this once happy country; and for a national debt, that perhaps will reach before it is settled $3,000,000,000, for which we shall be compelled to raise by a direct tax to pay the annual interest, and to support a standing army, with the expenses of the government of at least $300,000,000, without reducing the principal one cent. In short, they are the sum and substance of all the sectional villiany we have had, or ever shall have in this nation.

Lay off your sectional and partisan prejudices, and look the matter fair in the face, and you will see hundreds of millions of dollars being wasted to blind the credulous populace that they may load their sins on the backs of the innocent, while they are destroying and devastating the best government that ever has been or ever shall be on this earth, this side of the millenium. Indeed it was the foreshadowing of that blessed day.

I will requote the peace measures offered by Jeff. Davis of Miss. and Robert Toombs of Geo., that the reader may draw his own conclusions, by comparing the peace, love, harmony, and union we should now have between the extremes and throughout the entire country with the widespread ruin and destruction of human life, and the thousands of millions of hard earned property, with the devastation and consternation now widespread over our country, all of which would have been prevented had the following peace offerings been accepted by the republicans in power, or had the Crittenden Compromise been accepted by the same party.

" The Proceedings of the Senate Crisis Committee.

Washington, Dec. 26, 1860. The Senate Committee of thirteen had another meeting to-day, and discussed further the general subject of reconciliation; but nothing was adopted which would answer as a basis for permanent peace."

The (then) Hon. Jefferson Davis offered the following resolution, which he held to be necessary as an elementary principle of an adjustment that would satisfy the South, unless it was a division of Territories:—

" *Resolved*, That it shall be declared by amendment of the Constitution that property in slaves, recognized as such by the local law of any of the States of the Union, shall stand on the same footing in all Constitutional and Federal relations as any other species of property so recognized, and, like other property, shall not be subject to be divested or impaired by the local law of any other State, either in escape thereto or of transit or sojourn of the owner therein; and in no case whatever shall such property be subject to be divested or impaired by any legislative act of the United States, or of any of the Territories thereof."

The Republicans voting unanimously against the resolution, and all the others for it, it was lost by a sectional vote.

The following resolutions were then offered by the (then) Hon. Robert Toombs of Georgia, and were lost in the same manner as the above.

" *First*, That the people of the United States shall have an equal right to emigrate to and settle in the present or any future acquired Territories. with whatever property they may possess, including slaves, and be securely protected in its peaceable enjoyment until such Territory may be admitted as a State in the Union, with or without slavery, as she may determine, on an equality with all the existing States.

" *Second*, That property in slaves shall be entitled to the same protection from the government of the United States in all of its departments, everywhere, which the Constitution confers the power upon it to extend to any other property; provided nothing herein contained shall be construed to limit or restrain the right now belonging to every State to prohibit, abolish, or establish and protect slavery within its limits.

" *Third*, That persons committing crimes against slave property in one State, and fleeing to another, shall be delivered up in the same manner as persons committing other crimes, and that the laws of the State from which such persons flee shall be the test of criminality."

Now, for the sake of the common peace and happiness of the whole country, let us reason together and look this matter fair in the face, remembering that we all have the same interest at stake. We are all one people, east, west, north, and south, and every blow we strike the South, hits us just as hard as it does them, and *vice versa*. For God's and humanity's sake, let us now try to settle this matter like brethren. We can yet call a national convention and accept the offer; it is not even now too late. This union will never be fully restored without some such settlement. We may whip the South, but that will not bring peace and union back to our distracted country; but it will *consign us to an eternal despotism*, and destroy the last vestige of hope for the poor negro race in this country. We shall never know the great value of this *God-created Union*, until it is lost, and when once lost, it will be lost forever. *Human nature can be managed by Gospel means, but not by coercion.* The South want nothing but to be placed on a political equality with the North, where they would have the same protection and feel themselves entirely safe. Now see how easy it would have been to have prevented this widespread ruin. May the Lord save us *from such an interminable woe!* This settlement would not add one slave more to the number, nor increase the number of slave States, but would most undoubtedly result in making four or five of the border slave States free, and incalculably increase the liberty and happiness of the slaves in all the other slave States. It would end the controversy, and our peace and union would flow as a river until we should be engulfed in the Millennium.

As I have said, we may ultimately overpower the Southern States, but a standing army will have to be kept in the field, to keep them in subjection, which will eat out our very vitals, and this curse will be our doom throughout all time. It will place tyrants over us, and reduce us from a self-governing people to slaves, and force us to social, political, and domestic equality with African negroes. For God's sake stop and think before you take another step towards coercion, for I tell you the displeasure of Omnipotence will eternally rest upon us all, and our political glory will be extinguished forever, and the bright sunbeams of our national Union will cease to arouse the admiration of all the civilized nations of the earth, and to dazzle the eyes of kings, monarchs, or potentates of other lands. It will veil heaven in sackcloth, elevate infidelity, and send a thrill or howl of glory throughout deep, dark damnation.

I tell you that a union of these United States cannot be produced by war or coercion. A free Republican Union has never been nor never will be created or restored by coercion. Coercion and the sword are the legitimate weapons of monarchs, or the last resort against oppression; and monarchical or despotic governments are the only offsprings of coercion by the sword. Better for us a thousand times we had never broken loose from our mother country, better for us we had never tasted complete liberty, and felt the exhilarating influence of a true union of hearts. Yea, it would have been better for us had the blessed Lord suffered the destroying angel to have swept the whole nation at one dash from the occupancy of this part of his vineyard, while we were in a state of peace, and harmony, than it will be for us to attempt to reconstruct or restore our lost Union by coercion and civil war; for I tell you it will produce the very opposite and secure our nationtal, state, and individual ruin. The displeasure of Jehovah is already upon us, and unless we change our ideas of restoration in this matter, it will grind us to powder. And all this because the Great Giver of the unbounded and unlimited blessings we have enjoyed through our great and glorious union of States, charged us with a portion of an accursed race, for their good and our glory and benefit, and by whom all the States were equally blessed.

The South has been trying for more than fifty years to drive the negro question from the political arena, that the Union might be complete. They have offered to concede three quarters of their Constitutional rights on the question of slavery. Read the thirteen resolutions passed by a Southern con-

vention in 1850, at Nashville, Tenn., and their
proposition voted for in 1848, by a unanimous South
in both Houses of Congress, to extend the Missouri
Compromise through to the Pacific Ocean. You
will find them in the reports of 1848; but those
published above are sufficient to satisfy any true
Union man that the Southern States did not want
to break up this Union, but to save it in peace and
harmony. Now don't stop to denounce me as a
sympathizer with the Southern rebellion, for I tell
you I hate it more than you do who are willing to
destroy the Union to get clear of slavery. Look
over Davis's and Toombs's offers, as above, and just
think how different our condition would now be
had the party in power accepted that last offer,
though in that they asked for a great deal more
than they ever did before, but for nothing more
than their constitutional rights. Now, for humanity, union, and peace sake, stop and think before
you take another step to coerce the South, and let
us call a national convention and make those amendments to the national constitution. I don't mean that
we shall draw our armies from the field unless the
South should withdraw theirs.

I am told it is too late now to make any changes.
How are we to know that it is too late if we refuse
to make the offer? How came the majority in the
committee of thirteen to refuse when it was not too
late? Simply because it was a union saver and a
peace restorer, and a complete abolisher of the everlasting slave question from the halls of Congress,
and a preventer of any and every man from sad-
25

dling the poor unfortunate negro, and riding him into power.

The publication of this book may ride me off to some fort or dungeon; if so, I must submit to my fate. I know that I shall go there with a consciousness that I have done all in my power to prevent the collision between the North and South in the first place, and in the second, to save this great and glorious nation from an everlasting overthrow. I shall feel guiltless, and posterity will not rise up and curse me for what I have done. If I could be the means of convincing some good men of the great error of forcing or coercing men and women into a union (we had just as well undertake to coerce them to be Christians), or if I should be the means of convincing some of my Christian brethren of the different means necessary to establish despotic or monarchical governments, and a free republican union, I should feel happy locked up in some fort for my sins against abolitionism and infidelity. I have many good friends whom I love much, by whom I shall be stigmatized as a traitor to my country for this publication, but if they could see and know my heart they would not charge me with such a crime. I had rather be charged with murder in the first degree, or with highway robbery, and either one would be equally true and even more probable; for I look upon a traitor as being far worse than either. No patriot will interfere with the constitutional and lawful rights of any State, and he who does it is a traitor, and ought to be hung up by the neck until he is dead. True patriots are willing to yield to any man or set of men or States all of their lawful rights and a little more for the sake of the general good of their country; especially to save it from a civil war, and any refusal of the majority to yield to the minority all of their constitutional rights is treason, braggadocio, bullyism, and infidelity.

All abolitionists are not traitors in the true sense of the word, for I know some true men who are abolitionists, but not of the Garrisonian stripe. See what a condition we are in just by refusing the minority their Constitutional rights in our National Commonwealth, and how righteously easy it would have been to have prevented all this national and individual ruin. If our leaders had been true unadulterated patriots in the free States, all would now be happy and prosperous, east, west, north and south. *The South may soon be conquered in war*, but our glorious Union will never be restored with peace, harmony, and tranquillity, without some such concessions as asked for in the offers above.

I will close this chapter with a short quotation from a speech made by the Hon. John Q. Adams not long before his death, before the New York Historical Society.

How truly does he say, " but the *indissoluble link* of the Union between the people of the several States of this confederated nation, is, after all, not in the *right*, but in the *heart*," and also "*far better will it be for the people of the disunited States, to part in friendship* with each other, than *be held together by constraint*."

" In calm hours of self-possession, the right of a State to

nullify an act of Congress, is too absurd for argument, and too odious for discussion. The right of a State to *secede from the Union* is equally disowned by the principles of the *Declaration of Independence*. Nations acknowledge no judge between them upon earth, and their governments from necessity, must in their intercourse with each other decide when the failure of one party to a contract to perform its obligations, absolves the other from the reciprocal fulfilment of his own. But this last of earthly powers is not necessary to the freedom or independence of States, connected together by the immediate action of the *people*, of whom they consist. To the people alone is there reserved, as well the dissolving, as the constituent power, and that power can be exercised by them only under the tie of conscience, binding them to retributive justice of Heaven.

"With these qualifications, we may admit the same right as vested in the *people* of every State in the Union, with reference to the General Government, which was exercised by the people of the United Colonies, with reference to the supreme head of the British empire, of which they formed a part—and under these limitations, have the people of each State in the Union *a right to secede from the confederated Union itself.*

"Thus stands the right. But the *indissoluble link* of Union between the people of the several States of this confederated nation, is, after all, not in the *right*, but in the *heart*. If the day should ever come (may Heaven avert it) when the affections of the people of these States shall be alienated from each other; when the fraternal spirit shall give way to cold indifference, or collisions of interest shall fester into hatred, the band of political association will not long hold together parties no longer attracted by the magnetism of conciliated interests and kindly sympathies; and *far better* will it be for the people of the disunited States, to *part in friendship* with each other, than to be *held together by constraint*. Then will be the time for reverting to the precedents which occurred at the formation and adoption of the Constitution, to form again a more perfect Union, by dissolving that which could no longer bind, and to leave the separated parts to be reunited by the law of political gravitation to the centre."

CHAPTER VI.

Have the Friends or Quakers Produced this War?

I HAVE very often heard it said that the Quakers were all abolitionists, and consequently bad citizens. There is an impression throughout the free States, as well as the slave States, that the society of Friends were among the leaders, if not the instigators or originators, and perpetuators of all the schemes of abolitionism in the United States, and that they were contrivers and engineers of the underground railroad, and all other schemes of slave stealing ever concocted in this country. That their object is to get their labor for nothing, and I have often heard stories similar to the following told on them. That they would contrive to get the slaves to run away from their masters, and take them in their employ, and agree to pay them ten dollars per month, and board them for ten months, the wages to be paid at the end of the time. They worked them very hard, from the first of March to the middle of December, at which time they would inform the runaways that they had just got news that their masters were in the neighborhood after them, and that they must take the railroad immediately for Canada, or they would be caught; and frighten the

25* (293)

poor darkies out of their wits. They would have their tickets ready through to Canada, and pack up provisions enough to last them through, and then say they would send their wages as soon 'as they sold their crops; so the poor negroes would run into Canada penniless. But their Quaker friend would never send the wages. And in that way they would get their ten months' labor for their board, and about twenty dollars. The underground railroad would bring them another supply for spring, who would be carried through the same manœuvres, and run off in the same way, and so on, they would get their work done in that way for almost nothing.

These charges are false, and as slanderous as the charges of cruelties against the Southern slaveholders. The Orthodox Quakers have never meddled with slavery except in a lawful way, and that, I believe, has only happened in a few special cases, and then by lawful petitioning. There are no better citizens in the world than the Orthodox Friends; they have always attended strictly to their own business, and let other people's alone; which if all others here in the North had done, the present trouble would never been known or thought of, and the Quakers of North Carolina would be as happy today, as their brethren were twenty years ago in the North, and there would be a perfect business Union this day between the Quakers of the free States and the slaveholders of Charleston, South Carolina, and the slaveholders of the South would be allowed this day, and at all times, to travel through the free States anywhere, with their body bond-servants, unmolested; and Quakers would this day be in Charleston, from free States, attending to their business, and would be respected and loved there, as they are here at their homes.

Think of it. What a different state of things we should have to-day. And how quick peace would be declared, and everybody at their homes attending to their legitimate business, if every man would suddenly imbibe the principles of the Quakers in attending to their own business strictly and let other people's alone.

I have been intimately acquainted with the Society of Friends for thirty years, and have had a great many business transactions with them, some of long continuation, and some short, and have made as many settlements, and I can testify to their correctness and honesty in all their transactions in life. I have never known one to be troublesome or quar-·relsome in a single case. They believe in "rendering unto Cesar the things that are Cesar's, and unto God the things that are God's."

The Quakers are anti-slavery in principle and in fact; they are not slave-holders, and do not allow their members to own them, either directly or indirectly. But they are a law-abiding people, and are opposed to any interference with the laws of other States. They never have interfered with slavery beyond their own society; they say they are not responsible for the institution of slavery in this country. I have had many conversations with them on the subject, and some warm arguments; they differ with me on the divine institution of slavery, but many of them agree with me on many points. One is that the negro race is a lower grade of beings, and the two races never can be on an equality together in this world. And many of them say the slaves are better off where they are than they would be free. They are honest, upright, and sober, and are not apt to speak unless they have *something to say.* They are generally magnanimous, generous, and slow to anger; and very liberal where need be, and mostly kind in their dispositions. Of course they have some scabby sheep among them. But on the general they are outwardly all that pertains to a true Christian people, which must flow from a pure fountain within.

I don't know that I ever saw one angry, or the least excited. This gives them great advantage in debate, and they are mostly very respectful to the feelings of others. Upon the general, they are as near perfection as a society can be in all their walks in this world. And I believe, had they not *rejected the sacraments,* as a Christian society, they would now control a great part of this world, provided they had kept up their present principles as they have mostly done.

I am not a Quaker nor never was, and never had a relation that was. And I believe there was not one in the county in which I was born and raised. There were some in the adjoining county. I am not now connected with them in any way whatever, and I have no personal interest in them to influence me to speak for them. They take care of their own poor, and never allow them to suffer want. I never

saw one a beggar, or in the county almshouse.
They have their own asylums for the poor. I
think they are somewhat in error in their ecclesiastical arrangements. But, upon the whole, they
are the most upright, straightforward, and consistent citizens in this country.

I made a remark of this kind the other day to a
gentleman, and he said that could not be, for he
thought Passmore Williamson was a very meddle-
some man, and he was a Quaker. I told him I had
known Mr. Williamson for twenty-five years, and
knew he had not been a member of the Orthodox
Meeting for many years; therefore they are not
responsible for his conduct. Though I know nothing whatever against his character, but his fanatical notions of slavery, which I think have arisen
from great zeal without knowledge on that great
subject.

I have often thought that if the national Legislature were made entirely of Orthodox Quakers for
six years, we should have such an example set that
would do the nation good. I believe every article
and section of the constitution and laws would be
carried out and executed to the letter, even the
fugitive slave clause, for they are a law-loving, and
law-abiding people. They have, from George Fox
down to the present, made it a part of their religion
to respect the laws of the land. And yet they have
been subjects of great persecutions at times, even in
this country, and by professing Christians too. The
Puritans persecuted them to death in some cases, in
New England, where all the abominations have

been conceived and born, that have brought about
the awful crisis now in this nation, that perhaps has
ended the freedom and happiness of us all, in trying
to free those that God never intended to have temporal freedom. For when Noah said a servant of
servants he shall be to his brethren, He, Jehovah,
named no time this servitude should cease. He did
not say, until you are sufficiently punished, or until
you have repented, and have acknowledged your
crime against your old parent. But we are left to
suppose it will run through all time, and prevent
their freedom, and social equality. He has given
them a more loathsome and obnoxious appearance
to nearly all the senses of their brethren, the descendants of Shem and Japheth ; so much so, that social
and domestic equality is impossible, and their freedom would be the means of their extermination.
I have sufficiently discussed this point in the first
and second chapters, to which I refer the reader.

I say the Quakers have done nothing to produce
this war between brethren of the same family.

A great many people seem not to be aware that
there was a split in the Society of Friends in 1827,
on the atonement. Elias Hicks took the ground
that there was no more virtue in the shedding of
Christ's blood than that of a bull or a ram ; and he
had many followers; and the Orthodox Society was
cleansed thereby from fanaticism and discord. The
new societies are called the Hicksites. They are entirely independent of the Orthodox Quakers or Foxites. And the Orthodox are not responsible for any
doings of the Hicksites no more than they are for the

doings of Passmore Williamson, or any other anti-slavery fanatic. There are many Garrisonians among the Hicksites, and infidelity prevails among them to a very great extent, and in nearly all the infidel associations that come along, we find a large sprinkling of Hicksite Quakers, and at the public controversies that have taken place between Christians and infidels, we find very prominent Hicksite Quakers in attendance, and on the side of infidelity. The last controversy of the kind I attended was at Concert Hall, between Dr. Berg, D. D., of Philadelphia, and an Englishman named Barker who was once a minister of the Gospel of Christ; at which I saw a number, yes many of the disciples of Hicks seated through the house, and some on the platform, all of whom seemed to be on the side of infidelity. I was personally acquainted with a number I saw there of that class, all of whom seemed to exult more than any others whenever a hard blow would be let loose against Christianity by that celebrated infidel, by shouting, and stamping their feet, and clapping their hands, or pounding the floor with their canes. They followed this deserter from the Kingdom of God into the kingdom of the devil, the Sunday Institute, that was got up to blaspheme the name of the Son of God; they there worship at the feet of infidelity.

I cannot say that this self-styled society of Friends has had nothing to do with this awful calamity that is now afflicting this country from centre to circumference. For the only religion they seem to profess, is to oppose the atonement of our blessed Lord, and denounce slavery and slaveholders. They have dealt largely in the many publications that have so embittered the present generation of the free States against the slaveholders of the South and all the Southern people, except the poor negroes who are always better off and happier than the five-sixths of the poor people of the free States. I have heard some of them express themselves exultingly over the war now prevailing, and say many thousand lives may be lost, but the slaves would be set at liberty, and that would pay for all.

Those are the people that have given the Ortho-dox Quakers a bad name, a great many people not knowing that Apollyon had assailed the genuine ranks of the true Friends, and made many disciples, who formed themselves into a separate and independent society, and have closed the only door against themselves ever opened for eternal life. But among them are many useful citizens, and outside of their religious views of the atonement and their activity against slavery, they are much the same as the Orthodox.

The true Quakers are among the leaders in all the great improvements in the country. They have a great many rich men among them; and we have had the Copes, the Browns, the Woods, &c. &c., and they have not withheld their hands from any good thing. They are never hasty in any new improvement; but, when once started, they are untiring in their perseverance.

The Quakers, from George Fox down, have been opposed to war. In this they have been proverbial or celebrated for their opposition to all war and bloodshed, and the Quakers of the Revolution that entered the battle-field, were disowned, or excommunicated; they were called the fighting or free Quakers, and had their meeting house in this city at the S. W. corner of Fifth and Arch Sts.; but I don't think they have worshipped there for many years. It was said that they had to have Quaker preaching there a certain number of times every year, but they had no preachers. Yet some one of their members would go there at the appointed time, and go through the manœuvres. It was said the meeting house was left to them in that way. I do not vouch for those reports.

But I find a significant change has come over many of the Friends. The Hicksites seem nearly all to approve of the present civil war. This is strange, for they have always taken the ground that when attacked they would not resist by force of arms, but fold their hands and trust in the Lord for redemption. The disciples of Elias Hicks were celebrated for this kind of defence. But, strange to say, they seem to encourage the prosecution of this war to the hilt, to the steel, and to the death. And all the stories we ever heard told about the mildness of the Quaker in the time of an attack, showed them to be celebrated for compromise in order to make peace. And above all their great coolness when in the hands of an enemy of any kind, so that the worst of men have been made to love them, and offer terms of compromise, even when they had all

26

in their hands. Very many such stories have been told about them, to illustrate their cool wit and liberality to enemies and all others, under all circumstances of life. Therefore is it not wonderful that they should be opposed to any peace measures being introduced in order to settle the present trouble in some way to save the Union without the shedding of blood?

How are we to account for this among this class of Quakers? I don't say all of them, but many or most of them. Why did they and all others that went in for the success of the party now in power, say one year ago that there was no danger, that no attempt would be made by the South to secede from the Union, let who would be elected; that even South Carolina could not be kicked out of the Union. Such declarations were made by all the leaders of the successful party, and their followers, in reply to the declarations made by the opposition, that the success of the republicans would produce this trouble, unless they nominated and elected men who were known in the South not to be abolitionists. And why do they say now this trouble had to come anyhow, and let us push it through at the mouth of the cannon, at the point of the bayonet, and at the edge of the sword? Why did they then pronounce such anathemas upon us for foretelling these calamities? And now why do they denounce us as secessionists, and rebels against the government, because we tell them the only way to save the Union, and have a perpetual peace, will be to give the South her equal rights in the territories of the United States, and give them such guaranties as will make them feel safe in the Union with us.

I ask this question of all that I talk with who differ with me, and the only reply I get is: It had to be, and therefore there was no way to avoid it. I ask, have you tried any other way? Did we not tell you that your way would produce destruction to this heaven-like Union? And did you not tell us we were only sensationists, fools, and locofoco lick-spittles, and all such hard things? Now if we were such good prophets then, and foretold just what has come to pass, why not respect us now, when we tell you, under the same prophetic vision, that war will never save this Union? We may subdue the South, but I tell you again the white man has never yet been conquered nor never will be by force. He may be subdued by an overpowering force, and held in subjugation by the same; but he cannot be conquered. I mean he will never submit voluntarily, and love the place into which he is forced, or the power that compelled him.

Negroes can be conquered and made to love the power that holds them; it is congenial with their nature, and so of some of the mixed races. But the descendants of Shem have never been conquered into an affectionate submission, except by an equal compromise made in love, and by claiming them as equal in every particular. So if we want our Union restored, it must be done by peace measures offered in love, by acknowledging our Southern brethren to be our equals, and giving them their equal rights in all the territories that now belongs or may hereafter belong to the United States.

The time was when the extension of the Missouri compromise to the Pacific Ocean would have done, and saved us. But it will not now, I fear. If we continue to shout, no compromise with traitors, and determine to subjugate them, mark my words, our die is cast, and our doom fixed. Every republican that has studied the history of the questions that now divide us, knows well what would be the result of the success of the republican party. And when they persuaded the people that there was no danger in their success, they knew just as well as the devil did when he beguiled Eve, and said thou shalt not surely die, that death would be the result. That result was just what he wanted, and the emancipation of all the slaves is just what certain leaders of the republican party wanted, and still want, or there would be no trouble in settling this question. This is the answer to my question, and the only correct answer that can be given.

I would ask my Hicksite friends, what they expect to gain by the emancipation of all the slaves? Have you ever studied the human nature of the Anglo-Americans? Do you suppose for one moment, that he will ever be put on an equality with Africans, or allow them to have equal rights with the white man? If you do, you will be disappointed, for that day will never come? God never intended it should be so, and you never knew one, that went down to their level, that did not fall far below them, and was looked upon with disgust and contempt by all good citizens. What is that beautiful white girl thought of after she has become the wife of the African? Or what is that nice-looking and polite, chaste, and accomplished, white man thought of by all good people, who has chosen, and taken to himself a black, notty-headed negro woman for a wife? Think of it; this is the only way of being on an equality.

You say the white people of the South have children by their negro women. If they do, they take care of the mother and offspring. And so also do the white men of the North have children by black women, in much larger proportion to numbers than what is done in the South; and they leave mother and child to starve, or live upon the slops from the swill-tub provided for the hogs. We don't deny these facts, they are truths that stare us in the face daily. I would ask my Hicksite friends in what kind of esteem they hold men who do those things. If you find out who they are, are they not loathsome to your very soul whenever you think of them, and do you not hate and shun them wherever you see them? We know persons of strong passions and degraded by bad company and intoxicating drink, yield to such passions in the moment of temptation. But ask that man, if he is willing to be placed on a public and perpetual equality with the black man, and his very soul will revolt within him at the insulting question, while he will answer *no*.

I know some steps have been taken in New England towards a political equality. They are allowed to vote in some of those States, and in New York on certain contingencies. That has' been done for effect, and if all the slaves were emancipated, those liberties would be abolished in less than three years, and an animosity and prejudice would spring up against the poor negroes that would be more terrible than any slavery ever known on this earth. A large proportion of the liberties of the so-called free negroes of the free States, is the certain result of a hatred to the slaveholders of the South. Those liberties are given in some of the free States to try to prejudice the slave States, and to set the slaves against their masters. And I say again that the only safety in this country for the negro race, is to keep them in slavery; for universal emancipation will bring about a universal sweeping from American soil the entire colored race in some way. That will go hard with the poor negroes, and that awful conflict may commence where abolitionism did, and among those who have been the strongest opponents of slavery, will be found the first who will move to drive them out of the country.

I have many friends among the Hicksite Quakers, and I hold them in the high esteem, for when I was a stranger they took me in, and gave me my start in the world. But, alas! it now turns out too much like the cow that gave a large pail of milk, and when done, she up foot and kicked it all over. So I fear my friends have, by their conduct towards the South, aided largely in upsetting the pail that was so nearly filled. The Orthodox Quakers never have voted so nearly all one way as the Hicksites. They were mostly Whigs in Mr. Clay's time; yet they

were somewhat divided between the two great
parties, and last fall a great many of them voted for
John Bell, and a good many for Judge Douglas;
and even some for Mr. Breckinridge, and others for
Mr. Lincoln. So their vote was not a sectional one.
They are true to their country as a people, and
they do not make abolitionism their religion. They
embrace Christ as their only hope of salvation. They
were charged by some of being privy to the John
Brown raid at Harper's Ferry, Virginia, in consequence of which they made the following declarations, which will show that I have not misrepresented
them. I cannot but admire the principles set forth
in the declarations, however much I may differ with
them on a few points; but they nowhere call the
masters thieves, murderers, and robbers, simply
because they are slave-holders; but *friends,* in an
humble, affectionate, and Christian-like manner.
Which, if all other anti-slavery men had done likewise, our national peace would flow this day like
a river, and our Union and prosperity would be
limited only by the bounds of our country. By the
bounds of our country did I say? I should have
said unparalleled on the face of the globe. See the
declaration of the Foxites, who are the Orthodox
Quakers:—

"*At a Meeting of the Representatives of the Religious Society of Friends, in Pennsylvania, New-Jersey, Delaware,
&c., held in Philadelphia, Third Month 16th, 1860 :—*

"Several articles have appeared in the public Journals
within a few months past—some in the form of Letters, dated
and written in the plain style used by Friends;—and others as

proceedings of Meetings in which persons designated as Friends took part;—which articles seem to sanction the use of force to free the Slaves, and also to connive at efforts to subvert the government; and as those who are unacquainted with our principles and practices may be thereby led to implicate the Society in such views and proceedings, we believe it right, on behalf of those we represent, to disclaim any unity therewith, and to repel an imputation so unjust and injurious to the religion Friends have always professed.

" In compliance with the precepts of the Saviour of the world, which breathe peace on earth and good-will to men, and command us to love our enemies, and to do good to them that hate us and persecute us; our religious Society has steadfastly maintained a testimony against all wars and fightings, tumults, violence, and shedding of blood, and against forcible resistance to oppression, whether inflicted with or without color of law; and has believed it to be a duty to live peaceably under the authorities placed over us—to obey the laws of our country where they do not infringe on our religious principles ; and where they do, passively and patiently to endure the penalties inflicted on us.

" The Society of Friends has long borne a decided testimony against holding our fellow men in bondage, as being incompatible with the benign spirit of the Gospel, and contrary to the commands of our Lord Jesus Christ; Matt. vii. 12; John xiii. 34, 35; xv. 12, 17, &c.; and those members who once held slaves, long since set them free, and in many instances remunerated them for their labor while in bondage. This testimony is as dear to us now as ever; and we feel religiously bound to uphold it in the spirit of meekness and in that Christian love which craves the welfare of both master and slave.

" While convinced of the injustice and wrongs attendant on the system of Slavery, we cannot approve of, or sympathize with, any forcible or violent measures to obtain the liberty, or to redress the grievances of the Slaves ; but have counselled them to endeavor to serve with patience and fidelity while in bondage, to fulfil their Christian duties with propriety, and to commit their cause into the hands of a merciful and omnipotent Father in heaven.

" Whatever any persons, unjustly assuming the name or the appearance of Friends, may have said or done, which is inconsistent with these principles, is contrary to the faith and the practice of the religious Society of Friends, and cannot justly be charged upon it.

" Signed on behalf and by direction of the meeting aforesaid.

JOSEPH SNOWDON, *Clerk*."

I disagree with my Orthodox friend on the moral question of slavery in the abstract. That difference is caused simply by their confounding spiritual precepts and examples with temporal, though I do not know that they declare slavery to be a moral evil, but they strongly intimate the doctrine. The introduction of Christianity into the world was not intended to change a man's temporal condition in the world, but his spiritual condition only; so far as he would be improved by becoming a true Christian, he would be entitled to all the benefits thereof, by his increased worth. If he should continue to love and fear God, he would rise higher and higher in the scale of confidence, love, and respect; whatever his condition or situation might be in life. What is the greatest boon or blessing of this life? Is it not to have the confidence of all that know us, especially those who are concerned in us? What will drive a good man, or even a bad man to distraction sooner than to be sensible of having lost the confidence of his neighbors and friends, and especially those who have an interest in them? Righteousness is the only staff of pleasure, if it is unadulterated and constant, so that it becomes patent to all that know us.

The good slaves are the happiest people I have ever seen. They have privations, and great privations, it is true. And we have our privations. Theirs are singular, while ours are plural. While they are deprived of the liberty of working for whoever they please, they have no other concern in this world, but the salvation of their souls. Their bread, meat, drink, and homes are provided for them; they are not troubled about the future of this life in any way whatever. While we are far greater slaves than they. We are equally deprived of such liberties as we desire; and what is our concern about the future? How many white people are driven to distraction, and thrown into consternation at this time? Is it the case with the slaves, except those on or near the battle-ground? What are the pains and aches of the entire white population of the United States at this time, while the slaves of the South are fully provided for, and they feel no concern whatever, but to take care of their masters' property, and to prepare for heaven? What is the painful concern and solicitude of at least twelve millions of the white people of the free States, at all times, who are dependent on their daily labor for bread, and a home for themselves, their wives, and little ones. They are dependent upon their employers, and they know if thrown out of employment their families must suffer, for they have had to stint themselves and families in the necessaries of life, all the way through, to make their inadequate earnings keep them along. So if they lose their situations, they are thrown upon the cold charities of the world.

Compared to this, the slavery of the South is a bliss, it is a heaven and glory.

If our Saviour had fixed a temporal standard, or condition in this life for us to arrive to before we could embrace Christ as our Saviour, how many millions would be debarred, and sink into everlasting despair? But, blessed be his name, that is not the case. He is just suited to every man's case and condition in this life; and it is not required that any man should change his temporal relations in life, provided they are lawful.

We have an account of slavery since 2348 years before Christ, and slaves were the rightful property of their masters from that time until nearly 100 years after his ascension, and the entire Old and New Testament Scriptures were written after its introduction, and most of the patriarchs and prophets were slave owners. Yet, strange to say, not one single word was uttered against it in the whole book of God. Slavery still existed extensively in the time of the Evangelists and Apostles, and yet no one of the writers gives the slightest intimation that it was a moral evil. That book being the only moral guide ever given, and slavery being one of the fruits of the fall, or consequences of sin having entered into the world, therefore it is no more sin in itself than all other afflictions poor sinful men are subjected to in this world.

I will now close up with my Orthodox brethren, by telling a little story to illustrate their usual plan of interfering with slavery :—

Worner Miflin was an influential member of

Friends' meeting, and a man of talent and great moral courage, and a large amount of philanthropy. He was untiring in his efforts to get a master to set Joe, a slave, free. His frequent conversations and intercessions on behalf of Joe became annoying to his master; therefore he said to Worner one morning, that he was welcome at all times at his house whenever he visited Virginia; but I say now, you must never speak to me again about the emancipation of Joe, for that he should not do. Worner told the slaveholder he certainly would not, if it was unpleasant to him. But requested of the master to allow him to hold a conversation with Joe, and he would never mention the subject again. The master consented, and told him where he could see Joe at a certain hour. The master concealed himself near the spot, and Worner Miflen made his appearance, and said to Joe: I have seen thy master time after time to try to obtain thy freedom; I have done all in my power, but thy master cannot spare thee. I have called on thee to say, thy master is a very good man, and *thee* must be a faithful servant until the day of thy death. Love thy master, and obey him in all things; be not slack in thy duty to thy master at any time. And above all, never leave him without his consent, and let his will be thy will through life, and thou shalt have thy reward in heaven. Worner bid Joe farewell and left him.

At the dinner-table next day, the master said to Worner that he had heard all his conversation the day before with Joe, and I expected thee was going to persuade Joe to run away, but thy honor has so affected me, that I say to thee now, that Joe is a free man from this hour.

This is a complete illustration of the true principles of the Orthodox Friends—this is now their true character. Therefore, I say, if they had been the ruling power of the free States, we should now be in no trouble with our southern brethren. I have endeavored to give an outline of the true character of the true Quakers, and if I have in any way erred, they must pardon me, for I have aimed at right.

27

CHAPTER VII.

Do as you would be done by.

"Therefore all things whatsoever ye would that men should do to you, do ye even so to them; for this is the law and the prophets."—MATT. vii. 12.

I DON'T know that I ever had a controversy with an abolitionist on the moral question of slavery who did not quote the above text to condemn it, and to prove that the institution of American slavery should be abolished at once by church and state, because (say they), "*We, the people*," feel that we would not like to be slaves to the African race; and also to prove that if we refuse to give our influence for negro emancipation, we sin against both heaven and earth. They seem to take it for granted that negro slavery is a great moral evil under all circumstances, and no power of heaven or earth can make it otherwise, and think this precept is entirely one-sided in its bearing (*or say so at least*), forgetting that the slaveholders are partners in the great contest between the North and South of this country, and in the precept of our Lord above quoted. They forget that the slaveholder has a right to this text to shelter himself from the barbed arrows of abolitionists. For the slaveholders say, if the abolitionists would only obey this glorious precept, they would have peace and rest in all their borders. The abolitionists seem to think that this great moral precept was given exclusively for the benefit of the free States and negroes, and that "*We, the people*," have no protection under its beneficent hand from imposition and slander. Yet, if abolitionists could only be prevailed upon to obey this the best of all precepts, we should now have peace and harmony throughout this whole nation, instead of being on the verge of ruin by a most bloody civil contest. It would bring us to the very threshold of the great Millennium spoken of by Christ.

This text is in the words of our Lord himself, and no man can be his true follower and disobey it. If the abolitionists do not disobey it in all its requirements, no person on this earth does.

Suppose an abolitionist had a relative in Alabama, owning two hundred slaves, who should die, leaving all of his servants to his only heir, an abolitionist in Boston, what would you have the abolition heir to do, who should happen to be a very poor man? Your answer would be, free them or have nothing to do with them. Now, you know the laws of the South are such that the slaves must have a master to take care of them or to set them free, for none but a legal owner could free them, and without a legal claimant they would all be sold by the sheriff, to the highest bidders, which would scatter them to the four winds. Then, you say, let him go and take charge of them and free them. But you know the law does not allow them to be freed and left there.

Therefore you would be compelled, in order to free them, to take them to a free State. And if you should send them to a free State without equipping them suitably for the journey, and give them something to subsist upon until they could procure a livelihood, you would not be doing for them as you would be done by. And if you should conclude to send them to free States, it would cost you at least one hundred dollars each—that would amount to twenty thousand dollars. Suppose this amount should be raised to bring them away, and when you commence operations you should find at least two hundred more belonging to other men, who were wives, husbands, children, parents, brothers, and sisters of your two hundred slaves, what would you do then? To separate man and wife, and parents and children, would not be doing as you would be done by. To purchase them would be *dealing in human blood*, and if you should get over that point, it would take perhaps at least two hundred thousand dollars to purchase them. Suppose that amount could be raised, and you should find that their masters would not sell them, then would you separate man and wife by bringing yours to a free State? You know that this is one of your great objections to slavery; therefore, you could not do that, and *"do as you would be done by."* If you should resolve to have nothing to do with them, then all of them would be sold to the highest bidder. Parents and children, husbands and wives, would be separated never to see each other again. Let this abolitionist heir suppose himself to be a slave, and the husband of one of *his* women, who belongs to another owner, would he not have his master to purchase him, that he might go with his loved wife?

Now you must bear in mind that a negro husband, wife, child, or parent has the same protection under this glorious precept of our Lord, that the white abolitionist has. And no man has a right to claim what would infringe upon the moral or civil rights of others under this righteous law: "To do to others all things *whatsoever* you would have them to do to you." No man can be a Christian and disobey this counsellor, and an authorized Christian minister who does not respect this law, is simply a *moral devil*.

Suppose a murderer was arraigned before the court for sentence, and the criminal should say to the court: If your honor was in my place, and I in yours, I know you would have me to discharge you, and allow you to go out free, therefore you must do as you would be done by, and discharge me from custody, or you will be a criminal before God, and suffer eternal wrath for your disobedience in this glorious precept of his. This has just as much reason in it, as applying the precepts to the civil relation of master and slave. All that is taught by this counsel of Christ is, that the master should treat his slaves just as he would have them to treat him if circumstances were reversed, and he, a negro slave to one of them. Of course he would have his master to treat him the very best that could be under all the circumstances. So the mas-

27*

ters are all morally bound to treat their slaves the
very best that all the circumstances would allow, by
giving them good wholesome food sufficient for
their real wants, with comfortable clothing, and
never to put on them more than they can bear without injury, and not to injure them in any way whatever. When he has done this, he has fulfilled this
law so far as the law of master and slaves is concerned. If the master does not do this he will be held
to a fearful responsibility, and he will have to render
a fearful account in that great day of God. The relations of men are not to be changed to fulfil this·
divine precept.

This text is applicable to every transaction of
this life, and no man is required by it to give away all
of his property. But if we go out to sell a horse, we
must not try to make the purchaser believe what we
know is not the truth, in order to ·get more than the
value. "We must do as we would be done by," if
we were purchasing. The abolitionists are bound by
the same precepts ; that is, to do to the slave-owner
just as they would be done by if they were owners
of slaves. And he is bound to place himself, by
supposition, in a slave State with a large number of
slaves, for whose maintenance he is responsible, and
there ask himself the question, how would he have
men to treat him as a slave-holder. If he can make
up his mind that he would like to be called a tyrant,
thief, robber, and murderer, simply because he is a
slave owner, then he, as an abolitionist, has a right
to say hard things of the slave owner. He must
do as he would be done by if circumstances were

reversed; and if he does not do as he would be done by, he will be held to a fearful account.

A slave is bound by the same rule to do justice to his master in all things, just as he would have a slave to do to him if he had one, and if he does not render faithful service to his master, he will be held by the moral law as a *thief* and *robber*.

He who persuades or steals a slave away from his master, simply to get him away, has committed a crime, for which there is no punishment adequate. He does not only steal a man from his legal owner, but he runs him into a climate that is not congenial to his nature, and leaves him there to starve and die. Therefore, he is not only a man-stealer, but a tyrant and murderer.

It seems clear to my mind that if this precept of our Lord was understood by the whole Christian church as the abolitionists pretend to understand it, it would be fatal to almost every business interest on the earth, it would encourage all kinds of villainy and wrong, punish the innocent and let the guilty go free. It is a moral precept in which we cannot always judge another. Every man must be his own judge, and if every man was religiously honest, no man would then desire another to do for him what he would not do for another under the same circumstances. The abolitionists require the masters to do for their slaves what they (the abolitionists) would not do, were they placed under the same circumstances. And they have reason to believe that they require the master to do for the slave what the slave feels in his own heart he would not do for his master were circumstances reversed between him and his master.

The abolitionists have introduced a new code of morals, as unscriptural as that of Joe Smith, or the Spiritualists, and more productive of evil than the doctrines of the Mormons and Spiritualists. They are so palpably wrong that they do away with the code given by our Saviour and the apostles, and say its day has passed, therefore it does not affect society in general, and perhaps has been in some degree a benefit, because it calls out the morbid, the vicious, the licentious, the weak, misguided, and the fanatical, and in this way society is succored and purified by those doctrines of the devil. But the abolitionists remain in good society and try to instill their new code of morals into the minds of the pure, the virtuous, the unlearned in Scripture, and the unsuspecting and most pious, zealous portions of both church and state. They work with a zeal that is calculated to deceive. The manner of their proceeding is to agitate society by the question of slavery. They tell them of its great moral evil, that the slaveholders are murderers, robbers, and thieves, of the worst kind.

On the morning preceding the evening the Pennsylvania Hall in this city was burnt, I heard an abolition lecturer, by the name of Wright, tell a gentleman from Baltimore that Gen. Washington was a thief, robber, and murderer, simply because he (Washington) was a slaveholder. This doctrine is universally taught by abolitionists of the Garrison school, and their object is to throw firebrands into society, and to prejudice the North against the South, and the South against the North. They are guilty of treason, murder, and theft. Of treason, by dis-obedience to the laws of the United States, and by resisting the same with violence and deadly weapons; and of murder and theft by persuading the slaves to run away, "and if their masters pursue them and attempt to, arrest them, to kill them just as they would a dog, and to steal their master's horses and money, if they can get it, and make their escape." But the most glaring part of the theft is, stealing slaves from masters. I know men who do this thing and boast of the success they have had; and men who profess to be followers of our Lord. One told me, on a Sabbath afternoon, at his Sabbath school, that he had had as high as seventeen runaway slaves (run off from their masters by means of the under-ground railroad) hid in his garret at one time, all of whom they passed on to Canada on the railroad.

I am of the opinion that this crime ought to be made next, if not equal, to the highest crime known to our criminal code. To say the best of it, it is as bad as murder in the first degree. When a man premeditates a murder, he is likely to make up his mind to do it in the most expeditious way, that will prove safest to himself; therefore, does not torture his victim any more than he can help. But the underground railroad man does it in a more cruel manner. He first decoys his victim from his home, and does it by flattering words of freedom; he tells him of the cruelty of slavery—of its enormous wick-edness—the hardships he has to undergo, and when he is old and past labor, will be killed and thrown out. On the other hand, of the glories of the free States and of freedom; the happiness they will have, and of the rich fruits and abundant harvest of the free States; of political and social freedom; that he will be on an equality with his neighbors, and that the further he goes north, the better his condition will be—the greatest friendship and affection is shown to him. So the poor ignorant slave is completely deluded, and at once becomes dissatisfied with his condition, and anxious to be free.

I will here insert a report of an abolition meeting held in Boston the other day, and the wonderful exploits of a female conductor on the underground railroad. I have no doubt she was induced to think she was doing God's service by this cruel act. See as follows:—

"A FEMALE CONDUCTOR OF THE UNDERGROUND RAILROAD.— At the late Woman's Rights Convention, at Melodeon Hall, Boston, the most interesting incident was the appearance on the platform of the colored woman, Mrs. Harriet Tupman, who has been eight times South, and brought into freedom no less than forty persons, including her agēd father and mother, over seventy years old. She had a prolonged and enthusiastic reception."

The most noted point in this act of horror was the bringing away from ease and comfortable homes two old slaves over seventy years of age. Now there are no old people of any color more caressed, and better taken care of than the old worn-out slaves of the South, except the wealthy whites, who are few in number. A much larger proportion of the Southern slaves live to very old ages than do the colored people of the North, or free States. Why is it so? 1. Because they have regular employment or labor; 2. they have regular food; 3. they have but few, or no hardships, and are never overworked; 4. they are not dissipated, nor half so filthy in their living; 5. They are more cheerful and happy, and the climate is more congenial to their nature. The nature of the negro never was intended for the cold climates of America.

On the other hand, the colored people of what is called the free States seldom have regular employment; if they could have, they would not. They are exceedingly irregular in their food, and generally have that which is unsuited to health, being mostly refuse. They are very dissipated and filthy, and have little or almost no employment; and would not confine themselves to constant employment if they could get it. Those old slaves had earned their living while young, and a home for themselves when past labor, and had sat down at ease around the plentiful board of their master, whose duty it was to support them through old age, and see them well taken care of in sickness, and when dead to give them a respectable burying. This ignorant woman must have been persuaded and bewildered by flattery from some fiendish source, or she certainly would not have been guilty of such a diabolical act of wickedness and cruelty to her parents, who had a fortune laid up for old age, and had come to the time when labor had ceased to be required at their hands, and were entitled to a peaceful home with him whom they had served so many years, and where the laws of the State compelled him to give them that support righteously due them the balance of their days, and where they had friends to comfort and console them in declining life.

Can it be possible that so large an audience of white people can be found in so high a civilized community, professing so much love for the poor slaves, who could applaud such an act of wickedness and cruelty in a child to her parents, as this certainly was; and a thousand times worse than to steal young ones away! I admit it to be a great act of kindness to the master, or the estate that had them to support; and perhaps was a saving of some two hundred dollars a year to him or his estate. The notice does not say where she took them to; but we suppose as far north as she could get them, and altogether likely into Canada, where they have nearly six months of severe winter out of the twelve. I cannot conceive of a more wicked act towards parents. Confinement in the penitentiary for life would be "*inadequate*" to her crime, for stealing her old parents away from a good home and friends, and a living already laid up sufficient for all their wants; and from a warm climate altogether congenial to their nature, to a very cold one, and where there is nothing to depend on but their labor. And in a climate where the thermometer is in the neighborhood of zero four months out of twelve, and no master's wood-pile to go to; and no rich white man or woman to call them "Uncle Tom, and Aunt Lotta," whose fortune was protected by the laws of the State in which they had labored for their support. Yet an audience of white people professing love to the slaves, could applaud a being in human shape, for so cruel an act.

I have been in Boston many times, and at all seasons of the year, and most people I have talked with seemed to be Christians of some sort, and men and women of very large philanthropy, and yet how in that city of education and refinement such an audience can be culled out is more than I can tell, unless the underground railroad passes through Apollyon's Kingdom, for certainly they cannot be altogether human, or such exultation could not be had over such wickedness in June, 1860.

In the winters of 1851, 52, 53, I was in Boston, and could hardly go into a store or hotel without meeting some one with a subscription book that seemed to beg every one they met to subscribe some amount, to save the fugitive slaves in Canada from freezing or starving to death, and their stories of horror were enough to move the hardest heart; and now, in June, 1860, those devils incarnate could clap their glad hands and shout over the report of two old slaves, over seventy years of age, having been stolen and abducted from good homes in a southern climate, and brought to and turned loose in the frigid zones of the north, to freeze to death or starve with hunger. If the devil is any worse than that puritanic audience who assembles to hear the report of this wretched hard-hearted negro woman, I am sure it is a sufficient reason why I should strive to avoid his kingdom.

I will ask those Puritans if that was in keeping
28

with the golden rule of our Saviour, quoted at the head of this chapter, or which were the greatest sinners, this negro woman and the Boston audience, or the master of those two old slaves? Read the former chapters, in which I have fully set forth the moral questions of slavery, and then decide the above question.

Who would have supposed the descendants of the Puritans who landed on Plymouth Rock in 1620, and who had been driven from their native land by infidel tyrants, because they determined to worship God according to the dictates of their own conscience could have so fallen. It was thought to be a happy day when the Mayflower, with over one hundred of those Puritan saints, arrived at Plymouth Rock with open Bibles; but their descendants, like the good cow after she had given a large pail of rich milk, up foot, and kicked it over. Just so did the descendants of the Puritan saints, for it was soon discovered that they had imbibed so much of the tyrannical spirits of their fathers who had driven them from their native land to our shores for shelter; consequently they turned tyrants, and persecuted the Quakers of New England even unto death, because they desired to worship God according to the dictates of *their* own consciences, which differed in mode only from that of their Puritan brethren. This conduct of the descendants of the inhabitants of Plymouth Rock was sufficient to satisfy every intelligent Christian, that they had totally backslidden from that true Christianity that sustained them under similar trials in their native land.

Yet from the landing of those pilgrim fathers we date the birth of true Christianity in this country. But their sudden transition from infidel bondage to Christian freedom was too much for them, and they consequently overleaped the limits of religious liberty and soon became religious despots, and advocated the passage of such laws as would punish a man for kissing his wife on the Sabbath day, or expel him from church for happening to smile in church. And it was said they built their hen-houses so as to exclude the entire light of the sun, the brightest days, when the door was closed, and that they closed that door each Saturday night, and kept it closed until after twelve o'clock Sunday night, for fear lest the cocks would break the Sabbath by crowing, or the scratching of the hens for their little ones would cause anger in heaven. Therefore it was hardly to be wondered at in the summer of 1860, that their posterity should all assemble at Melodeon Hall, in the city of Boston, to worship the goddess of liberty in the shape of a poor deluded negro woman. And sing and shout with the loudest acclamations of glory and honor to her for the performance of as cruel an act as ever was performed by a child towards parents.

Did those religious fanatics " do as they would be done by ?" Did they "render unto Cesar the things that were Cesar's, and unto God the things that were God's ?"

But those demoniacs were harmless to both church and State, as long as both kept them at a distance; but when both opened their doors to them officially, and invited them in for their money and votes, our die was cast and ruin sealed. And when they were placed in power by the Constitutional votes of " We, the people," the blessings of heaven were withdrawn from us, and we are now entering a gulf of strife in which fraternal blood will flow as rivers, and unless we speedily spue out those Puritanic saints (devils) from power we shall speedily be plunged into the most terrible despotism ever known on this earth, yea, under the fangs of whose power every man and woman will be imprisoned who may refuse to worship the "goddess of liberty" of Melodeon Hall, Boston.

Those deluded Puritanic successors have now succeeded to power, and the coronation took place the fourth of last March, and now we see the fore-shadowing of a national overthrow more terrible than any history has yet recorded. The enormous amount of fraternal blood that will be shed during the present (republican) administration will cause the whole civilized world to wonder if there is any such thing as Christianity. How else can it be, when the descendants of the Puritan saints, who are now leaders of the so-called Christian ministry throughout New England, have, by trampling upon the Constitution and laws of the United States and by the foulest slanders ever heaped upon any people on the face of the earth, so completely alienated the hearts of our Southern brethren from us, that nothing but the overpowering grace and love of God can ever reunite the two extremes of our great country, without which our government is no more than a rope of sand. Take grace and love from the Christian church, and let such hate take its place as now exist between the North and South of our country; how long do you suppose the church would stand?

There is but one road to a political salvation for us, and that is for all those Northern abolition fanatics to stop short, and "do to all others as they would have all others to do unto them." "For this is the law and the prophets." Without these Christian principles shall be fully established, there can be no such thing as a government by the people. *Any attempt to force the South to love us will be certain destruction to our great national fabric that was marked out and planned for us by no other finger than God's own finger; therefore the slander and hatred.* But let us restore the government by the principles embraced in the above text, which were the principles by which it was first formed, the only principles on which it ever can be restored, and *without which it would not stand if restored.* If the free States had always treated the South according to the principles embraced in the above text, there would not be one secessionist this day south of Mason's and Dixon's line. As long as we lived by those principles we were inflexible, and all the powers on the face of the globe combined could not have affected us in war, because we were all, "*We, the people*," and God was our King. We were all one people, and the laws bore the same relation to the poorest hard-working man in the nation, as they did to the President of the United States, and he was only equally protected

28*

with the poor industrious man and no better, and owned no more law than the poor man.

But the Chicago platform has been substituted for the Constitution and laws of the United States. Therefore the office holders are our supreme rulers. The Chicago platform is a rebellion by the free States against the Constitutional and lawful rights of all the slave States. The great Daniel Webster of Mass. declared all such proceedings to be treason against the United States government, in a speech he made at Albany, in 1851. Yet the Melodeon Hall of Boston was filled to overflowing by an infidel crew culled out of that city of education and Puritanism (a city that contains many as true, and as good loyal, national men as are in the United States), who clapped their glad hands, and shouted, "Glory to a black Goddess of liberty," not only for having committed treason against the United States government, but against the State governments; and for a theft of over $50,000 worth of property, besides robbing her aged parents of homes, where they had plenty of this world's goods, and friends without limit, and brought them into a country, heartless and cold towards the negro race, *especially old worn-out ones.*

Now I ask all candid men to look at this congregation of traitors a little; and see if the South had not reason not only to be insulted, but alarmed to the extreme, when they learned that enough such men and women could collect at Melodeon Hall in Boston in 1860, to densely fill it, who would laugh and shout over such wickedness, in a poor weak-minded negro woman, in trampling upon the rights of the South with impunity. What could be more insulting, after having lost over $50,000 worth of property by that deluded negress, than for a large congregation of white and well educated people of Boston to endorse such an imposition on the Constitutional rights of the slave States? Had we any right to expect anything but a rebellion against a government that refuses to protect them against such outrages on their rights?

Suppose some negroes of the South had gone into Massachusetts, and run off $50,000 worth of horses, and landed them safe in South Carolina, and two or three thousand citizens of Charleston had collected and endorsed the operation by loud applause, and concealed the property from the owners, as the Bostonians did the forty negroes, what would the Yankeys have thought and said? Then suppose this game had been going on forty or fifty years without abatement, and even constantly on the increase, until millions of dollars worth of our horses had been run off, and when we should go for them, we should have found seven or eight of the slave States had passed laws that completely forestalled the Constitutional laws of the United States and made it next thing to impossible for us to recover our property; and in addition to that, they should have turned a large gang of negroes loose against our free white citizens, and mobbed them out of the State, or shot them dead on the spot, for going down there to recover their own. What should we have thought of it? Should we have

borne with it for fifty years? Now I ask all candid men to look this thing fair in the face, and
answer me the question, should we not have rebelled against the government long before this, if
the circumstances had been reversed as above?

It is all nonsense to say the South has done
any worse than what we should have done under the
same circumstances. The fact of the matter is: certain leading men in the free States have been aiming
to produce a rebellion for forty years, and had the
South not loved the Union a thousand times better
than the Melodeon Hall assembly, they would have
seceded ten or fifteen years ago. Every man and
woman who has studied human nature to any extent,
and had a thorough knowledge of the movements of
the abolitionists or disloyal people of the North or
free States, have been looking for this rebellion to
to take place since 1850; for as soon as the fugitive
slave law was passed by Congress, in that very year,
some of the free State Legislatures amended their
personal liberty bills so as to overthrow or defeat
its action, if possible. Several of the free States
rebelled at once by Legislative acts against the law
of the United States, passed for the security of the
South. This assertion is proved by the personal
liberty bills passed in several of the free States.
If you do not agree with me that this rebellion
was forced upon us by the free States rebelling
against the Constitution and laws of the United
States, I shall *yield all hope of* this great Union
ever being restored, and shall look for a military
despotism to be permanently established, that is

now only temporarily upon us. There were not only free State laws passed against the national laws, but associations were formed all over the free States to defeat the Constitutional laws of the United States, many of whom pledged their lives that those laws never should be executed in their respective neighborhoods; and employed the free negroes and fugitive slaves to aid them in the execution of their treasonable designs. And perhaps one-half of all New England pulpits constantly echoed the loudest declamations against those laws, and the rights of the southern people, attended with the foulest slanders ever heaped upon any people, by any man or set of men. I say, under these circumstances (in connection with the success of that very party in the national election of 1860, on a platform containing the clearest treason which the whole party was pledged to sustain at all hazards), we had no right to have looked for any thing else but a rebellion and a civil war. *We have brought it on ourselves by not doing "as we would be done by."*

I will say, in conclusion, that the South did not desire to rebel against the government of the United States, only so far as the United States officials refused to protect the slave States in their Constitutional rights by not making them equal with the free States. They only intended to rebel against the executors of the national government (and all others) who were chosen from that class of people who had declared themselves against the civil institutions of the slave States. As Seward (now

Secretary of State) said, "slavery must and shall be abolished, and *we can do it.*" Mr. Lincoln said one year before his nomination, that "this is a world of compensation, and he who would be no slave, must own no slaves. He who denieth freedom to others deserves it not for himself, and under a just God he shall not long retain it."

Between sixty and seventy republican members of both houses of Congress endorsed with their own signatures and by their own hand in 1859 the following sentiments:—

"*Ineligibility of slave-holders.* Never another vote to the trafficker in human flesh. *No* co-operation with slave-holders in politics. *No fellowship with them in religion.* No affiliation with them in society. No patronage to slave-holding merchants. No guestship to slave-waiting hotels. No fees to slave-holding lawyers. No employment to slave-holding physicians. No audience to slave-holding parsons. No recognition of pro-slavery men except as *ruffians, outlaws, and criminals.* Abrupt discontinuance of subscription to pro-slavery newspapers. *Immediate death to slavery*, if not immediate, unqualified proscription of its advocates during the period of its existence. A tax of sixty dollars on each and every negro in his possession at the present time, or at any intermediate time between now and the 4th of July, 1863," &c. &c.

This is a correct quotation from Helper's book, that was endorsed by nearly all the republican members of both Houses of Congress. This, taken in connection with the John Brown raid that was arranged to take place just at the right time to produce the greatest and most alarming effect upon the minds of the people of the slave States, did produce an alarm and consternation unsurpassed. Those republican members of both Houses of Congress who did not endorse Helper's book with their signatures, mostly defended those who did by all the powers they possessed. Let any candid man read the quotation above, then turn to another page of the same, and read the names of all the endorsers of those sentiments, and get a copy of the Congressional Globe of that Congress, and see how strong most all other republicans endorsed them in their speeches, and denounced all who dared to condemn those sentiments. This is not a thousandth part of what has been said and written against the Southern people by leading men of the North.

Now, think of human nature, and tell me, had we any right to expect anything but secession and rebellion in a country like this, where the government was with the people? And just as sure as God lives, we shall be humiliated, unless we speedily stop our rebellion and persecutions against the Southern State rights, and give them all that was conceded to them by the adoption of the Constitution in 1787. The Southern people have never interfered with us, nor with any Constitutional law of the free States. I know a few leaders of South Carolina attempted to nullify a national law in 1832, and all other Southern Statesmen nullified them, and would this day still do the same to all such, had we not nullified the Constitution of the United States and the laws of Congress passed for the protection of the lawful institutions of the slave States, by the laws of many of the free States. I ask candid Christian men to say whether we had a right to look for anything but national, State, and individual overthrow, and social ruin.

Whom has the present national executive called around him for his supporters and guides? Why, those very men who cordially endorsed the above declarations in Helper's book, and none others. Only think of it! Read the sentiments over again, and suppose yourself to have been a Southern slaveholder, and then remember that the very men who endorsed those sentiments had succeeded in 1860 in the election to the Presidency of one who had so recently declared in writing to that party, that he who refused to free his negroes should be made a slave himself, and that speedily. Could any family, social circle, or any volunteer association or combination either religious or political, hang together under such circumstances? Look at it and bring it home to yourselves. Remember that the President has surrounded himself with the most ultra of the endorsers of Helper, and exhausted his patronage with them; and will give no man an office of the most paltry kind, who refuses to endorse Helper entire; and by so doing he has laid a sickle with two edges at the root of the best and most wholesome government ever formed since the one for our first parents in Eden. Every Christian man and woman, who knows anything of human nature, knows that a volunteer government must be voluntarily sustained, or fall into ruin. But Mr. Lincoln was selected by the endorsers of the above declaration from Helper's book. Read over the quotation again, and in view of all these circumstances, say whether we had a right to have expected anything else than the threatening circumstances which are thickening before us.

Don't stop to accuse me of being a secessionist, traitor, disunionist, or a sympathizer with rebellion, for there is not the slightest shadow of truth in the declaration, unless rebellion against the abolitionism of the free States be treason.

Let the present administration and all other abolitionists, including the worshippers of the black goddess of liberty of Melodeon Hall, Boston, "do as they would be done by;" then we shall have peace throughout our great and glorious country, and the Union be restored in less than a month.

"Therefore all things whatsoever ye would that men should do to you, do ye even so to them; for this is the law and the prophets."

The words of Jesus Christ. Don't forget to notice the words in the text, " *all things whatsoever.*"

I wrote about two thirds of this chapter in 1860, prior to the Presidential election, and the balance soon after the firing upon the American flag by the rebels at Charleston. This is the reason why it first speaks of prospective; then the appearance of present strife between the North and South.

CHAPTER VIII.

Correspondence between Mrs. Mason of Virginia, and Mrs. Childs of Massachusetts. Mrs. Childs' Scriptural Quotations to sustain Abolitionism.

MRS. SENATOR MASON wrote Mrs. Childs last fall, soon after the John Brown raid in Virginia, on the impropriety of the interference by Northern people, with the lawful institutions of the South, to caution abolitionists not to place the southern people into such imminent danger, by trying to get up servile insurrections in the South. Mrs. Childs answers in a long letter, justifying herself in her ungodly insurrectionary work, in teaching southern slaves that they are as good as their masters, and should be insubordinate, and by charging the southern slaveholder with the most infamous and foul crimes that ever were charged to the hearts and hands of human beings. She quotes largely from Miss Grimkee, said to be a daughter of Judge Grimkee of South Carolina, who came North (she said) to get clear of the sound of the lash, and bemoanings of the tortured slaves, that did not cease to sound in her ears from six in the morning until late in the evening.

I have unfortunately lost fifteen pages of my manuscripts, in which I replied to the awful slanders

(338)

therein made; and as I have lost the letter of Mrs. Childs also, I have to restore them from memory. Therefore, can give only an outline of one or two stories. One was, that it was so common to whip slaves to death, that it was no more noticed than killing an animal, and that for the slightest disobedience. That it was an every day occurrence to strip men and women naked, and tie them up to a limb by the hands, and draw them up until they were on tiptoe, and then give them five hundred lashes, and let them stand in that position for many hours, after having bathed them with salt and water, and then give them five hundred lashes more, and salt them again, and let them hang for some hours more, and cut them down. They frequently died under this torture, and no account taken of it.

Again; after tying up men and women in the same position, they would take a large paddle made for the purpose, with holes through it, and paddle their naked bodies with it; every hole in the paddle would raise a blister, at each blow, until the whole surface of the body would be a complete jelly, and then they would throw on the salt and water, for still greater tortures; and that they frequently died under this mode of torture also, but no account taken of it by the authorities, and if they should happen to notice it, it would be passed over by a sham trial, and the parties discharged, or never call it up for trial.

I have no doubt some could be found in the North weak enough to believe such enormities in crime. And I might believe such stories under some cir-

cumstances. But no thoughtful person would believe this one told by Miss Grimkee. I have
travelled a great deal over this country, and have
not yet seen the party or parties who were willing to
amuse themselves at so dear a rate. Every man or
woman will count the cost of their pleasures. But
I do not believe that any man in his right mind
could enjoy such cruelties and tortures, even if it
cost them nothing in dollars and cents. And if the
believers in Miss Grimkee's book will take a cow
skin, and give a tree five hundred lashes as hard as
they can lay on, and then give it five hundred more
in the same strain, they will find themselves very
tired when done, and will conclude there is too
much labor for the trifling fiendish pleasure it might
be to them, when we remember that the people of
the South are not so fond of hard work. And that
such flogging may cost the owner $1500 each, for
he could get that sum for the slave at any time if
sound.

Is it possible, that any man or woman is fool
enough to believe any such stories? Who would
believe any one raised in the South could tell so
monstrous a falsehood? It would be hard for me
to decide which I would prefer to be guilty of: the
believing of such unnatural and foul slander, or to
be the originator of it. For I think I should commit as great a sin by one as the other. It is hard
for me to believe any man or woman credulous
enough to believe such monstrosities, and cannot
persuade myself they believe it when they tell it,
unless reason has been confused. And if such

things were sanctioned in the Bible, all such as Mrs. Childs and Miss Grimkee would take the opposite track, and deny the truth of all such statements. What, a man to purchase negroes at $1000, $1200, and $1500 each, and then whip them to death, or maim them so that they would be of no use whatever? Would you believe that a man would purchase a thousand dollar horse and then whip him to death, or allow it done? I thought Miss Grimkee's murderous stories were sufficient to murder themselves; though I am inclined to believe she only intended them as a burlesque on the monstrous abolition stories told and written by the thousand by other unscrupulous persons. And yet Mrs. Childs, of Wyland, Massachusetts, seizes upon them in her reply to Mrs. Mason, with an air of boast that would seem to a credulous mind to be sincere, and quoted the whole story, as though it had been the *Gospel of God our Saviour.*

I still have the part of this chapter embracing Mrs. Childs' quotation from Scripture to sustain herself and Miss Grimkee, and to condemn slaveholders, which is sufficient of themselves to satisfy any man that reads the Scriptures for the truths therein contained, that the abolitionists know better, and that with the fact that they care nothing for the suffering of the poor free people of color, either North or South. And the hypocrisy of the Rev. Dr. Cheever, and all others that are laboring to abolish slavery in this country, ought to satisfy any observing mind that it is not the slaves, or slavery, or slaveholders they care about; it is evident they have

29*

other objects in view than the abolition of slavery. Then what can their object be, you ask? It is for the abolition of the Constitution of the United States and the union of States, that the *"Liberator" says is in " league with hell."* (The Liberator is the organ of the abolition party.)

Why should they want to break up such a country and government as this that is the ante-chamber of heaven? I ask the inquirer, why did the devil say to Eve *" thou shalt not surely die ?"* was it not to prevent the Kingdom of God from ever being established on this planet, where he (the devil) had reigned, perhaps, many millions of years without a competitor? I answer that the abolitionists have the same object in view that the king of darkness had when he spoke to Eve, and said, " thou shalt not surely die." They hate God, and righteousness, and this government, because it is so God-like in its formations and aims, and (they) being the true Aping sons and daughters in spirit of the same old Apollyon. They take upon themselves every form of Christianity that they may effect the destruction of the Constitution of this great and glorious government, that he, their master, the devil, may reign supreme and without a rival on this globe of ours.

I do not wish to be understood to say that the abolitionists are the only infidels on this continent; for there is another set in the South called fire-eaters, who are the legitimate offspring of the abolitionists of the North, and they might be called the children of the devil, for they are co-workers with the abolitionists in the work of the destruction of this, the best government known under heaven. A government formed by God himself; for it was not in the heart of man to form such a one; and no one in the Convention of 1787 intended to make it just what it is. But He interfered, and would not allow them to agree on any other form, and no one of them seemed pleased with it at the time. Every article in it seemed to be the result of compromise between the conflicting parties in the convention. And they at one time came to a dead lock, being completely gamed, and could not move one inch further. Here was a perplexing dilemma. No one seemed to see light. Some proposed to give up and fall back on the Articles of Confederation. And they sat and looked at each other with despair. And it was only when they saw that they could do nothing else, that a proposition was made to send for Bishop White to come and offer up a prayer to Him who saw their dilemma, and held them fast. The good Bishop arrived with his Bible in hand, took his stand on the platform, opened the holy book, read a chapter, and called upon them to unite with him in prayer. He knelt down, and with uplifted hands and heart, he stated the case to the great God of the universe, and implored his mercy, his blessing, and his direction in the great dilemma they had fallen into, and to lead them in the path of Union and love. When he was done, every-thing seemed changed. The sunlight of hope broke through the dark cloud that had benighted them. The spirit of love was visible in each face, and the Christian spirit of compromise was felt in every heart. From that time, each member of the convention seemed disposed to yield in part for the sake of an agreement, that the Constitution might be formed and adopted for the sake "of a more perfect Union" than that of the Confederation which was nominal and without ligaments. And they had little or no trouble after that prayer was ended. They formed the Constitution; that is to the United States just what the Bible is to the Christian church. And woe be unto that party, or State, or confederation of States that shall attempt its destruction.

I have digressed too far from my subject, and will return after saying that if all the contending parties would now send for such a man as Bishop White, and in the same spirit that he was sent for, all contentions, disputes, and divisions would end in a week.

Some persons may think I use very severe language towards Mrs. Childs, Miss Grimkee, and other great apostles of abolitionism. But if they saw the consequences ahead as I do, they would say— say on, for God's sake, and awake the people that they may see the deep black gulf of civil or servile war that they are surreptitiously leading the nation into. But instead of giving us encouragement in foretelling the troubles and pointing out the way of escape to the rock of safety and universal *peace* and *union*, they cursed us with bitter curses, and told us we were hirelings of the democratic party, and were working under false pretences, to enable them to elect their candidate to the Presidency. Many of the old Whig, American, and the

People's parties having united themselves with the Republican party, who had dropt the name of aboli- tion, free soil, and anti-slavery, and taken the name of Republican; which was about as consistent as it would be for an African negro to drop his title and take that of Anglo-Saxon. It was surreptitiously taken, and for purposes of deception. There were a few thousand in the North who saw the trick, and refused to take a part in the union with the Repub- lican party; who in order to destroy and defeat our movements to save this country from civil or servile insurrection, war, and anarchy, or an everlasting despotism. We were accused of, and called every- thing bad, and nothing good.

I wrote this chapter long before the election of Mr. Lincoln, but by some mishap, as before stated, I lost the first fifteen or twenty pages of manuscript out of forty-four, and now rewrite a part of it, after the election, from notes I made at that time; there- fore, I cannot avoid alluding to facts as they then were, and as they now are. When we told the peo- ple what would be the result of the success of the republican party in the election of 1860, we were called fools—cursed fools—locofoco *lick spittles*, whom they hired to do their dirty work, negro traders, pro- slavers; and at least three hundred thousand men of the free States united in those declarations, and that to vote for the Constitutional Union party would only be voting for the locofoco party, when they knew in their hearts that it was not so; and the most of them only did it that they might succeed in electing a

President by an exclusive sectional vote of the free States against the slave States.

They were told by thousands of the best men in the free States what the result would be. But the leading Republicans only spit at us, and threw their dirty water upon us. And the same leaders after having secured the offices, and robbed the State treasury of this State of at least $500,000, and other corporations and associations of $500,000 more by extortion, and the sale of their votes and a signature with the State seal, turned around and charge us Union loving men with being secession-ists and rebels against this glorious government, that would be a heaven-like Union was it not for abolitionism; and we are so strongly threatened with the hemp, that I, for one, conceit I almost feel the rope around my neck, and simply for proposing measures to try to settle this question without a most inhuman, unnatural contest between brethren of the same family, when, once fully inaugurated and seated, will be one of the most bloody ever known on this earth; and when we have conquered them, it will be found that they are not subdued. And even if we should subdue them and bring them into the traces of the Union again, what will be the state of society? Will fifty years bring us back again to where we were prior to the John Brown raid in Virginia? See how demoralization has spread already.

Talk even to some of our Christian ministers on the subject, and see if they exhibit anything of the spirit that was in our Lord while he sojourned here

below. No; you will find them full of fight and
the spirit of revenge. I talked with one not long
since, who at once bristled up, his eye filled with
vengeance, and he said he would see the *Union flindered to atoms before he would yield one tittle from the
so-called* republican principles. So the Christian
church generally are becoming more or less demoralized by the contest even now. If that is the
case now, what will it be when this war shall be
ended by the force of. arms, and our fathers, our
sons, and our brothers have been slain? Shall we
love the South as we did before? Will there not
be a bitterness of feeling that will not be wiped out
only when this generation has been forgotten, and
every page of history obliterated that shall truly
record its scenes? Our children's children will be
more or less tainted with it. What a history it will
be to hand down to our children, and grandchildren,
and their successors. Of course they will take it
for an example or precedent; will it be such as our
Lord left on record for us?

The abolitionists want to break up the union of
States. I for one cannot now, nor ever shall, consent
to a division of these States into two separate kingdoms. All I asked for is, that all honorable and
Christian means should be used before force, to try
to settle the dispute, without a resort to arms. We
have a record to cleanse, which ought to be done before we ask our brethren to correct theirs. Let us
first "cast the beam out of our own eye, that we
may see clearly how to remove the mote from our
brother's eye." We have laws in a number of the

free States in direct opposition to the Constitution of the United States. This is enough to make the South to feel that she has the right to appropriate the whole instrument to herself, and to establish an independent government on its principles. After we have given them all their lawful rights under the Constitution, and then if they still refuse to co-operate with us in the Union, I would then say make them do it at any cost.

I have been told so often in debates on the dangers this Union was in, by ultra republicans, that *they would let the Union slide.* This was a very common expression through the campaign of 1860, and even a member of Congress from the third district, I am told, said that he would see this government split to atoms before he would yield one inch from the late republican platform. If this is the spirit that is to be shown by the party coming into power, terrible will be the result. It is not to be wondered at if the South should take the Constitution and appropriate it to their exclusive use, when members of Congress abandon it, and take the Chicago platform in preference, and say they would see the Constitution flindered to atoms before they would yield one principle of said platform.

Now in the name of heaven, what are we to expect, when we find that members of Congress have no respect for the Constitution of the United States, and take a party platform for the government of this nation, adopted by a set of office seekers, who are thirsting for power, place, and the public crib? May the Lord save the people! Slavery has been made the machine for all this. What a convenience is made of the old patriarchal institution when there is not one word found on Scriptural record or reason that shows slavery to be a moral evil.

Modern emancipationists say there are a great many sins not named in the Scriptures of truth that we know to be sins, and the sin of slavery was ne-glected or forgotten. I would ask if there is any *sin* named in the Scriptures of truth that is not condemned by the writers of the moral law? If slavery be a sin, it is the only one that was so ex-tensively spoken of without having one condemna-tory sentence passed against it. They say card-playing was not mentioned, and many other sinful games. But card-playing is not mentioned at all, and it is evident did not exist in the time of the apostles. But no one will pretend to say that slavery did not exist, even as far back as Noah, Moses, Abra-ham, Isaac, and Jacob, and notwithstanding this, there is not a single declaration or precept made directly or .indirectly against it. But swearing, or taking God's name in vain, lying, stealing, murder, adultery, fornication, and drunkenness, and all such are de-clared to be sinful and forbidden by the moral law, all of which were extensively practised in those days. For the evidence of which I will refer the reader to the first two chapters of this book.

St. Paul never told the owners of slaves that they must set them free, or that they could not enter into the Kingdom of Glory hereafter; not the slight-est intimation of the kind was given. Yet there was a moral connected with slavery as with every-
30

thing else. If a master treats his slaves as mere
beasts of burden, and refuses to look upon them as
men, he is a moral rebel, and will be held as such;
and God will judge him accordingly. But tells the
masters how they must treat their slaves, and re-
minds them that they have a master in heaven.
The master must remember his slaves have the
same infirmities caused by the same transgressions,
and in addition to that the servant has the curse
put upon Canaan to bear, caused by the sins of Ham
against his father Noah, therefore they are to be
bond-servants forever; and they merit the sympathy of their masters; and do not deserve to be
treated merely as beasts of burden but as an unfortunate man that is of great use to the world,
made up of flesh and blood, soul and body, just as
the white man is, and that it is sufficient to be a
slave without being ruled with a rod of iron. That
they must not be stinted in food and raiment, and
he must make them as comfortable as circumstances
will allow. The servants are affectionately told
that they must render unto their masters due service, that by so doing they please God, and that it
will be counted in righteousness. That their time
belongs to their masters and must not be wasted,
and if it is, it will be counted in unrighteousness.
So the duties of each are equally set forth by St.
Paul, and both will be held equally accountable
for their doings towards each other, in the great and
final day of reckoning.

But the Apostle nowhere teaches that the servant is to be placed on an equality with his master

in this world. But the supremacy of the master is set forth everywhere in the Bible. Yet the apostles of abolitionism teach another and different doctrine. They tell the slaves to be disobedient to their masters, and *not* render unto them good service, for none belongs to them; that their masters are *thieves*, murderers, and robbers, therefore run away, steal their masters' money, and their horses to make their escape, and if their masters attempt to stop them, kill them as they would a mad dog. When he gets him away from his master who respected him, and cared for him, and watched over him in sickness, dressed his wounds, and soothed his heart under pain, he leaves him among strangers in a cold climate, without money or friends, and he at once becomes an object of charity, but soon finds that there is no response. He is sick, and no doctor, no nursing mistress's soothing hand to wipe the sweat from his or her heated brow. No master's pocket to lean upon, nor wood pile to resist the piercing northwester. And that his hypocritical pretended abolition friend is always distant in the time of need. He is left to starve and die; and no one to drop a tear upon the plank, brick pavement, or virgin earth on which he may be stretched to die.

Now I ask which teaching of the two is the most *Christ-like, or human, and common sense-like?* Tell me which is the most merciful, the teachings of St. Paul, or that of the abolitionist? Throw off your prejudices; look the subject fair in the face; think of the common lot of the whole human family, and make up your mind from sound unbiassed reason

and common sense, and say which is the most God-
like, or which is the most demon-like. I must be
allowed to think every candid seeker of the truth
will say St. Paul's doctrine is the most Christian-
like and reasonable. I think it would be better for
him who takes so strong a stand against the Bible
and the United States government to be careful.

I have said enough about the usefulness of slaves
in previous chapters, to which I refer the reader.

Through the fall from Eden the whole earth was
corrupted, and the torrid and frigid zones, the blast-
ing winters, the burning summers, and all that is
unpleasant was produced through the sin of Adam,
and so, also slavery, for usefulness in the tropics.
Man is in fault, therefore he must submit to the
direful and variegated consequences. The African
race, as slaves, are one of the offsprings of sin, *but
not sin in itself*, and his lot is before him, and he
will have to submit. And if the Anglo-Saxon race
attempts to change the decrees of God, God may reverse the curse; and terrible will be the day when
negro slaves shall become the masters of those who
have interfered with God's arrangements among
men—better for him he had never been born. He
may look upon the highwayman, the pickpocket,
the burglar, the swindler, and the deceiver and robber of the widow and orphan with contempt, hatred,
and condemnation, and even feel that such persons
would be a blackening disgrace to a midnight assas-
sin's gallows ; but I look upon him as their equal
in crime, and will stand on the same ground in the
day of judgment, and perhaps on a higher scale of

crime than any others, for he just as much robs men of their own, as the pickpocket does when he slips his hand into his neighbor's pocket and steals his money and appropriates it to his own use. The slave is held by the same moral law to render faithful service to his master, not as a man-pleaser, but "with singleness of heart, doing the will of God." His time righteously belongs to his master, and if he wilfully wastes it, by neglecting to do duty to his master as a good servant, he robs his master of what belongs to him just as much as a pickpocket would in stealing another man's money, and is equally guilty before God, and will be so judged by the moral law, and he who persuades him that his master has no right to claim his labors, and tries to dissatisfy his mind with his condition as a slave, and persuades him not to render service, is worse than a thief, for he not only encourages robbing the master of what belongs to him, both legally and morally, but he is a traitor to the laws of his country.

How men professing Christianity, and say they are called by the Holy Ghost to preach the everlasting Gospel of God, can be modern abolitionists, I cannot understand. I can well see how infidels can be followers of Wm. L. Garrison, especially those who deny the Bible being the word of God, and know nothing of the nature of the negro; but those who embrace the Scriptures as the revelation of God, know they have no right given them in that book to declare slavery to be a sin against God. Therefore it is a new code of morals started up for which there is no warrant given in the Scriptures, and is as demoralizing as the doctrine of Joe' Smith, or those of the Spiritualists; and all such have done ten times the mischief to both church and state that could be done by the Mormons or Spiritualists. The Mormons separate themselves from all others, and unite themselves as a separate people, and openly declare Joe Smith a prophet and great high priest; but the abolitionists remain in good society, and there promulgate their doctrines of infidelity, and split up churches and good society, distract neighborhoods, and whole State Legislatures, and have now well nigh destroyed our national government, and are likely to plunge us into a civil war in the prospect of which they now exult, and say, better this should all take place a thousand times than that slavery should be allowed in any part of this country.

It was and is, as I have said before, a very common reply to the declaration that the Union was in danger, *"let the Union slide."* There was no expression more common through the late political struggle by republicans, than *"let the Union slide,"* and *"I would see this Union and government split into a thousand atoms, before I would yield one letter from the Chicago platform."* Leading men of the abolition stripe did thus reply whenever they were warned of the infinite danger the Union was in by the course they were pursuing in politics.

I have known professing Christians for more than twenty-five years, who have been laboring to obliterate the Constitution of the United States, that they might be able to separate this great Union, that the slaves of the South might clear themselves of their masters; and ministers of the Gospel have proclaimed those doctrines from the pulpit, and denounced slavery, and slaveholders as murderers in a most vehement and vindictive manner, right in the teeth of all the patriarchs, prophets, our Saviour, and the apostles, all of whom encouraged slavery and slaveholders, from Noah to St. Paul; and Paul never failed in a single instance to declare the right of the master to the earnings of their slaves, and plainly told the slaves that they must be diligent in their service to their masters. That in so doing they were doing service to God; that he must not waste his master's time, for he cannot do this and be a child of God, and not the least intimation given anywhere to the contrary.

I presume Dr. Adam Clarke's opinion will have some influence on most minds, or ought at least. He being a foreigner, and so much opposed to slavery, that he said there was no punishment adequate to the sinfulness of slavery. Please examine his opinions at full length on all the following passages of Scriptures. John Wesley said some hard things against slavery, but at the time he said it, it is certain he had little or no knowledge of American slavery, but had a full knowledge of the British slave trade, which was then the sum of all villainies. There is not a doubt but Wesley and Clarke both alluded to the cruelties of British slave trade, that was not prohibited but carried on by that government to an enormous extent at that time.

For a long while after Wesley passed his terrible anathema against slavery he ordained slaveholders in the West Indies, and set them apart for the ministry of Christ, and baptized their children, knowing them to be slaveholders, and that the children would be heirs to slaves, and not one single word expressed against it by Mr. Wesley..

Dr. A. Clarke, and all others whom I have consulted, show clearly in their commentaries that American and English slavery is the same as existed in the time of the apostles, and the great probability of its existence throughout all time. But they do not attempt to turn a single passage of Scripture to condemn it as a moral evil or sin against God, notwithstanding their great personal opposition to slavery, and when Dr. Clarke said there was no punishment adequate to the crime of slavery, he must have had reference to the British African slave trade, and not to common slaveholding, such as is legalized in our Southern States, and recognized by the Constitution of the United States. No true follower of our Lord, who reads the New Testament, and is capable of understanding it, will embrace this false code of morals, that slavery is a sin against God under all circumstances. Mrs. L. Maria Child, of Wayland, Mass., in her letter to Mrs. J. C. Mason, wife of Senator Mason, of Virginia, herein alluded to, quoted eighteen passages of Scripture in reply to, or as an offset to some very appropriate passages quoted by Mrs. Mason, in her letter to Mrs. Child. Mrs. Child is said to be a lady of uncommon talents, possessing great knowledge of the Scriptures, and is held up as the great champion of this new moral code of Garrison, Wright, Abe Kelley, and others.

Therefore it is evident, if she has produced nothing from the Holy Scriptures that proves slavery to be a moral evil, it cannot be done. I will now examine her quotations and see how much they prove.

She commences as follows:—Heb. xiii. 3d.

" Remember them that are in bonds, as bound with them; *and* them which suffer adversity, as being yourselves also in the body."

This certainly has no reference to common sla- very, but refers to those who were in prison for preaching the gospel of God our Saviour, and not the slightest allusion to common legal servitude, or involuntary labor, for an individual or master; but that they should feel for those in prison as they would have those to feel for them if circumstances between them were reversed. I will refer to A. Clark on this verse.

2d quotation, Isa. xvi. 3, 4 :—

"Take counsel, execute judgment; make thy shadow as the night in the midst of the noonday; hide the outcast; be- wray not him that wandereth.

" Let mine outcasts dwell with thee, Moab; be thou a co- vert to them from the face of the spoiler : for the extortioner is at an end, the spoiler ceaseth, the oppressors are consumed out of the land."

These two verses have not the slightest allusion to slavery as found in our Southern States. But Judah had been invaded by the Israelites, and defeated, slaying one hundred and twenty thousand men, nearly ruining his kingdom. When Judah began to recover, and becoming more prosperous, he seemed to be called upon to receive and protect the fugitive Moabites, that, perhaps, were scattered in the time of battle. I think any candid person will say there is no application to American slaves in this quotation, nor to fugitive slaves from the South. The context makes the text quoted clearly something else.

3d quotation, Deut. xxiii. 15, 16:—

"Thou shalt not deliver unto his master the servant which is escaped from his master unto thee. He shall dwell with thee *even* among you in that place which he shall choose in one of thy gates where it liketh him best: thou shalt not oppress him."

This quotation doubtless has an allusion to some sort of slavery. Dr. A. Clarke says this "is a servant who left an idolatrous master, that he might join himself to God and his people. *In any other case it would have been injustice to have harbored the runaway.*" It is clearly set forth in Scripture that a legal owner of a slave has a moral right to claim his service anywhere, and ought not to be prevented from taking him back to where the law made him a slave, and any laws passed by the free States to prevent a man from another State recovering his slave that has run away, is a crime. We have just as good a right to pass a law making it legal to take every Southern man's money from him that comes into our midst, and appropriate it to our own use; or seize their vessels and appropriate them to ourselves, or to protect a mob in doing it, as we have to protect them in rescuing a fugitive slave from his legal owner or his agent. The several quotations I have made from St. Paul's letters to the churches make this clear.

4th quotation, Prov. xxxi. 8–9:—

"Open thy mouth for the dumb in the cause of all such as are appointed to destruction. Open thy mouth, judge righteously, and plead the cause of the poor and needy."

Those verses, perhaps, allude to poor persons accused of crime, who have not the language to plead their own cause, nor the money to pay counsel. And no application to American slavery can be drawn from it by any course of reasoning whatever; for the slaves of the South are not oppressed, nor "dumb," nor "appointed to destruction," neither are they "poor and needy."

5th quotation, Isa. lviii. 1:—

"Cry aloud, spare not; lift up thy voice like a trumpet, and show my people their transgression, and the house of Jacob their sins."

This verse is also foreign to the subject, and contains no allusion whatever to the subject matter in dispute.

6th quotation, Col. iv. 1. I will refer the reader to what I have said on this text, in Chapter II. of this book.

7th quotation, I think will satisfy the reader that Mrs. Child was not honest, and has undertaken to do what she knew she could not do, that is, to support a bad cause by the Holy Scriptures. She quotes from Matt. xxiii. 8th and 10th. Why did she not quote the 9th also? I will quote the 8th, 9th, and 10th, and every reader will see clearly why she left the 9th out.

" 8th. But be ye not called Rabbi: for one is your Master, *even* Christ; and all ye are brethren.

" 9th. And call no *man* your father upon the earth: for one is your Father, which is in heaven.

" 10th. Neither be ye called masters: for one is your Master, *even* Christ."

I think comment on the above is not necessary, for every reader will see that there is no reference to common American slavery, and the teaching of our Lord in the above verses has no allusion to the relation of master and slave, but to the Head of the Church; that he himself is the Head, and no one else can be, and it would be treasonable for any one else to attempt to place himself there. Therefore they are forbid calling any one master besides Christ himself.

Why did Mrs. Child quote the 8th and 10th verses of the above chapter, leaving out the 9th? Simply because in the 9th we are forbidden to call any one our father upon the earth, because we have a Father in Heaven, which is Christ Jesus. How perfectly ridiculous it would be for us to forbid our children calling us father, because of the language of our Lord in the 9th verse, and it is just as ridiculous to say a slave should not agree that his owner is his master, and therefore refuse to call him master; and Mrs. Child has just as good a right to forbid the relation of parents and children under the moral law of the 9th verse, as she has to forbid the relation of master and slave, because of the precept contained in the 8th and 10th verses. And from those three verses it would be just as consistent with common sense or moral law, to establish a party or association to prevent parents from controlling their children, or to run the child off on an underground railroad from his or her parents, as it is to oppose the relation of master and slave from anything contained in the above quotation.

Children are held as the property of their parents by the civil law, and if there was not a civil law giving the parents the full control of their children until they are twenty-one years old, they could not compel them to remain with them for any period. In this country the age is fixed at twenty-one years for the parents to have full control of their children. In Spain I think the law fixes the maturity of the child at twenty-five years; and if I am not mistaken in some countries they are held by the civil law under the control of the parents a much longer period. The right of the parents to control their children and put their earnings in their own pocket, is sustained by the moral law, as well as the civil, and I believe by all the civilized nations of the earth; and I don't know any association that has ever been formed to oppose the moral and legal claim of the parent to the child during his minority.

Yet the 9th verse above, according to Mrs. Child's reasoning, forbids the lawful relation of parent and child, and that the child should not call any man his father; or in other words, should not submit to the government of its parents; for this doctrine is just as fully taught in the 9th verse as the anti-slavery doctrine is in the 8th and 10th verses. For slaves are held by the same human laws to the mas-

31

ters that children are to parents. And if the doctrine of the abolitionist is sustained in the 8th and
10th verses, then no parent can, under the moral law,
sustain a claim upon his children. And according
to the abolition creed and teachings, no civil law
should be respected when that law interferes with
the liberties of any part of the human race.

8th quotation, Matt. vii. 12 :—

"Therefore all things whatsoever ye would that men should
do to you, do ye even so to them ; for this is the law and the
prophets."

I don't know that I ever held a conversation on
the subject of slavery with an anti-slavery man who
did not boastingly quote this passage from our
Lord's exhortation. This certainly is one of the
most sublime precepts of the whole gospel code;
and if every man would only take it upon himself
to follow it, or be governed by it, troubles and
disputes between men would be at an end, and the
South would not be under the necessity of making
laws to prevent the abolitionists from stealing their
slaves, which would be a most glorious achievement
for this whole country.

The meaning of this text is obvious to every unprejudiced mind ; and every slave-holder would be
willing to enter into a covenant with all modern
abolitionists to keep this precept to the strictest
letter. But abolitionists seem to think that they
are not bound by this precept, and that it is a rule
that only works one way, and seem to forget, while
they require the masters to set their slaves all free
under this precept, that the masters are calling upon

the North under the same rule to let them alone. There is only one rule to explain this passage, and that is as follows :—" Do as you would be done by."

In order to decide righteously on this, you must reverse your circumstances and place yourself entirely where the slave-holder is, with all the concomitant circumstances through which he became, and still is, a slave-holder, and then ask yourself the question, *how would you have Northern abolitionists to treat you* on the subject. This is the only righteous rule by which we can come to a righteous application of this text.

This brilliant precept of our Lord ought to silence every true follower of His on this negro question, except those who, after having reversed situations with the slave-holder as above, and then makes up his mind that he would have the abolitionists to call him a thief, robber, and murderer, and run his slaves off to Canada on the underground railroad by $10,000 worth at a time. Even then that man has not the right, according to this precept, to call all the slave-owners robbers, thieves, and murderers, and to steal the slaves away from their masters, and then let them starve and die among strangers, because it would not be a reversion of circumstances as they are. I think all honest unbiassed minds will agree with me on this quotation.

I will respectfully refer Mrs. Child and her followers to the first five verses of this chapter, and hope they may be read with prayerful hearts.

Quotation 9th, Isa. lviii. 6 :—

" Is not this the fast that I have chosen ? to loose the bands of wickedness, to undo the heavy burdens and to let the oppressed go free, and that ye break every yoke ?"

Dr. A. Clarke says this verse alludes to the slave trade; but I cannot see any allusion to that business; for I do not believe a greater crime can be committed than to buy human beings, and drive them through the country like cattle, and sell them among strangers, without respect to the treatment they may receive. I believe men will be held responsible at the bar of God for all such crimes. When a man has more slaves than he can make useful to himself, it is his religious duty to choose a master for that servant, with the same care he would for his own child that he wanted to send away to learn a trade. He should know the man to be a good man to his servants. And if he sells his negro to whoever shall give the most for him, without respect to his future welfare, he will be held responsible to his Maker in the great day of accounts. The servant's future welfare should be looked to, and not the highest price that could be got.

I believe this verse has reference to the moral conduct of the Jewish nation; they made loud professions in public that they did not practise in private, and they were very overbearing and selfish. They perhaps taxed the people more than they were able to pay, and binding burdens, and laying them on other men's shoulders, too intolerable to be borne, such as they were not willing to touch with the end of their finger. And no doubt they extorted duties from surrounding tribes, over whom they had, by supreme power, extended their government, that was more than they could pay. The slave trade could not have been included in this precept.

Every American who has read the Declaration of our Independence, will have some idea of oppression, and the opium war between England and China some few years ago will have some idea of the bonds of wickedness alluded to in this verse.

Quotation 10*th*, Joel iii. 3.

" And they have cast lots for my people; and have given a boy for a harlot, and sold a girl for wine, that they might drink."

This verse certainly has reference to treatment to the Jews while in captivity. Their sons and daughters were traded off for wine and necessaries of life, and they were used for the most brutal purposes. It has no reference to common slavery of the Africans.

Quotation 11*th*, Prov. xiv. 31.

" He that oppresseth the poor, reproacheth his Maker; but he that honoreth him hath mercy on the poor."

This verse is so foreign from the question at issue, that I am surprised that Mrs. Child should have quoted it. The slaves in the southern States are not oppressed; they are fed and clothed, and the happiest people I have ever seen, and have no concern about the future of this world whatever. Their masters attend to all their business for them, and feed and clothe them. They are not oppressed, for they want nothing. But he who persuades the slaves to run away from their masters is a thief and an oppressor of the poor in the strictest sense of the word; and he that winks at it is no better.

31*

Quotation 12*th*, Prov. xx. 22, 23.

"Say not thou I will recompense evil; but wait on the Lord, and he shall save thee.

23. Divers weights are an abomination unto the Lord, and a false balance is not good." "

Whatever Mrs. Child sees in this quotation to condemn 'slavery or slaveholders she can enjoy it; I can see nothing touching the subject whatever. But I would advise Mrs. Child to be careful that she does not make out a false balance in her own favor, for such things are an abomination to the Lord.

Quotation 13*th*, Jer. xii. 13.

" They have sown wheat, but shall reap thorns; they have put themselves to pain, *but* shall not profit. And they shall be ashamed of your revenues, because of the fierce anger of the Lord."

This verse is quoted also to condemn slaveholding, but I think the reader will see that it condemns the abolitionists just as much as it does slaveholders and a great deal more.

Quotation 14*th*, Eph. iv. 28.

"Let him that stole steal no more; but rather let him labor, working with *his* hands the thing which is good, that he may have to give to him that needeth."

I think Mrs. Child ought to call the attention of all the underground railroad companies to this text, and urge the Christ-like precept home to their every heart; for if she can prevail upon all people, white and colored, male and female, North and South, to respect this text, we shall have but little trouble on the slave question. Remember that man stealing is a great crime against God.

Quotation 15*th,* Isa. x. 1, 2.

"Wo unto them that decree unrighteous decrees, and that write grievousness *which* they have prescribed,

• 2. To turn aside the needy from judgment, and to take away from the poor of my people, that widows may be their prey, and *that* they may rob the fatherless."

Those verses, no doubt, allude to certain laws made for extortion. "Unrighteous decrees and grievous writings" has reference to taking the laboring classes or surrounding tribes, that had been overpowered and made subjects, and then taxed them · more than they were able to pay, which is condemned throughout by the Holy Scriptures, but it is a very different thing from American slavery. A slave gets more for his work than any other laborers, generally; he has his board and clothes, and a house to live in, and his doctor's bills are all paid. His wages goes on while sick, even his nurse is paid, and all his tobacco bills, and taxes by his master; and he gets all this for doing · about one-half the work that any white man does that works at all; and it is no matter if he (the slave) has a wife and ten children, they are all supported by the master, and he does not have to work one minute more on their account, and he takes "no thought for to-morrow," and has no concern about the future. He is not called upon to provide for winter or lay up for sickness. The only concern he has is to prepare for death and judgment, and there is reason to believe that many thousands are laying up for themselves a very large fortune, where it cannot be taken from them. I will repeat that they are the happiest people I have ever seen. But oppressive rulers will have a large account to settle some day, and that is the class alluded to in the above quotation. They taxed them more than they were able to pay, and. many times, under all such oppressive laws, their personal tax takes nearly all the man's earnings, and he is left without support to his family. There is no such oppression in our southern States. But if abolitionists ever get the power, we shall learn by sad experience the meaning of this text.

Quotation 16*th*, Job xxx. 13, 14 :—

"They mar my path, they set forward my calamity, they have no helper.

"They came *upon me* as a wide breaking in of *waters ;* in the desolation they rolled themselves *upon me.*"

These verses had reference to war, no doubt, either to cutting off retreat, or obliterating the guides for an attack. The 14th has reference to a besieged city, a storm, fight or slaughter. There is not the slightest allusion to slavery such as is found in our Southern States.

Quotation 17*th*, Job xxii. 9, 10, 11 :—

"Thou hast sent widows away empty, and the arms of the fatherless have been broken.

"Therefore snares *are* around about thee, and sudden fear troubleth thee ;

"Or darkness *that* thou canst not see; and abundance of waters cover thee."

I think these verses have a strong allusion to dishonesty or hardness of heart, and would bear much harder upon the conduct of the underground railroad company, than upon a large majority of the slave-holders. There is nothing in the three verses that condemns slavery, or slave-holding.

Quotation 18*th*, James v. 4 :—

" Behold the hire of the laborers who have reaped down your fields, which is of you kept back by fraud, crieth: and the cries of them which have reaped are entered into the ears .of the Lord of Sabaoth."

The precept in this verse is a good one; it has reference to laborers, and clearly sets forth that it is not honest to hire a man, and after he has done your work, to withhold his wages. This is a sin of the worst kind. But a slave is not meant, for he gets the worth of his labor. If you pay the voluntary laborer all off at the end of every day, the four-fifths of them have to limit themselves in all the necessaries of life, and the larger the family the smaller the allowance, and a large majority of them cannot satisfy their wants, and with this they have constant fear of being thrown out of work, and their wives and children left to starve. But not so with slave laborers. They do not have to limit themselves in food, they have no fear of being out of employ, and it is no matter whether they have a wife and twenty children, or no wife and no children, their concern about this world is the same. Their bread is sure, and their pay certain.

I think it will be admitted that Mrs. Child was driven to some extreme for Scripture, to have made those quotations. To say the most of them, but little could be got out of them that has any refer-

ence whatever to the matter in dispute. They bare
on all alike, they are general terms and not special.
Mrs. Child is said to possess a talent far above
mediocrity, and yet she has not produced one single
passage that proves slavery (in the abstract) to be a
moral evil. Her friends say she is fully conversant
with the Scriptures from the beginning to the end;
yet after all her boast of "favorite passages of
Scripture" to sustain abolitionists, she has produced·
the above eighteen passages, and there is only one
or two of them that has any reference to slavery
whatever, and according to the best authorities they
just as much prove that it is wrong to hire a man,
and pay him his hire in silver, as it does to own
African negroes, and give them all the necessaries
of this life; and it proves no more. So clear are
the Scriptures on this subject that hundreds of extreme abolitionists have rejected them *entirely*, because they do not condemn slavery.

It is clear from the New Testament, that the
Christian church is not to interfere with civil questions. Her mission is to point out the ways of truth
and righteousness, and make men as happy in this
world as circumstances will permit, and to show
them the way to eternal glory. Therefore our Lord
refused to decide civil questions, as in Matt. xxii.
15th–22d. The Pharisees took council how they
might entangle our Lord, by getting him to decide a
question that did not belong to the Christian church
that was maturing at that moment. Whether they
knew the effect of getting him entangled in State
matters or not, the great wicked spirit did know

that it would overthrow the mission of the Saviour of the world; and our Lord knowing that, he carefully avoided giving his opinion on the subject.

" The Pharisees sent unto him their disciples with the Herodians, saying, Master, we know that Thou art true, and teachest the way of God in truth, neither carest Thou for any *man:* for Thou regardest not the person of man. Tell us therefore, What thinkest Thou ? Is it lawful to give tribute unto Cesar, or not ? But Jesus perceived their wickedness, and said, why tempt ye me, *ye* hypocrites? Show me the tribute money. And they brought unto him a penny. And he said unto them Whose is this image and superscription ? They say unto him Cesar's. Then saith he unto them, render. therefore, unto Cesar the things which are Cesar's; and unto God the things that are God's."

Now it seems clear to my mind that our Lord refused to answer this question directly, to show us that the church has nothing whatever to do with civil institutions, that do not interfere with the rights of conscience, and allow all men to worship God according to the dictates of their own judgments. And so far as I have learned, the masters of the Southern slaves have not at any time attempted to control the conscience of their slaves, or forbid them to serve the Lord, in their own way; and a large majority of the masters pay liberally to have the gospel preached to their slaves each week; and I believe they are not charged with dictating to their conscience, and the slaves are not required to work on the Sabbath day, and are taught that they should worship God according to the dictates of their own conscience.

I will refer the reader to Paul's Epistle to Philemon, and I hope Mrs. Child and all other abolitionists will read the whole chapter with attention.

It seems that while Paul was imprisoned in Rome for preaching Christ, he did not cease to preach the gospel; and under his preaching, a servant by the name of Onesimus was converted by Paul, and becoming a true child of God, he made it known to his spiritual father, "St. Paul," that he was a fugitive slave from the service of one Philemon. Onesimus became a great comforter to St. Paul, after his (Onesimus) conversion. Yet as soon as Paul learned that Onesimus was a fugitive slave, and had a Christian master, he rested not until he got Onesimus off to his master Philemon, with the epistle alluded to; though he needed Onesimus much to wait on him, but he could not consent to keep him there without his master's (" Philemon") permission. Therefore he started him with the letter to his master, and by that letter he intercedes between Philemon and his fugitive servant Onesimus, thereby to get Philemon to pardon his servant, and if he would do so, and take him back to his service, he (Paul) would pay for whatever Onesimus might have taken from his master previous to his flight. See 18th verse. "If he hath wronged thee, or oweth *thee* aught, put that on mine account."

How does this contrast with modern abolitionism, the underground railroad, the negro *female conductor*, and the Boston congregation alluded to in a previous chapter.

In reference to the church, I think this epistle does settle the question, and clearly demonstrates that the church has nothing to do with slavery, only to see that her members, if slaves, should be faithful to their masters, and the masters to their slaves. The teachings of the New Testament are too clear to be misunderstood, and I believe every good man, who seeks for truth only, will understand it so; and instead of making trouble between master and slave and running the slaves off on the underground railroad, and persuading them to steal their master's property, or kill him if necessary to make their escape, will teach the slaves how they should best serve their masters, and be the most useful to them; that they cannot be true Christians, and wilfully neglect one duty to their masters. This was left on record by St. Paul; therefore he who teacheth otherwise is an infidel; and I think I have proved satisfactorily to every candid Christian man and woman that every circumstance connected with the African race down to the present day, fully sustains the preaching of St. Paul and proves that the descendants of Canaan were to be slaves or subordinates through all time, from Noah's declaration after the flood, over 4200 years ago, that Canaan should be a *"servant of servants to his brethren."*

APPENDIX.

I WAS charged with deception soon after the John Brown raid in Virginia, for my opinions, and was called a fool when I said the success of the abolitionists to national power would produce a civil war in this country, and destroy the Union of States.

This I said in the winter of '59 and '60· How stands the matter on this the first day of October 1862 ? I add this little appendix merely as a re-membrancer. I am not disappointed in the result, neither do I think anybody else is who had given human nature and abolitionism an impartial study.

I will now close this volume by giving two letters from the pen of the Hon. Wm. Bigler of Pennsyl-vania, who was called upon in writing, by a number of his constituents, for the information given in the letters; I hope they may be examined with scruti-nizing attention, for they are written by one who knew the facts.

LETTER I.

CLEARFIELD, September 29, 1862.

GENTLEMEN : I am in receipt of your letter, and with plea-sure proceed to comply with your request. In doing this I shall endeavor to be brief, though it must be obvious that any thing like a full history of the proceedings of the United States Senate on the resolutions familiarly known as the Crittenden Compromise, and the occurrences incident thereto, cannot be compressed into a very short story.

You can all bear me witness that in the addresses I have made to the people, since my retiracy from the Senate I have not sought to press this subject on their consideration in any party light—I have held that the government and country must be saved, no matter whose folly and madness had im-perilled them—that we should first extinguish the flames that are consuming our national fabric, and afterwards look up and punish the incendiary who applied the torch; but as the subject has been brought before the community by a distin-guished member of the Republican party, for partisan ends, and statements made inconsistent with the record, it is eminently proper that the facts—at least all the essential facts —should be given to the public.

It is not true that some republican members of the Senate supported the "Crittenden Compromise" and some opposed it.

They opposed it throughout, and without an exception. Their efforts to defeat it were in the usual shape of postponements and amendments, and it was not till within a few hours of the close of the session that a direct vote was had on the proposition itself.

On the 14th of January they cast a united vote against its consideration, and on the 15th they did the same thing, in order to consider the Pacific railroad bill.

But the first test vote was had on the 17th day of January, on the motion of Mr. Clark, of New Hampshire, to strike out the Crittenden proposition and insert certain resolutions of his own, the only object manifestly being the defeat of the former. The yeas and nays on this vote were as follows:—

Yeas—Messrs. Anthony, Baker, Bingham, Cameron, Chandler, Clark, Collamer, Dixon, Doolittle, Dirkee, Fessenden, Foot, Foster, Grimes, Hale, Harlan, King, Seward, Simmons, Sumner, Ten Eyck, Trumbull, Wade, Wilkinson, and Wilson —25.

Nays—Messrs. Bayard, Bigler, Bragg, Bright, Clingman, Crittenden, Fitch, Green, Lane, Latham, Mason, Nicholson, Pearce, Polk, Powell, Pugh, Rice, Saulsbury, and Sebastian —23.

So Mr. Clark's amendment prevailed, and the Crittenden proposition was defeated. On the announcement of this result the whole subject was laid on the table.

This was the vote on which some six or eight Senators from the Cotton States withheld their votes, and of this I shall speak hereafter.

It is true that, within a few hours after these proceedings, as though alarmed about the consequences of what had been done, Senator Cameron moved a reconsideration of the vote by which the Crittenden proposition had been defeated.

This motion came up for consideration on the 18th, and to the amazement of everybody not in the secret, Senator Cameron voted against his own motion, and was joined by every other Senator of his party. The vote is recorded on p. 433 of 1st vol. *Congressional Globe*, and is as follows:—

Yeas—Messrs. Bayard, Bigler, Bragg, Bright, Clingman, Crittenden, Douglas, Fitch, Green, Gwin, Hunter, Johnson of Arkansas, Johnson of Tennessee, Kennedy, Lane, Latham, Mason, Nicholson, Pearce, Polk, Powell, Pugh, Rice, Saulsbury, Sebastian, and Slidell—27.

Nays—Messrs. Anthony, Baker, Bingham, CAMERON, Chandler, Clark, Collamer, Dixon, Doolittle, Fessenden, Foot, Foster, Grimes, Hale, Harlan, King, Seward, Simmons, Sumner, Ten Eyck, Wade, Wigfall, Wilkinson, and Wilson—24.

This vote was regarded by many as conclusive against the

Crittenden proposition, for the reason that the Republican Senators, after full deliberation and consultation, had cast a united vote against it. I shall never forget the appearance and bearing of that venerable patriot, John J. Crittenden, on the announcement of this result. His heart seemed full to overflowing with grief, and his countenance bore the unmistakable marks of anguish and despair. The motion of Senator Cameron to reconsider had inspired him with hope—strong hope ; but the united vote of the Republican Senators against his proposition showed him too clearly that his efforts were vain.

The final vote was taken directly on agreeing to the Crittenden proposition on the 3d of March—one day before the final adjournment of Congress—and is recorded on p. 1405 of the Congressional Globe, second part. On this vote every Democrat and every southern Senator (including Mr. Wigfall, who voted against the reconsideration of Mr. Clark's amendment), voted for the proposition, and *every Republican against it.*

As for the Cotton State Senators who withheld their votes on the 16th of January, so that Mr. Clark's amendment might prevail, I have certainly no apology to make for their mischievous and wicked conduct on that or any other occasion, but if they are blameworthy for withholding their votes, and not sustaining the Crittenden proposition, what shall we say of the Republican Senators who, at the same time, cast a solid vote against it, as I have already shown ? It was no half way business with them—they aimed directly at its final defeat. Some of the southern Senators, on the other hand, who had withheld their votes on the 16th (Messrs. Slidell, Hemphill, and Johnson of Arkansas), by the 18th had repented their error, and cast their votes to reconsider and revive the Compromise proposition ; but the Republicans persisted in their hostility to the end.

Nor is it true that the votes of the Cotton State Senators with those of all the other southern Senators, and those of all the northern Democrats, could have saved and secured the Crittenden Compromise. They could have given it a majority, but everybody knows that the Constitution requires a vote of two-thirds to submit amendments to the Constitution for the ratification of the States. These could not be had without eight or ten Republican votes. But suppose the Constitution did not so require—what could it have availed to have adopted a settlement by a mere party vote ? It was a compromise between the two sections that the exigencies required. The Republican was the dominant party in the North, and no compromise or adjustment could be successful, either in the

Senate or before the people, without their active support. They constituted one of the parties to the issue, and it would have been folly—worse than folly—to have attempted a settlement without their sanction and support before the country.

But no one can misunderstand the real object of the Republican orators in parading the fact that six or eight Southern Senators had, at one time, withheld their votes from the Crittenden proposition. It is to show that the South was not for it and did not desire a compromise, and hence the Republicans are not responsible for the horrible consequences of its failure. On this point the testimony is very conclusive, and I shall give it at some length, please or displease whom it may. If Republicans choose to take the responsibility of saying that they were against the proposition and determined to make no settlement, however we may lament their policy, no one could object to that position, as matter of fact; but they will forever fail to satisfy the world that the South was not fairly committed to a settlement on the basis of the Crittenden proposition, or that the Northern Democrats would not have compromised on that ground had they possessed the power to do so. I am aware that there are plenty of Republicans who would still spurn to settle with the South on such conditions, as there are also radical fanatics who would not take that section back into the Union even on the conditions of the Constitution. They certainly can have no complaint against my views and sentiments.

When Congress assembled in December, 1861, it was obvious to every one who was at all willing to heed the signs of the times, that the peace of our country was in imminent peril, the natural consequences of a prolonged war of crimination and recrimination between the extreme and impracticable men of the North and the South. The anxious inquiry was heard everywhere—" What can be done to allay the agitation and save the unity and peace of our country ?" Amongst those who were willing to make an effort to compromise and settle, regardless of sectional, party or personal considerations, consultation after consultation was held. The first great task was to discover whether it was possible to bring the South up to ground on which the North could stand. Many and various were the propositions and suggestions produced. But it was finally concluded that the proposition of the venerable Senator from Kentucky (Mr. Crittenden) was most likely to command the requisite support in Congress and before the people. These, together with all others of a similar character, were referred to a select committee, composed of the following Senators :—

Messrs. Crittenden, Powell, Hunter, Seward, Toombs, Doug-
32*

las, Collamer, Davis, Wade, Bigler, Rice, Doolittle, and Grimes—five Southern men, five Republicans, and three Northern Democrats. The Southern and Republican Senators were regarded as the parties to the issue, and hence a rule was adopted that no proposition should be reported to the Senate as a compromise unless it received a majority of both sides. All the Southern Senators, save Mr. Davis and Mr. Toombs, were known to favor the Crittenden proposition. On the 23d of December, this proposition came up for consideration, and it became necessary for Messrs. Davis and Toombs to take their positions in regard to it, and I shall never forget the substance of what both said, for I regarded their course as involving the fate of the compromise. Mr. Davis said, "that for himself the proposition would be a bitter pill, for he held that his constituents had an equal right with those of any other Senator to go into the common Territories, and occupy and enjoy them with whatever might be their property at the time; but nevertheless, in view of the great stake involved, if the Republican side would go for it in good faith he would unite with them." Mr. Toombs expressed nearly the same sentiments, and declared that his State would accept the proposition as a final settlement. Mr. Toombs also, in open Senate, on the 7th of January, used the following language:—

"But although I insist on this perfect equality in the territory, yet when it was proposed, as I now understand the Senator from Kentucky to propose, that the line of 36–30 shall be extended, acknowledging and protecting our property on the south side of that line, for the sake of peace—permanent peace, I said to the committee of thirteen, as I say here, that with other satisfactory provisions I would accept it." [Page 270, *Cong. Globe*, 1st.]

In addition to my own testimony of what occurred in the committee of thirteen, I present extracts from speeches of Mr. Douglas and Mr. Pugh, bearing directly on this point:—

On the 3d of Jan., in the course of an elaborate speech, Mr. Douglas used the following language:—

. "If you of the Republican side are not willing to accept this nor the proposition of the Senator from Kentucky, pray tell us what you will do? I address the inquiry to the Republicans alone, for the reason that in the committee of thirteen, a few days ago, EVERY MEMBER FROM THE SOUTH, including those from the Cotton States [Messrs. DAVIS and TOOMBS] *expressed their readiness to accept the proposition of my venerable friend from Kentucky, as a final settlement of the controversy*, if tendered and sustained by the Republican members. Hence the sole responsibility of our disagreement, and the only difficulty in the way of an amicable adjustment, is with the Republican party." These remarks were made, as I well remember, before a very full Senate—in the presence of nearly, if not quite . all the Republican and Southern Senators, and no one dare to dispute the facts stated.

Mr. Pugh on the 2d day of March, in the course of a very able speech, remarked:—

"But suppose that Senator does promise me a vote on the Crittenden proposition : 1 have followed him for three months; I have followed my honorable friend from Kentucky [Mr. Crittenden] for three months ; I have followed my friend, the Senator from Pennsylvania, [Mr. Bigler] for three months ; I have voted with them on all these propositions at a time when there were twelve other Senators in this chamber on whose votes we could rely; and what came of it all? Did we ever get a vote on the Crittenden proposition? Never. Did we ever get a vote on the peace conference proposition? Never. Did we ever get a vote on the bill introduced by the Senator from Pennsylvania [Mr. Bigler] to remit these propositions to a vote of the people? Never. They were not strong enough to displace the Pacific railroad bill, which stood here and defied them. in the Senate for more than a month. They were not strong enough to set aside this plunder bill you call a tariff. They were not strong enough to beat a pension bill one morning. For three long months have I followed the Senator and others, begging for a vote on these questions; never can we get it; never; and now I am to be deluded no further; and I use that word delusion certainly in no unkind sense to my friend.

"The Crittenden proposition has been endorsed by the almost unanimous vote of the Legislature of Kentucky. It has been endorsed by the Legislature of the noble old Commonwealth of Virginia. It has been petitioned for by a larger number of the electors of the United States than any proposition that was ever before Congress. I believe in my heart, to-day, that it would carry an overwhelming majority of the people of my State, aye, sir, and of nearly every other State in the Union. Before the Senators from the State of Mississippi left this Chamber, I *heard one of them, who now assumes, at least, to be President of the Southern Confederacy, propose to accept it, and to maintain the Union, if that proposition could receive the vote it ought to receive from the other side of this Chamber.* Therefore, of all your propositions, of all your amendments, knowing, as I do, and knowing that the historian will write it down, at any time before the first of January, a two-thirds vote for the Crittenden resolutions in this Chamber would have saved every State in the Union but

South Carolina. Georgia would be here by her representatives, and Louisiana also—those two great States which, at least, would have broken the whole column of secession."

Mr. Douglas, at the same time said in reply, " I can confirm the Senator's declaration that *Senator Davis himself, when on the committee of thirteen, was ready at all times to compromise on the Crittenden proposition. I will go further and say that Mr. Toombs was also ready to do so.*"

But if this testimony were not in existence at all, do we not all know that the great State of Virginia endorsed this proposition and submitted it to the other States as a basis of a final adjustment and permanent peace. It was this basis on which that State called for the Peace Conference which assembled soon thereafter.

It was also endorsed by almost the unanimous vote of the Legislature of Kentucky, and subsequently by those of Tennessee and North Carolina. But it is useless to add testimony. The Republican members of the Senate were against the Crittenden proposition, and the radicals of that body were against any and every adjustment. When the Peace Conference had assembled, and there was some hope of a satisfactory settlement, it is well known that Mr. Chandler, Mr. Harlan and others urged their respective Governors to send on impracticable fanatics as Commissioners in order to defeat a compromise.

In what I have said I have not intended to extenuate or excuse the wickedness of the secessionists. Bad and impolitic as was the policy of the Northern radicals, it furnished no sufficient reason for secession, rebellion, and war; but I believed most sincerely then as I do now, that the acceptance of Mr. Crittenden's proposition by one-third of the Republicans in Congress, at the right time, would have broken down secession in nearly all the States now claiming to be out of the Union; and it might have been accepted without any sacrifice of honor or principle. So far as the common territory of the United States was concerned, it proposed an equitable partition, giving the North about 900,000 square miles, and the South about 300,000. No umpire that could have been selected would have given the North more.

If, then, it was a material interest and value we are contending for, it gave us our full share; if it was the application of a political principle the Republicans were struggling for, it allowed the application of their doctrine to three-fourths of the estate that belonged to all the States and all the people. It expressly excluded slavery from 900,000 square miles, and allowed it in the remaining 300,000. The Republicans, it is true, had just elected a President, and were about to take possession of the Government; but still the popular vote in the several States showed that they were over a million of votes in the minority of the electors of the United States. Being a million in the minority, if they secured the application of their principles to three-fourths of all the territory, was that not enough? Could they not on that have boasted of a great triumph?

For a time these arguments and considerations seemed to have weight with the more moderate and conservative of the Republican Senators. Indeed at one time I had strong hopes of a settlement. But the radicals rallied in force, headed by Mr. Greeley, and the current was soon changed. We were then met with the argument that the people, in the election of Mr. Lincoln, had decided to exclude slavery from all the territory, and that the members of Congress dare not attempt to reverse that decision. We then determined to go a step further and endeavor to overcome this obstacle; and it was to this end, after consultation with Mr. Crittenden and others, that I myself introduced a bill into the Senate providing for taking the sense of the people of the several States on the Crittenden proposition, for the direction of members of Congress in voting for or against its submission for the ratification of the States, as an amendment to the Constitution.

This was an appeal to the source of all political power, and would have relieved the members of all serious responsibility. The vote of the representative would have been in accordance with the votes of his constituents, either for or against the proposition. The only objection made was that it was somewhat irregular and extraordinary: But the same men could not make that objection at present. Too many extraordinary things have since been done by their chosen agents. I believed with the Senator from Ohio, as I believe still, that the proposition would have carried a majority in nearly all the States of the Union, but it shared the fate of all other efforts for settlement. Would to God our country was now in the condition it then was, and that the people could be allowed to settle the controversy for themselves under the lights of eighteen months' experience, of war and carnage, and countless sacrifices of national strength and character.

Very truly, your obedient servant.

WM. BIGLER

LETTER II.

CLEARFIELD, PA., November 1, 1862.

MY DEAR SIR : In reply to your favor of the 30th ultimo, I have to say that you have been rightly informed. I do not intend to be a candidate for United States Senator at the coming election, and have so expressed myself to friends on all proper occasions. I have a number of reasons, public and private, for this course, one of which is that the Eastern and Northern sections of the State, make special claim to the Senator, at this time, on the ground that we have one in the West recently elected, and cannot reasonably claim both for so long a term.

The other question you ask, "what can be done to save the country," is not so readily answered. The usual response is, God knows. Few of our best thinkers seem to have any clear views on the question; and it is not even certain that the Administration at Washington has a well defined policy to that end. I have some thoughts on the subject which I do not hesitate to give you. They may seem to you crude, and on some points even novel and startling; but they are the result of some reflection.

The sword is the only agency at work. But the sword cannot do all. It is an agent of destruction. It can tear down but cannot build up. It may chastise and silence the rebels in the field; but it cannot make a union of States; it cannot restore confidence and fraternity amongst a people estranged and alienated from each other. If the war was against the leaders in the South only, as many at the beginning supposed, then the sword might put them down and the masses could return to their allegience. But the conflict turns out to be with the whole mass of the people within the revolting States, old and young, male and female, numbering many millions. With such a power, sooner or later, we shall have to treat and negotiate. The sword alone will never restore this people to the Union.

You well know that when the present calamities menaced the nation, I was for peaceful means to avert the blow. Then our present suffering and sacrifices could have been avoided, and as I believe, the unity of the States preserved for generations, without the sacrifice of principle, or honor, or conscience on either side; passion, prejudice and fanaticism only would have been required to give way; and I still think, nay, I am sure that other means beside war are necessary to save our country—our whole country—from present afflictions and impending ruin.

I know how easy it is to talk about war and carnage; about stratagetic positions and brilliant victories; about the prompt subjugation of the South by the North; even how pleasant it may be to some to float in the common current of excitement and passion; and especially how unpleasant, if not unsafe it is to stem this tide. But the time is coming, if it be not now, when the public man who would render his country a substantial service must do this. He must look at the whole work before us, and strike for the right regardless of clamor or consequences to himself personally.

We have had war for eighteen months, the like of which the world has seldom witnessed before. To sustain which a national debt of startling magnitude, which must hang over posterity long into the future, has already been created, and more than a quarter of a million of invaluable lives sacrificed, on the Union side alone, in addition to the many thousands that have been crippled or diseased for life; and yet but little, if any substantial progress has been made in the good work of re-establishing the Union, or even of maintaining the Federal authority within the revolting States. Has not then, the experiment of war, as a means of extricating the country from its present deplorable condition, been already tested—tested at least to such an extent as to prove its utter futility unaided by other means.

It was a happy thought of President Lincoln, expressed in his Inaugural, that if we went to war we could not fight always; "and when, after much loss on both sides and no gain on either, you cease fighting, the identical old questions as to terms of intercourse are again upon you." This prophetic and highly significant sentiment shows that even Mr. Lincoln, before the war began, anticipated the time, in case it did begin, when it would be necessary to put the sword to rest, at least for a season, in order to resume the identical old questions about intercourse and settlement. It does not seem to have occurred to him that the sword could do the whole work, but that inevitably we would have to come back to the original point to compromise and settle. If then, we cannot fight always; what amount of fighting is necessary to render it proper to prepare to cease, or suspend in order to consider terms of reconciliation. There has already "been much loss on both sides and no gain on either," and whilst the time to cease fighting may not be yet, the period has surely come when other means besides the sword should be employed in the effort to save the government and country. Certainly the object of the war, and the extent to which it is to go, should be definitely known to the country. If it be intended to subjugate the States in rebellion, and hold them, not as States in the Union, but as conquered provinces, then the sword must be kept in constant motion, and war and carnage must be the order of the day. New levies and fresh supplies may be properly raised, for it will require a formidable army in each of the seceded States to execute and maintain this scheme. If extermination be the object, then the sword should have unrestrained license to deal death and destruction amongst the rebels, in all parts of their country, regardless of sex, or age, or condition. But neither of these purposes, if practicable, would re-establish the Union, although there might remain a Union composed of certain States. But, when the Union is re-established, the South as well as the North must be in it; the family of States must exist as heretofore, else it will not be the Union about which we have talked so much and for which so many brave men have offered up their lives. The physical triumph of the North over the South in the field, as the North in the end, may triumph, is not the whole of the task. The States must be brought together; the feelings of the people of both sections must be so constrained and moderated, that they can fraternize and live together, else the Union is gone forever. To subjugate the Southern States and so hold them, could subserve no good end for either section, and in no way, that I can discover, advance the welfare of the North; for so long as the South was so held their hate of the North would increase, and whilst the North so held the South, it could do but little else; meanwhile its material interest must languish and die. But, in addition, such a work is utterly inconsistent with the genius of our institutions and could scarcely fail to lead to their utter perversion and ultimate overthrow, adding to the calamities of disunion, the sacrifice of free government. Conquest and empire, however magnificent, could not compensate for such a loss.

To exterminate the inhabitants of the South, would be a deliberate emasculation of the Union, rendering its reconstruction at once impracticable and hopeless, and involve a work of barbarity, from which the Northern people would shrink in horror. The existence of the Southern States, in some form, with their inhabitants, and on some terms of intercourse, is highly essential, nay, I will say, indispensible to the welfare of the North. I am, therefore against extermination, and against the policy of holding the Southern States as conquered provinces. This ground can be so easily maintained on purely selfish considerations for the North, which will occur to all, that I need not trouble you with their presentation on this occasion. I am for re-establishing the Union as it was, or making a Union as similar as practicable, the States to be equals, and to be sovereign to the extent the States now are, each to have and enjoy such domestic institutions as it may choose, and, were I in Congress I should sustain that measure of war and that only, that would clearly tend to the accomplishment of these ends; but no war of subjugation or extermination.

I know it may be said in reply to all this, then let the Southern people lay down their arms and come back into the Union, and all will be right again. Would to God they could be induced so to do! There is no guarantee in reason that I would not be willing to grant them. But do we see any indications of such a return to reason and duty? I can see none, and I expect to see none, so long as the sword is unaccompanied by agents for settlement and peace. When our army went to Mexico it was accompanied by a peace commission in order to embrace the earliest opportunity for settlement. In God's name, I would ask, should we do less when engaged in a war amongst ourselves? It is idle, and worse than idle, to delude ourselves about the nature of the conflict in which we are engaged. We cannot make a Union by force alone, though we may triumph over the South in the field, and we may as well look the complications square in the face as not. The first question is, do we intend—do we desire, to have all the Southern States back into the Union, on the terms of the Constitution? If we do, then it is seen that they are to be the equals of the Northern States, in rights, sovereignty, and dignity. Does any one believe that such a relation can be established and maintained by the sword alone? Should a certain number of the States subjugate and humiliate the others, then they could not live together as equals and friends, for the subjugated are always the enemies of the subjugators. When all the States, therefore, resume their former relations, or new relations of Union and intercourse, it must be the act of all, if the settlement is to be complete and permanent.

I have heard a great deal about patching up a dishonorable peace—about the humiliation and disgrace to the North, involved in any and every proposition for settlement, and there is nothing that is said about the affairs of the country for which I have less respect. It is even held by some that he is a disloyal citizen who seeks to re-establish the Union by other means than the sword. How absurd! The sword has been at work; its agency has been tested—vigorously and terribly tested, and how stand the States now that should be in harmony? The sad response is, where they were when the war began, arrayed in grim and relentless hostility.

33

Then, why spurn other agencies to aid in the good work? In the words of Mr. Lincoln we cannot fight always, and we should not fight longer, unless we can do so as a means of ultimate union and permanent peace.

What, then, can be done? and I regret that all that should be done cannot be accomplished promptly. The States now in the Union should be in Convention, or have delegates ready to go into Convention, in order to reaffirm the present constitutional relations amongst the States, with explanations on controverted points, or to make such new relations as may be found necessary to bring together and retain all the States. The State Legislatures could petition Congress for such a Convention, as provided by the Constitution, and Congress could make the necessary provisions for it, before the close of the coming session. Such State legislatures as do not meet in the regular order could be specially convened; and when the necessary number of States petition, it is obligatory on Congress to comply. The body thus constituted would be competent to adjust and settle all the complications which now beset us. In the midst of war, then, we should be prepared to make peace. Whereas, when the time comes for settlement, in the absence of such a body, it might be found that we have no competent authority in existence to do the things that may be necessary. Neither Congress nor the Executive, nor the two together, have rightful authority to change the old or to make new relations amongst the States. Congress may submit amendments to the Constitution for the ratification of the States, and I believe the present calamities of the nation could have been averted in that way in the winter of 1861; but now the disorders of the country are probably too complicated to be reached in that form.

Meanwhile, the President and Congress should prepare the way for settlement; indeed, by consulting the people through the ballot-box, they might make a settlement, to be ratified by the States thereafter. Let the President propose an armistice, for the purpose of considering some programme of reunion and settlement, in which the feelings and rights of the masses in the South shall be duly appreciated and provided for. Invite them to come back on the conditions of the Constitution, with explicit definitions on controverted points, or on new conditions with the fullest assurance of justice and equality when they do so come. Let him do this, and challenge the rebel authorities to submit such propositions as may be agreed upon, to an unrestrained vote of the citizens of the Southern States, as he will, at the same time, submit such propositions to a vote of those of the Northern States, with the understanding that if a majority of slave States, and a majority of free States accept the proposition, its conditions should be binding until ratified or superseded by the States. Suppose the Confederate authorities reject this, or any similar proposition, no harm could ensue to the Northern cause. Such action would only leave them in a worse light before the world, and the Government at Washington in the better. The preliminaries for such a movement could be readily arranged by commissioners selected for that purpose.

It may be said that we are constantly inviting the Southern people to lay down their arms, and come back into the Union and this would seem to be conclusive; but it must not be forgotten that they rebelled, because, as they say, the party now in power at Washington, would not permit them to enjoy, in peace, the real conditions and covenants of that Union, and that there is no evidence that they would fare better now. Beside, he has studied human nature to a poor purpose, who cannot discover that unconditional submission involves a degree of humiliation, to which they will never come so long as they have any means of resistance. In the effort to gain back even the masses, their passions and pride, and self-respect, may be wisely considered. We must give them some new ground; some pretext, if not complete and substantial guarantees, before we can expect them to entertain the idea of forsaking their present leaders, and embracing the old Government.

I am fully aware of the indignation and even contempt with which these suggestions will be perused, by some, in both sections; but I care not; are we not engaged in an effort to re-establish and maintain the Union, and are not the seceded States to compose part of that Union? Then why not endeavor to rescue them from destruction, and cultivate good relations with them?

When the family of States again exists as heretofore, they must become our brethren and our equals in every particular. What pleasure, then, can we have in their destruction or humiliation. If there be any friends of the old flag and the old Government within the seceded States, they should cultivate the same spirit toward the North. The absent element of a substantial Union is fraternity amongst the people, and that can never be furnished by the sword. Again, in the words of Mr. Lincoln, "there has been much loss on both sides and no gain on either," and the identical old question as to terms of intercourse are upon us, and we should seek so to adjust them as to re-establish the Union on an imperishable basis.

But, it may be asked, is this a war for the Union? Are we sure that those in authority intend nothing else? They certainly profess nothing else, and I attribute to them nothing else. If the war is not for the Union, and is not directed with sole reference to that end, then it is the most stupendous fraud that has ever been practised upon the world. We all know, however, that many, very many of its partisans will not be satisfied with that issue. It might be very important, therefore, to the salvation of the country, when the time for reconstruction comes, if ever it should come, to have the soundings on this point taken in advance. I should like exceedingly to see a popular vote taken in the North, especially in New England, between the proposition to receive all the States back into the Union, on the terms of the Constitution, which makes the States equals and alike sovereign, each with the right to have such domestic institutions as it may choose; and a proposition to recognize the independence of the Southern Confederacy. It might be interesting, as well as instructive, to unveil the hypocrisy of a certain school of politicians who have clamored so zealously about the war for the Union. It is painfully apparent that notwithstanding this clamor, they do not intend that the Union shall exist hereafter on the terms of the Constitution, if it is to embrace all the States. The ratio of slave representation, and the rendition of fugitive slaves, are features of the Constitution which they condemn and abhor. Between the maintenance of these and the recognition of the Southern Confederacy, many of them, in my judgment, four to one, would prefer the latter. Their aversion to these clauses of the Constitution were a primary cause of the alienation and hostility of the South, and I fear they would not yield that aversion now to render the Union what it once was. Let Mr. Lincoln try this question if he would solve the problem of the nation's embroglio.

Do not understand me that I would yield the sword or any other means to render the Union what it was. What I mean is, that if the Union, and that only is the object, the sword will never find the belligerents in a better condition to consummate that work than they are now, and that other agencies should be promptly employed. I yield to no man in devotion and loyalty to the Union as it was, and to the principles of government transmitted to us by our fathers. The maintenance and perpetuation of these shall be the object nearest my heart, whether I be in private or public life.

With much esteem, I remain, yours truly,

WM. BIGLER.

To S. D. ANDERSON, Esq., Philadelphia, Pa.

I fully concur in all of the above sentiments,

JOHN BELL ROBINSON.

www.ingramcontent.com/pod-product-compliance
Lightning Source LLC
Chambersburg PA
CBHW040144270326
41929CB00024B/3355